WALLS

Hiltgunt Zassenhaus

WALLS

Resisting
the Third Reich —
One Woman's Story

With a new Foreword
by Katherine Paterson

BEACON PRESS *Boston*

Beacon Press
25 Beacon Street
Boston, Massachusetts 02108-2892

Beacon Press books
are published under the auspices of
the Unitarian Universalist Association of Congregations.

99 98 97 96 95 94 93   8 7 6 5 4 3 2 1

Library of Congress Cataloging-in-Publication Data

Zassenhaus, Hiltgunt.
[Baum blüht im November. English]
Walls : resisting the Third Reich—one woman's story / Hiltgunt
Zassenhaus ; with a new foreword by Katherine Paterson.
p.   cm.
Originally published: Boston : Beacon Press, 1974.
ISBN 0-8070-6345-2
1. Anti-Nazi movement—Biography. 2. Zassenhaus, Hiltgunt.
I. Title.   II. Title: Resisting the Third Reich—one woman's story.
DD256.3.Z3413   1993
943.086′092—dc20
[B]   92-40910
CIP

FOREWORD

How CAN I TELL YOU about this book? Why is it so important to me that you read this story?

As a nation, we face enormous problems that call for concern and action from all of us. Yet the refrain I hear from young and old is much the same: "Well, what does it matter? There's nothing anyone can do. The problems are too immense. It's all I can do to look out for myself and my own family." *Walls* reminds me that it was into just such a scene, one of economic hardship and lawlessness, that Hitler came to power. He promised stability, prosperity, law and order.

"No nation is immune from a Hitler," Hiltgunt Zassenhaus said in 1974 when this book was first published. "I used to think he was a purely German phenomenon, but now I know that is not true. America has never had a Hitler, thank God, but one can appear whenever there is a climate of apathy, indolence, and fear."

Zassenhaus first published this memoir of her young life in response to an America racked by the Watergate scandal and the OPEC-engineered energy crisis. "There seems to be," she said at the time, "a tendency to isolation and retreating to their own backyards." If this testament to the power of individual conviction and action was needed in 1974, how much more is it needed today when apathy, indolence, fear, and, above all, cynicism grip our populace like some paralyzing disease.

This is a book about faith that impels acts of incredible heroism, and yet the author often confesses how close she came to losing sight of the spiritual convictions of her youth.

This is a book about hope that endured for twelve dreary years of war and oppression, and yet fear and despair haunt its pages.

This is a book about love that can transform the world, and yet the temptation to build walls of prejudice, fear, and hatred against not only the oppressors but also one's own cowardly neighbors is nearly overwhelming.

You may read this wonderful book in several ways: as a hair-raising adventure, as a testimony to the mysterious workings of Providence, as an account of one determined young woman's defiance of an evil regime.

But the chief way I read it is as a warning. As I read, I see too clearly in myself and my neighbors the deadly tendency to remain uninvolved — that same apathy that benumbed the vast majority of good German people who neither adored Hitler nor resisted Naziism.

I can't tell you how to read this book. That will be your own choice. But I can tell you that by choosing to read *Walls* you are letting yourself in for an experience you won't forget.

Katherine Paterson
September 1992

PROLOGUE

With the exception of public figures, I have changed the names of most of the people described in this autobiography. Many of them are still living, and I felt it was the content of their actions (or lack of them) which was important to share — not their identities. I have not changed the names of Frederik Ramm, Olav Brunvand, Bjoern Simoness, or the Reverend Svendsen. Their stories are well-known in Norway and illustrate the struggle for freedom which must root in your own heart and mind.

I WAS ON MY WAY TO BERLIN and we would soon be landing. I had not been back for almost twenty-five years, not since that night in winter 1945 when I had been on the run hiding from the Gestapo . . .

I was enjoying the flight. High above the man-made boundaries of the earth, the blue sky stretched endlessly, and I felt free . . .

For a moment I closed my eyes. I had not intended to go back to Germany, not ever. But on my recent trip through Europe, word had reached me from a publisher in East Berlin. "We want you to come," he had written. "We have a special assignment for you."

Special assignment? Had it not been for those words, I would have ignored the letter, but they struck a chord from the past. I became curious and, on the spur of the moment, decided to go.

It would be only a short call, just one day. By tomorrow I would be on my way back to the United States.

My ears started to buzz. We were going down. I could not spot the wall which separated East Berlin from the West. From the plane Berlin looked like any other big city — just one huge cluster of streets and houses, dotted with the dusty green of late summer.

Still, we had to be over the East. Streets and open spaces looked deserted; the only sign of life was an occasional car.

Then the scene below changed abruptly. Vehicles jammed the streets; parking lots overflowed with cars. We were over West Berlin and only minutes later touched down at Tempelhof Airport.

"How long will you stay?" the desk clerk at the hotel inquired.

"Just for tonight," I said and set out for East Berlin.

*

The Wall would not be any obstacle for me. I had an American passport. But, as I entered Checkpoint Charlie, I was not so sure.

They took my passport away; and, when at last the official returned it, he kept looking alternately at me and my photo, apparently doubting whether we were one and the same.

Two other officials joined him. Why had I come, where would I go, and how long would I stay?

"We have to examine your luggage," they said.

"I have none," I replied.

They asked for my purse, opened it, and held it upside down, so that its contents spilled over the desk. I stared at their faces, amazed to discover that they all looked alike. I glanced away. Had I not learned that before? Hadn't they always all looked alike?

"We are only doing our duty," one of them said. They handed the purse back to me.

When I finally could pass on, I entered the land of the Wall. Friedrichstrasse once had been a thoroughfare of Berlin. Now it ended at the Wall, and the road was deserted as far as my eyes could reach. The houses were vacated, and a church, split open by the bombs of World War II, had never been rebuilt. A brick wall now barred entrance to it.

One cab was parked near the underground station. I got in, telling the driver where I wanted to go.

"There is no such street anymore," he said. "They have changed its name." He pushed the gas pedal so hard that the car jumped ahead with a jerk. "Yes, they have changed it — everything has been changed."

It was an uneasy ride. The road was full of bumps and holes. Yet the driver, unchallenged by traffic, did not even attempt to avoid them, and drove on sullenly. But I caught him glancing at the mirror above, obviously curious.

"Where are you from?" he asked at last.

"America."

"America?" he repeated as if I had mentioned the moon. After a pause he observed, "You speak German well."

"I was born and raised in this country."

4

". . . and got out when there was still time?"

"Not quite," I replied.

We had arrived at the publishing house, a huge building, almost like a tower. It had large shiny windows and walls of white marble.

"Property of the Party," the cab driver commented dryly before taking off with a jerk.

On either side were wide open spaces, covered by reddish dust — the rubble of World War II, razed to the ground by big machines. Some weeds were pushing through — and a bluebell here and there . . .

I turned away from the dust and looked up at the marble. What was life like behind its walls? Inside, there was no plush lobby, only a bleak hall, a floor of wooden planks. In a far corner I saw an open booth with a phone on a small table and behind it an old man, shabbily dressed. It was noon. With a tin spoon he was stirring something in a mug before him. I recognized the smell of the mixture — chicory and water.

"The comrade is expecting you," he said, when I asked for the Chief Editor.

The elevator was out of order, and I climbed the five flights of steps to his office. Heavy carpets covered the floor.

"We want your story," the Editor began. "Our youth should find out what you did during World War II, but," he paused for a moment, "you have to make certain changes."

I smiled in disbelief; then I asked, "Is that the special assignment you had in mind for me?"

"Well," he said, "one has to adapt . . ."

He called in his assistant, a young woman with horn-rimmed glasses and short, straight hair. He called her "Comrade."

"Let's sit down and discuss it," he suggested, obviously trying to be pleasant.

"I have read your story," the assistant started quite eagerly. "God was mentioned five times. He has to go out!"

"You seem to have done your work as an individual," the Editor observed. "That's unacceptable to our way of thinking. You'll have to state that you belonged to an underground organization. We believe only in collective action."

My eyes went to the window. From up here I could see the Wall.

"You are right," I said quietly. "I was not on my own — God was there all the time."

The Editor got up and paced the floor.

"You don't seem to understand!" he exclaimed.

"I think I do," I replied, suddenly remembering other days when I had been told that very same thing.

We did not come to any agreement. I left, and, walking down the stairs, was surprised to discover that I felt no emotion, not even anger, as if what I had heard and seen today could no longer touch me. I had cut my ties and my past was a closed book.

There was no cab outside, so I walked. I walked briskly, and, sliding my hand into my pocket, I touched my American passport — only twenty-four more hours, and I would be back in the United States. But then I stopped abruptly. I had come to "Unter den Linden," once Berlin's most fashionable boulevard. In the distance I could see a huge monument of the past: the Brandenburg Tor, and also something I had missed all day — people! Many people. They were gathered in front of the monument, standing shoulder to shoulder, forming a human wall.

The spaces between the pillars of the Brandenburg Tor had been filled in with concrete, making the monument part of the Wall. East German soldiers with guns over their shoulders, faced the crowd.

Only then did it occur to me what today was — the thirteenth of August 1969 — the eighth anniversary of the Wall!

In the heavy silence you could hear fragments of music coming from West Berlin . . . rock 'n' roll.

Suddenly out of the stillness a child's voice asked, "Mother, what is behind that wall?"

"People," she answered.

"People like us?"

6

"People are the same everywhere. They cry and laugh just as you and I."

"But why then is there a wall?" the child persisted.

I watched his mother's face close, as if she had drawn a curtain between herself and her child.

I knew that "curtain." I had seen it before. That woman's face told me that my past was not a closed book. I would never forget . . .

○

Walls . . . walls of cement, brick, and wire — and walls that could not be seen or touched — invisible walls built by prejudice, fear, hate, and what is worse, indifference. Walls that blocked our minds and rendered us insensitive to the pain inflicted on others.

These were the walls of the Third Reich — the walls of a people who took freedom for granted and in doing so lost it.

I grew up inside these walls, and saw people succumb to terror. But I also saw people rise above their fear and defy the forces of destruction. They were the people of the "hidden" Germany — a Germany the world knows little about.

Many of these people perished. Many of them are dead. I want them to live on, for they gave me hope that the walls separating man from man one day will fade so that people will cease destroying each other and join to serve life.

For me, the Third Reich meant windows glued over by swastikas and bonfires in which "reverence for life" went up in flames. It meant empty façades — all that was left of a people silenced by their fear of Hitler and choked by the smoke of burning cities.

But, for me, the Third Reich also meant a family who stood together in their opposition to Hitler, a father who taught his children to live by their convictions and a mother who said, "Only what you give, you'll have."

Hitler's Germany happened many years ago, but it could happen today. Again we are living in a world torn by some of the same forces that either activated or paralyzed the German people. We must identify with them in their bewildered confusion, for although Hitler is dead, he is still alive. He will live on as long as the walls remain . . .

PART ONE

1

THIS HAPPENS TO BE MY STORY. Only in a book are there a beginning and an end. When you are alive and seventeen, you can't recognize the beginning, and you are so sure it will never end.

One morning in winter I awoke, and I could see no sky through my window. The room had a dim, yellowish, almost sulfur-like light. The window glass was covered with thick, yellow paper, printed over and over with swastikas. Overnight our house had been dimmed by unknown Nazi hands.

This was in Hamburg, Germany, January 30, 1933. Adolf Hitler had come to power.

Two SS–men came the same day and asked for my father. As he was sick at that time, they let him stay; but a few months later he was without a job. He had been the principal of a girls' high school; he was a historian and had written an anthology on the history of christianity. He also had taught and written about Albert Schweitzer's "reverence for life" — a philosophy not tolerated by the Nazis.

That day he said; "From now on our house will be a fortress, where we will live and think, as we did before." My mother added, "It will last only a few months."

It lasted twelve years.

2

I WAS LATE FOR SCHOOL that morning of January 30, 1933. I had tried to get the glued paper off the window, but it stuck. I did not want to give up until I had scraped off at least one of the many black swastikas. But, digging back and forth with my knife, I had cleared only two lines which looked like a cross and through them I could see a touch of the blue wintry sky.

My favorite teacher, Miss Brockdorf, had the first class. She taught German and history, and just the day before we'd had a heated discussion comparing democracy and liberalism with totalitarian systems.

Not only that, but the month before Miss Brockdorf had assigned me to attend a rally where Hitler had spoken. It was the first time I had heard him speak, and afterwards I put down my impressions. "The loudness of his voice can silence you, but it cannot convince," I had written. In the early morning hours, with the conviction of my seventeen years, I ended my essay with the words, "Hitler is a psychotic!" Miss Brockdorf had graded my paper with "A", and asked me to read it to the class.

This morning, when I entered the classroom, I noticed that she was pale. She asked why I was late; but, when I started to tell her, she interrupted me curtly with a "Never mind." There was something in her face, something I saw later in the students, too. When I told them what had happened to my home, it was as if a curtain had fallen over their faces. Their faces went blank. They became quiet and turned away. Only my best friend, Inge, stayed with me and whispered, "Be careful!"

I was startled. Caution was a thought I had associated only with traffic. All I wanted to do was go home. When school finally ended that day, I rushed down the staircase. Miss Brockdorf stood at the bottom and stopped me. She motioned me into her office and carefully closed the door. My essay was on her desk. "Take it and burn it," she said. She stumbled over her words, when she added, "The things we believed in until now . . . we must forget . . ."

I had known Miss Brockdorf better than any other teacher. Not only had she taught me in school, but for more than two years she had invited a small group of students who had special interests in literature to her home for weekly meetings. We called it our "Private Book Club."

She lived with another teacher, who had been my favorite in junior high. Together we had read the great works of literature, covering a ground as wide as Stevenson and Goethe all the way to Thomas Mann. She had interpreted Dr.

Jekyll, who, when he had released his innermost thoughts, turned into Mr. Hyde. She had helped us understand why Goethe's Faust was driven to the edge of suicide when he made a pact with the devil. With her we had read Thomas Mann's *Magic Mountain* — about the man who, turning away from a conventional way of life, found himself.

"What about our club?" I asked her. Again her answer was, "You must forget about those books, too. Everything has changed."

At home only the outside had changed. Inside it was the same. My father told us that day, "Maybe now is the time when our beliefs will be tested, to see if they will hold."

His warning was to become true. In school we had to read Hitler's *Mein Kampf*; and one day Miss Brockdorf asked me, "Should you think objectively or subjectively when it concerns your country?" She looked at me intently, as if she were urging me to give the answer she expected from me.

"Objectively," I answered without hesitation. She became impatient with me and said, "You just don't seem to understand."

Soon a new order was announced. At the beginning of each class, when the teacher entered, we had to stand up, raise our right arm, and say, "Heil Hitler." I made up my mind that I would not. I thought it might be the first step to further concessions. In fact, I did not even take it seriously; we recently had read a drama of Schiller, and I reminded my friend Inge of the way its hero Wilhelm Tell had dealt with the oppressor who had overrun his country. When the tyrant placed his hat on a pole and ordered that everyone passing by was to bow, my hero had defied him. But Inge answered, "Why don't you do what I do? I raise my arm and just mumble something."

I decided not to do even that. There were thirty in the classroom; and when Miss Brockdorf entered, it sounded loud and distinctly, "Heil Hitler." I stood by the window; she looked at me. After the class she called me, "You know of the new order, and I have to insist." She added in a low voice:

"Please don't make it so difficult for yourself — and for me."

I went home and talked with my parents, but I got no advice. All they said was, "You must decide for yourself."

The next day all eyes were on me. The girls were standing with raised arms, but their heads were turned in my direction. Miss Brockdorf's face was ashen when she said, "Why do you force me to go further?" I was summoned to the principal, who said that I would have to be expelled if I did not give in. He gave me a day to think about it and said he would be in himself to see that I followed the order. I spent a sleepless night. My father asked me, "Do you feel it is worth the consequences you might face?" I realized that it could mean I would have to leave school. It could be the end of my education.

In school the next morning, I was badly shaken, and I would have preferred to run. But I knew there would be a tomorrow, and I had to find an answer today.

Miss Brockdorf entered, and behind her the principal. It was one of those first spring days — the windows swinging into the room were open and the trees blossomed with the first green of life. I was angry and at the same time fearful that if I compromised I might do something for which I would later despise myself. All eyes were on me; and while I again heard "Heil Hitler" loudly and distinctly from the other girls, I made a desperate movement with my left arm into the air. It struck the open window. It was done with such force that the glass was broken, and a large piece of it went into my arm. A scream went through the class, as blood started to pour down my arm. I was rushed to the hospital. Hitler was forgotten; and, from then on, no teacher entering class looked in my direction. They simply ignored me.

3

THAT SUMMER VACATION in 1933 I decided to leave Germany. I was aware that I could not be gone forever, but I wanted to get away for just a few weeks. Anywhere would do. I looked at the map, and the nearest border from Hamburg was

Denmark. My parents understood and let me go. Inge, my school friend, went along; and, with rucksacks on our backs, we crossed a border for the first time in our lives.

I drew a deep breath. Outside Nazi Germany the air seemed purer and the sky bluer. Suddenly I began to realize I had lost something I had not even missed — freedom and what freedom meant. I saw it in the faces of people whose smiles seemed happier. I did not understand Danish; but when I heard people speak to each other, there was no curtain between them. There was not that certain movement of the head to which I had become accustomed in Germany in the past months — that turn of the head to both sides and behind to make sure no one could hear, that inquiring look, before addressing a person — and that deadly silence, which might be the only answer.

Inge and I walked along the highway, passing fields and meadows and the straw-thatched, white-walled Danish farm-houses. Happiness came over me, and I started to sing. How good it was to be alive, just to be, and not to think of yesterday and tomorrow.

Suddenly thick black clouds covered the sun, and it began to rain. There was lightning on the horizon and from the distance we heard rolling thunder. We took refuge under a huge oak tree at the edge of the road.

Quite unexpectedly an oncoming car came to a stop where we stood. A woman with white hair was at the wheel. She leaned out of the window and said something we could not understand. Her eyes smiled; they were blue, the bluest I had ever seen. Then she asked in German, "Where do you want to go?"

"We are looking for freedom," I answered for both of us.

Again she smiled. She opened the door and said, "Get in."

While she was driving, she started to sing in a low voice. The rain was pouring down, hammering against the windows; and the wipers in front cleared only a little view. But I did not attempt to look out; I observed our unknown friend. To my seventeen years she seemed old, at least fifty. There was a peace and kindness about her, as if she were still a child who had never experienced evil. Again a feeling of happiness came over me. I got drowsy and fell asleep.

When I awoke, it was dark. The car was slowing down and I looked out. We were near the ocean. The moon was just coming up, and I thought it was larger than I had ever seen it before. The night was very still; a soft light fell on the water like a golden bridge. "We are home now," said our friend, "and I want you to be my guests."

The car had come to a halt in front of a large iron gate. Hiproses were climbing over the gate — they were blooming, and their faint fragrance blended with a tangy taste from the sea.

I was still not quite awake nor quite sure whether I was dreaming or not. I heard voices. One especially stood out, and in the summer night I saw a young man coming toward us, dressed all in white. He opened the car door and said in German, "Welcome home, Mrs. Jeppesen"; and, with a quick glance at us, added, "Who did you bring home this time?"

"Make them feel welcome," she answered. "They are looking for freedom."

As it turned out, we were not the only ones from Germany.

Mrs. Jeppesen was the widow of a wealthy Dane, who lived in a house the size of a mansion. It was surrounded by many cottages where artists and intellectuals were invited to stay. Mrs. Jeppesen made her selections with an almost childlike intuition — on the spur of the moment. If she liked an artist's work, she would write and invite him. If she heard of an intellectual in need, she would offer him asylum. If she met a person who caught her interest, she immediately extended an invitation as she had done with us.

This summer most of her guests were refugees from Germany; Eduard Bruns was among them. He was the one who had greeted us first. He was an artist, about thirty years old, who had belonged to one of the most progressive and liberal art groups in Germany. Shortly after he had left, members of his group had been arrested. He told us his story that very first night while we walked on the beach.

It was a mild summer night, and we stayed by the sea until

the moon faded away and a rosy horizon announced the dawn. Eduard's attention had focused on Inge and I became increasingly silent. My mind was in turmoil. How much had happened in twenty-four hours. Only that long ago I had crossed the border in my search for freedom. It had taken me only a day to lose it again. A bewildering and peculiar feeling came over me, one I had never experienced before: I had fallen in love.

It was as if I had just come alive and had discovered the world only today.

We stayed three weeks. The days were spent on the beach with the other guests. They were long days for me. While Inge and the others held endless discussions about Hitler and the Nazis, always speculating how long it could possibly last, I thought of nothing but Eduard. I lived only for him. Not only did the events in Nazi Germany seem unreal in Mrs. Jeppesen's protected world; for me they did not even matter. For hours I listened to the cries of the sea gulls and watched those tiny bushes of hiproses and their pink blossoms, growing for miles in the white sand of the beach like a string of pearls. In the afternoon we searched for driftwood, and at night we all gathered around the fire. Not till then would Eduard join us.

All day he worked in his studio in one of the cottages. I found out that each morning he walked more than a mile to a newspaper stand. Soon I, too, was on my way and managed to act surprised when I met him. He would sit on a bench near the newsstand, studying the paper meticulously; and whatever he found would determine his mood. "It will last only a few more months," he said one morning.

One day he invited me into his studio and showed me his paintings. They were beautiful. I said so, and he wanted to know why but I dared not answer. All I wanted to say was, "Because they are yours, and I love you!"

It must have been written all over my face, because he got annoyed and said, "Oh, you are just a schoolgirl."

He turned away and continued to work. His canvas showed a sandy road up a hill with fields on both sides and small white straw-thatched farmhouses. The sky was as you find it only in Denmark — a vague blue with a few gray clouds. Finally he turned his head toward me, smiled, then took the brush and, with a quick movement, painted some musical notes into the sky.

"What is beyond the hill?" I asked.

"Our tunes are different," he answered. "For you, your home and a future; and for me, sea gulls and the ocean."

"I hate the Nazis as much as you do," I insisted.

"Go home," he answered. "They are not threatening you. You are still so young that you can adjust."

Eduard had put me in my place. I had no choice but to accept it. Yet, much to my surprise, he asked me again the following day to come to his studio. "I have decided to paint your picture," he told me.

I was more than willing, for while he painted, he talked, and by listening I came closer to him than I had ever dared hope. He never again mentioned Hitler. He talked about himself and soon he began to show me how to look at paintings.

"They are like people," he said. "To like or to dislike them is not enough. Ask yourself why? Try to understand them; judge them on their contents and not on your own feelings."

While our sessions continued, I found happiness, but I also felt a growing sadness, for as the painting progressed, I saw myself as he saw me. The canvas showed a schoolgirl of seventeen years, sitting very straight, without a smile on her face. He pointed at the picture one day and said, "For your young age you are much too preoccupied with the Nazis."

On our last night Mrs. Jeppesen asked us to spend the evening in her living room by the fireplace.

A new girl had joined us, an actress with long black hair over her shoulders and a beautiful face. She spoke in a soft, purring voice; and when she walked, everybody looked at her. I did not mind "everybody," but it hurt when I noticed Eduard's eyes.

That evening we decided to try our hand at acting. A writer suggested a scene in which a young girl, happy and secure in her love, comes home and finds a letter from her lover saying he is leaving her forever.

The newcomer, the real actress, volunteered to start. It did not take long to convince her to take the lead! She vanished and a few minutes later danced in, singing a little song. With incredible grace and imagination she acted out first the happiness and then the despair of a deserted girl. My own frustration grew by leaps and bounds. Eduard had not once looked toward me. He seemed unaware of my presence and was watching her every movement — completely absorbed by the performance and, I thought, by the girl herself.

I was desperate. How could I ever be able to outshine so much grace and beauty? Besides, I could not compete with this girl — she was older than I, an advantage only appreciated at seventeen.

I saw myself reflected in the glass door: a cornflower-blue cotton dress, white socks and sneakers, and a red scarf around my head. This was how Eduard saw me — just a schoolgirl!

Then it was my turn. Eduard lit a cigarette and turned half away. I stepped briefly out of the room. When I came in again, something happened inside me — something which took hold of me completely. I did not take the time to act happy, discovered the letter, glanced at it and then pulled off my left shoe and threw it at Eduard. I hit him at the temple close to his eye.

I heard the startled scream; I saw Eduard turn and put his head against the wall. His cigarette fell to the floor, and for a moment I thought the earth would split open. I was stunned. Then came remorse and, most of all, fear; fear of what was inside me, of what had led me to act so violently. Once more I glanced at Eduard who was now silently leaning against the wall with his head buried in his arms. I saw only him. No one else in the room mattered. Never had I loved him so much as I did then. All I wanted to do was to run over to him and beg his forgiveness, but something inside stopped me.

I opened the glass door and stumbled out into a pouring rain. With a shoe on only my right foot I limped through the heavy, wet sand back to the cottage where Inge and I had our rooms.

I did not undress but lay down and pulled the cover over my head; and where the pillow had not been soaked by the rain from the open windows, it now got wet.

I did not think about Eduard and the pain I had caused him. I thought of myself, and an agony of doubt swept over me. I felt totally inadequate, something I had never felt before. I had been so secure in my family's love and approval and in my own little world.

There I had been taught to accept or reject others by standards determined by ideology only. Now I recognized intangible, undefinable qualities — qualities that made Eduard so unattainable for me, and this girl so desirable to him.

Whatever they were, I seemed to lack them. I was a failure with no way out. I wanted to die and began making plans for my funeral. While outside my cottage wind, rain, and ocean were in turmoil, I visualized Eduard — a lonely figure — standing by my open grave; and before I knew it, I was shedding bitter tears of sympathy for his loss.

I must have dozed off. Was I dreaming or was there a knock at the door? I thought I heard Inge's voice; but there was another one, too. My door opened and somebody entered. Eduard was at my bedside.

A sharp twinge went through my heart — Heaven itself had descended on me. He bent down, kissed my eyes, and I heard him say, "Good-by, Hiltgunt, and — take care."

Then he was gone.

When I woke up, the sea was calm and the sun stood like a red ball barely above the horizon, casting a pink glow into my room.

On the table beside me was my missing shoe — it was not a dream after all. I had been forgiven. I was filled with a joy so complete that the whole world and even I myself looked good and right.

It was still very early when we left. Only Mrs. Jeppesen was up. She smiled and asked, "Will you be back again?"

I did not answer; but she said, "Whatever happens, remember—as long as you live, each year there will be a summer."

4

THOUGH MY GRADES had become increasingly poor, I somehow managed to graduate from high school. Graduation, I came to see, would have been impossible without Miss Brockdorf's help. Outwardly she had rejected me time and again, trying to force me into accepting the new rules and ideas. But later I found that she had held long conferences with the other teachers on my behalf.

When I thanked her on the day of my graduation, she did not answer but silently pressed my hand; and I saw tears in her eyes.

Had she helped me out of sympathy with my father? Already in the beginning of 1933, soon after he was forced to resign from his teaching position, he had shown the first signs of a gradually worsening illness that had been diagnosed as Parkinson's Disease.

Hans, my eldest brother, studied mathematics. My brothers Guenther and Willfried were in medical school. Now I was to join them at Hamburg University. My mind had been made up ever since that summer in Denmark. I had decided to study Scandinavian languages.

In Germany a new law had been passed: only students who participated in Nazi activities would get scholarships. That left us out. We began to wonder how we would manage to pay our tuition.

Together we made an all-out effort. Expenses were cut to a minimum. There was meat only once a week, and when my mother had divided it into six equal portions, the plate seemed rather empty, but less expensive food would do. We moved into a much smaller house. Fortunately, it still had a room for each of us, even if there was space for only a bed and a chair and a table. It was all we needed — and soon our house became a beehive.

Day in and day out for the next four years a small army of children of all ages would arrive to be tutored by us; even my mother tutored. Laughingly, we sometimes called them "Tuition" and "Groceries." The student sat on the chair by the table, and the teacher sat on the bed!

During summer vacation we took jobs. These should have been carefree years, and there were moments of happiness, but always in a rather subdued way.

Five years of Nazi regime had taught us an attitude we had not known before. We had learned to be cautious in all our actions. During the first year we had seen the books burned in bonfires throughout the city, books such as those my father had written, containing the very ideas and thoughts which had governed our lives until then. More than the flames I remembered the fanatic stare in the eyes of the men who had burned them.

We had also discovered that there was a definite method in Hitler's seeming madness. He attacked only one group at a time. First the members of parties that had previously opposed him. Then, the intellectuals at the universities. Much later he turned against prominent church leaders, and finally the Jews. He attacked each as a minority group. And with the ingenuity and slyness of the primitive, he apparently sensed human behavior patterns and exploited them. He counted on the apathy of the individual, who would react only if he himself were endangered.

We had learned to fear the ringing of the doorbell after dark. Friends had disappeared, picked up in their homes by the Gestapo in the middle of the night. They had not returned, but we had seen the letters from the Gestapo — form letters, informing the families that death had ensued due to a "sudden illness."

We knew better and — though later it would be denied — many knew. There was a concentration camp on the outskirts of Hamburg. High walls topped with barbed wire surrounded it, but the screams could still be heard.

I started to probe into myself. Under the Nazi system I,

too, had aquired the ability to withdraw into a world of my own, a world created only for myself.

Every day I took long walks. At night, in my dreams, I would search back to a sandy white beach with tiny bushes of hiproses. I longed for a vague blue sky with light gray clouds. I dreamed of those musical notes, which Eduard once had painted into the sky of his picture. Somehow, I could not let go of that tune.

I would wake up in the middle of the night, haunted by fears. The beams of light from an oncoming car, touching the darkness of my room, would cause me to break out in sweat; and when I heard the sound of the approaching motor, my mind would rush through the day gone by. What had I said or done which might have given reason for suspicion? Long after the car had passed and the stillness of the night had again closed in on me, I kept turning and tossing, with my ears pounding. I was sure one night our doorbell would ring, as it had done for so many others.

I had little faith in tomorrow. No longer could I remember when I had last prayed. In my childhood God had been real to me: not only did I pray to him at night, when my parents were sitting at my bedside; I could also speak with God after they had left and it was dark in my room. I was convinced that I was the only one who mattered to Him, and at times I would drive hard bargains with Him and make all kinds of foolish promises. If I got what I wanted, I conveniently forgot the promises. I could not visualize His face, but I was always aware of His presence. With my eyes closed I used to imagine His huge, dark blue coat embracing the universe and me; and when I pressed my eyes tightly against my arms, I could see thousands of stars twinkle in the blueness of His coat.

That had been a long time ago. Now I differed little from those who, out of fear, accepted the system. In my silent opposition I had become just as fearful.

Deep, deep back in my mind I sometimes thought of Eduard. I had not heard from him. But one Christmas a large parcel arrived addressed to my parents. No note was attached; but even before it was unpacked, I knew what it was. From then on, whenever I looked at the painting on the wall, noting the serious expression of the schoolgirl, I wondered whether Eduard had really believed it when he suggested, "You are young, you can still adjust . . ."

Our life at home had not changed. We lived for those hours when we were alone, my parents and we four. My father, whose face had become mask-like due to his Parkinsonism, was still unbroken in spirit and never failed to encourage us. My mother, whatever might happen, managed to instill hope in us: the first forsythia on the table to tell us that spring was coming, fresh strawberries in July from a nearby farm to let us know that summer was here, or the bittersweet smell of baked apples in the fall. The Christmas season, which began early in December, never ended before most of dreary January had passed.

5

IN THE SUMMER OF 1938, I got my degree. Since an academic degree in Scandinavian languages was quite a rarity, I was presented with the "Seal" of the City of Hamburg even though I was only twenty-two. The seal meant a lifetime appointment as an official interpreter to the Court of Hamburg. It was given to me only because the man who had previously held it was ready for retirement. The seal was just a small and rather unsightly rubber stamp. I had no way of knowing that one day it would become the key to opening prison doors otherwise barred.

I did not rent any office, but continued as before in my room at home. A typewriter was all I needed to translate official documents. I also began to give private lessons in the Danish language.

6

ELIZABETH LEVY was my first student. She was a pianist. Even though she could not have been older than I, her dark hair already showed some gray. Her eyes looked sad, and the worn-out expression in her thin face reflected sleepless nights.

She seemed to be in a great hurry to learn Danish. "I plan a trip in the near future," she said rather vaguely. The rest of her story I could guess. She was Jewish.

We had our first class in the living room of my home. Elizabeth acted rather remote. Whenever I said anything not related to the Danish language, a curtain fell between us.

It was a day in June. The hawthorn tree in front of the house stood in full blossom, and through the open window came the sounds of early summer.

I liked her immediately and looked for a way to let her know it. My eyes fell on the piano which stood at the window. As she was ready to leave, I asked, "Would you play for me?"

She looked startled, but after a moment of hesitation she said, "What would you like to hear?" "Mozart," I answered and told her a story from my childhood.

When I turned nine, I got a hat, made of straw and circled with daisies. It was my first hat. It was summer, and the rain poured down so I could not walk outside to show it off. But I found a way out. Our piano always had stood in the living room by the window, which faced the street. My brother Hans, then very young, was an accomplished pianist. When he played Mozart, passers-by would stop just to listen, and I was convinced that my hat would well compete with him. I sneaked into the living room, closed the door carefully, opened the window, and started to bang on the piano. I had not yet learned to play and, what under the hands of my brother had turned into harmony, now filled house and street with noisy discord. Passers-by indeed looked up, but in disgruntled wonder.

Elizabeth laughed, and how young she suddenly looked! The ice was broken and she sat down and started to play. After a few moments of listening I knew that she was a great artist. It was so beautiful I forgot everything around me.

But suddenly in the middle of a passage she stopped. "Pull the curtains," she anxiously whispered.

It was then I noticed that people had gathered on the street and were listening intently. At the abrupt end of the concert they began to applaud and lingered on with the hope it would resume.

But behind the curtain there was only silence. We waited until the people had gone before Elizabeth left.

That same afternoon in the yard I saw our neighbors, standing on their side of the fence. Elderly people, they whispered to each other, looked at me and whispered again. At last they seemed to make up their mind and motioned for me to come close. Although we were all alone, they continued to speak in low voices, emphasizing over and over again that they did not want to get involved. They said they wanted to live in peace with their neighbors and again repeated that they did not want any trouble.

"You should be more careful," they said.

It took some time before they finally admitted that, the day before, two men had come to their home.

"It was the Geheime Staatspolizei, and they wanted to know whether you associate with Jews."

Gestapo.

We had several Jewish friends. Which one did they have under surveillance? Or had they started to take *our* activities under scrutiny? There was not yet any law against seeing Jews, but there were unwritten rules — stronger and more threatening than anything printed on paper.

It could not possibly concern Elizabeth. She had only been here for the first time today. But from now on we decided to see our Jewish friends at their homes and only at nighttime.

Elizabeth lived in another part of the city. It was dark when I arrived the following day. Two flights of steps led to a modest apartment. She waited for me in the hall. It was small and barely lighted by an electric bulb, dangling freely on a cord.

There were two pieces of luggage, ready to go. Elizabeth followed my eyes. "I am waiting for my passport," she said.

I understood. I knew it could mean waiting for only a few days or it might last for months. Jews were still allowed to leave Germany, but it was entirely unpredictable who would be given a passport or when.

Her parents were dead and Elizabeth lived with her grandparents. Her great musical talent had been discovered when she was a child, and since then she had been in training as a concert pianist. Shortly after Hitler came to power, the conservatory asked her to leave. She had continued with private tutors, and all of her grandparents' savings had gone toward her education.

The largest piece of furniture in the small living room was an open piano. On it was the photo of a very young girl — with large, smiling eyes and a happy face.

"It was taken some time ago," Elizabeth said. She sounded almost apologetic.

There was room left for only a small table and a few wooden chairs. My steps sounded hollow, as the floor was without a carpet. On the wall was a picture of a young man in the uniform of a German officer. Beside his photograph in a frame was the Iron Cross.

"Your father?" I asked.

"He died in World War I."

The living room opened into the bedroom, and there was just enough space for three beds. On the wall was a rack with old clothes, evidently in the process of being altered. Elizabeth's grandfather was a tailor. His workshop was behind the kitchen. His back was bent; but when he came out to shake hands with me, there was no curtain between us.

I went every night. As the weeks passed by, Elizabeth learned Danish rapidly, but the expression on her face became increasingly worried.

Then one evening when I arrived, she was crying and laughing at the same time. In her hand was the passport. Mrs. Levy stood in the living room. She was wiping her eyes. She had put a white cloth on the table and there was coffee and cake. Mr. Levy interrupted his work and joined us.

On this last night we were sitting together like old friends.

It was then I noticed a radio in the corner. It was almost new and stood in peculiar contrast to the wornout shabbiness of the other belongings.

"We bought it for Elizabeth," Mrs. Levy explained, "so she could listen to the symphony concerts on the radio."

Nothing more was said, but I understood. Although Jews were still permitted to attend concerts, Elizabeth had stayed away — her Jewish features made her the target of cold rejecting stares.

"One day Elizabeth herself will be heard over the radio," I said attempting to break the silence.

I got no answer and I wondered whether we all thought the same. Would they live long enough?

Had I ever been in Denmark, Mrs. Levy finally inquired. I said I had, and that it was a good country. I had found freedom there, I said, and then I ventured to ask, "Wouldn't you want to leave with Elizabeth?"

She looked at her husband, took his hand, shook her head sadly, and answered, "It's too late for us. It is here we belong, whatever happens."

Elizabeth followed me out into the hall. Tomorrow she would be gone, she and two pieces of luggage. She was allowed to take along whatever she could carry herself.

She shook hands with me. Her voice sounded sad when she asked, "Will you keep an eye on my grandparents?"

I would try, I promised.

"Tak!" she said, using the Danish word for "Thank you." Then her face lit up, as if something occurred to her.

"Don't leave yet," she said and stepped back into the living room.

She returned with the radio and handed it over to me.

"We want you to have it," she said. "Maybe one day in the future *you* will hear me play . . ."

7

I was twenty-two. I felt left out. I yearned for a life I thought I would never get back. Life for me was a moon at the ocean, large as I had seen it only once . . . the fragrance of hiproses blended with the tangy smell of the sea. Yet no matter how hard I might try to visualize Eduard's face, it would not return, and one day it struck me that time had come between us and that I was in love with a memory.

My frustration was growing. Why could I not be like everybody else? What had made me different from my neighbors? They seemed happy and content with their pictures of Hitler in their living rooms.

Why could I not accept what I was unable to change? After all, what had I to fear for myself? I was not Jewish; as yet the bell of our door had been spared by the Gestapo and it did not seem to matter that none of us had joined the Party.

Why not let go, just let go? I stretched my arms out into the warmth of the night and felt my hands getting wet from a summer rain. It was one of those rains which would bring no relief. Far away music drifted in from a neighborhood tavern where people danced night after night, but the distant siren of an ambulance almost drowned it.

I thought of my father and his illness. What would happen to us if he died? I had never seen anybody die; death was something I knew only from books or had seen acted out on a stage, but I could not imagine what it was like in real life.

I buried my face in my pillow, thinking that between death and my father there was still Dr. von Berg.

He was our physician, and since 1933 he had come each Tuesday night. He arrived at seven o'clock, so promptly one could set one's clock by him. He had taught internal medicine at the University of Hamburg and his lectures had been renowned for clarity and precision, but in 1937 he had been forced to resign from his teaching position when he made no effort to join the Nazi party.

All that was known at that time about Parkinson's Disease, he knew. Although he had told us from the beginning that there was no cure, he somehow always succeeded in giving us hope. What medicine could not do, he did with his heart.

My father lived from one Tuesday to the next; we all did. Dr. von Berg would sit at Father's bedside with my mother opposite him. Some distance apart, at the foot of the bed, we children would stand, watching silently.

I wondered why he carefully examined my father each time, though he must have known that, whatever the result, it could not alter the course.

I observed how he anticipated our unasked questions.

"Your father is better this week," he would say; or, suggesting another medicine, he might add, "I am sure this will give him relief." Another time he would tell us about new efforts being made to find a cure.

I noticed that he never left without asking my father a question in his field — a religious or philosophical question — and I noticed, too, how my father in answering seemed to come back to life.

Dr. von Berg had been an officer in the German army in World War I. Although I knew him only as a civilian, I always visualized him in an officer's uniform because of his manner. He never discussed politics; and at times I sensed that, by ignoring current events, he wanted to erase a reality he refused to recognize.

He had never sent us a bill. I wondered why he gave us his help so generously? Was it his way of expressing his silent opposition? What gave him the patience and strength to instill hope when there actually was none? As the years went by, my admiration for him grew — as did my interest in medicine, the way he practiced it.

It was early September when he took us aside and told us, "Your father is getting worse. His muscles are getting more rigid. You must try harder to make him walk."

We took turns, my brothers and I. For hours every day we walked with my father along the Elbe river. It was the same path we had walked in earlier days when he had talked about the history of mankind and taught us in his particular way how to "walk on our own."

Each step was now a struggle for him; but, if we encouraged him to walk long enough, the spasms and rigidity of his muscles would ease and, on his way home, he would sometimes feel so much relief that he could talk.

One afternoon he reminded me of the story of the dance around the golden calf. "What truth!" he commented. "Haven't we seen ourselves what happens if we don't have the courage of our own opinion?" He was more lively than he had been for a long time and, with apparent irrelevance, he added, "We must try to give your mother all the help we can."

I wondered what he meant. When we got home and I saw how pale and exhausted she looked, I realized how preoccupied I had been with myself. I started to ask questions but her face closed up and she turned aside.

Now I noticed that she was often gone for hours, sometimes all day long. Taking my father's advice I began to help with all the daily chores, while Guenther and Willfried took over his care.

I had told my mother about Elizabeth. She had asked, "Have you been back to see her grandparents?"

I had never been back. Only once had I called them to find out where in Denmark Elizabeth lived. I had written a letter to her, but she had not answered.

○

One night in October my mother took me along when she went to visit our lawyer, Mr. Cohn. He was Jewish and an injury during World War I had left him with a limp.

While I talked with his wife, I noticed that my mother took him aside, and I saw her hand him a paper while talking in a very low voice. She sounded urgent and I was able to catch a few words. "It is late," she said. "You must leave."

"I cannot be happy anywhere else," he answered.

But she must have succeeded in convincing him that life for Jews in Germany would soon become unbearable; the next month, November 1938, my mother sent Willfried and me to the station to see them off. It was a gray day and there was a nip in the air. The wind was coming up, pushing along clusters of leaves in the gutter.

The station was crowded with Nazi SS troops, but I paid

31

no attention because the train bound for Paris was almost ready to leave.

We rushed along the platform, hurriedly glancing into each compartment until we finally found them. They were alone, sitting each in a corner, with their eyes closed as if all life had left them.

We dared not talk to them in public, but we knocked at the window and pressed our faces against the glass. I pulled from my purse some violets, wrapped in white paper and lifted them to the window. We clasped our hands moving our lips as if saying, "Good-by."

They looked at us without smiling.

We stood still until the last of the train had disappeared into the fog. We had witnessed the sentence of two people condemned to go on living.

                             ○

I stayed in town that day to do some work for the Court. When it turned dark, the fog changed into rain. It poured down steadily.

On my way home I saw groups of men on every block. Troops in black uniforms with the SS insignia on their lapels. They whispered among themselves, moving restlessly, as if waiting for something. In the mist of the rain the white street lights gave their faces a ghostlike appearance, and in their eyes I noticed that fanatic stare I had seen once before.

Again the undefinable fear filled me. I sensed something was about to happen.

The next morning we knew. An all-out raid had been made on all property owned by Jews. Synagogues were invaded and burned down, glass was broken, and doors were trampled in. Stores were looted and destroyed. The merchandise was floating in the canals of Hamburg. Private homes and apartments were raided, and any Jew they trapped was beaten and arrested.

Although most of them were released after a few days, it was now obvious that it was only the beginning. But around me life seemed to go on as always. Despite what happened, people stood idly watching or turned casually away. I could not tell what they thought or felt, but I heard no open protest.

It had been carefully planned. None of the troops who actively participated in the raids and arrests were from that community. Whole units of SS–men had been moved in from other localities to avoid any second thoughts, doubts, or personal involvements.

"You have taught us much," Willfried said to my mother one day, "but you never told us there are evil people."

My mother paused before answering. At last she said, "Let us not think about that. Let us answer the evil with good."

8

IT WAS CHRISTMAS 1938. We knew it might be the last one we would spend together. Looking at my father I could see the change for the worse. On the political scene it was obvious that war was pending.

For Willfried and me Christmas began on December 23rd, the day we set out to get our tree. It was growing on Mrs. Manning's farm, and I had picked it out early in summer, following its growth through the seasons.

The old woman's farm was nearby; a few acres she worked all by herself. She lived alone and in more than one sense she was like a forgotten island where time and events had passed unnoticed. At least that was what I thought.

Strawberries, cabbage, potatoes, and apples were her only companions. She was of an undeterminable age, but under the blue scarf she wore around her head summer and winter I could spot some white hair. She was almost deaf, and her hearing aid was a horn of nearly an arm's length; but I had not seen her use it. Whichever vegetable we wanted, she let us take and jotted down what we owed.

Her farmhouse was an old shack, actually nothing more than one room. But, as time progressed, she had built additions in all directions for storage, and the original shack looked like a fortress, towering over the outer forts. The four walls were stacked up with heads of cabbage to the east, a pile of potatoes to the west; the north side was protected by a heap of black coal; and entering the shack from the south, one was surrounded by a mountain of apples.

Mrs. Manning had no radio, and newspapers for her meant wrapping material. I sometimes thought, with almost a feeling of envy, "For her Hitler does not even exist."

That winter night, when we arrived, she was watching for us. She had cut our tree; and, when she saw us coming, she held it up into the air like a candle. Putting the tree down, she beckoned Willfried and me into her inner sanctuary.

On the glowing red stove I saw apples baking. Willfried and I looked at each other; they smelled good and the sizzling of the juice promised us a treat.

"Sit down," Mrs. Manning said, motioning us to a table; it was in one of the corners, with built-in benches. The green hanging lamp above it spread a soft light. The warmth from the nearby stove made me a little sleepy; and, with the outer "forts" and their walls shielding off any sound from the road, I felt protected and at ease, as if I were in another world.

Mrs. Manning brought us the apples with sugar and cream. There was silence until we had finished.

Then she raised her horn to her ear and asked, "Do you speak English?" Out of her pocket she pulled an envelope, containing a postcard and a letter. "It is from my son."

The postcard showed a figure, which to me looked like an angel holding a torch in her upraised hand. Below it was printed, "America, The Land of the Free."

I looked at it again, for I liked those words.

"It is the Statue of Liberty," Willfried explained.

It was my first meeting with America. Before, it had been but a spot on the map, as far away and as unknown to me as the moon.

"How long has your son been there?" Willfried asked.

"Since 1933 . . . ," she hesitated before she continued. "He got away, but his father was killed."

"In a camp?"

She nodded, but her face told us that she did not want any

34

further questions. She took up the letter and held it tight to her, as if somebody might try to take it away. "When I was left alone, I thought my life had come to an end," she said. "But today my son writes that he wants me to join him in America."

The idea was nothing but a dream as long as Hitler was in power. Not that they were Jewish, but the Gestapo had them on their lists. They knew her husband had been anti-Nazi and that her son had escaped. As if guessing our thoughts, she added, "I will have to wait, but I want to learn English now. Will you teach me?"

I promised I would and asked, "What is America like?"

"I don't know," she answered, "but they have no Hitler."

○

Our Christmas tree never looked prouder or greener to me than this year, with a fragrance of pine as only a tree taken directly from the soil can have. The morning of Christmas Eve Willfried and I trimmed it with white candles and red apples, which also came from Mrs. Manning's farm. The only ornament was on top of the tree — a Christmas angel in white, and I found myself thinking that she somewhat resembled the Statue of Liberty.

As it turned dark snow began falling. It was as it always had been; while my mother made her final preparations, my father and we four waited in his study. Then at last there was the sound of the Christmas bell — my mother opened the door of the living room, and there was our tree standing at the window near the piano. The candles cast a glow over the apples, and the angel on top swayed in the warmth of the lights. We led my father to the armchair; Hans sat down at the piano, and we formed a circle around my father to sing "Silent Night."

We had not even pulled the curtain, for it snowed so hard that you could see neither in nor out. A golden reflection of the candles flickered in the black shining wood of the piano, but did not give enough light for the Bible which my father had opened. It did not matter. As long as I could remember he had read the Christmas story to us; he knew it by heart.

The candles on the tree were burned halfway down before we turned to our presents. There was a package for me from Denmark. I tried not to show my excitement. Eduard had sent it.

I recognized the painting at once: the white, straw-thatched farmhouse with the road leading uphill, and the notes in the sky. All that Eduard had written was the question, "Have you found your tune?"

              o

As the New Year began, I started to teach Mrs. Manning English, and these weekly nights in her lonely shack were happy. Her difficulty in hearing made it hard to communicate, but she never tired of holding her horn to her ear; and, as the ice melted on the road to her farmhouse and the first green was showing, she was able to speak some English. More than that, her tightly closed lips would at times show a smile.

One day I brought Mrs. Manning a map of America. We looked for New Jersey, where her son was living. On my map it covered a space much less than an inch.

"In which town does your son live?" I asked.

"Elizabeth," she answered.

I looked up. It struck me to hear the name and it must have shown on my face.

"Do you, too, know somebody over there?" Mrs. Manning inquired.

I got hold of myself. There was no logical explanation and I answered vaguely, "I used to know somebody by the name of Elizabeth."

We learned all that could be known from an encyclopedia about America, and in my eagerness to bring Mrs. Manning closer to her son I soon found myself intrigued with a world which until now had been unknown to me.

We knew how many inches of rain were falling on New Jersey throughout the year. We read all about those big cities near the state, New York and Philadelphia. But my encyclopedia had not told me what I wanted to know most — what about America's people?

The only person in America I had heard of was Mrs. Manning's son. There was another one — at least for me she had come alive. I had looked at her again and again — it was the Statue of Liberty. The postcard was now on the wall in Mrs. Manning's room. My eyes went again to it. I wondered whether people in America knew what was happening under the Nazis; and, if so, did they know we needed to be rescued?

9

THE HAWTHORN in front of our home was in full bloom, and through the open window the sounds of summer came again. I was standing beside the piano, listening to a letter my mother was reading to me. It was from England.

"I would like our daughters to meet," Mrs. Thompson, an old friend of my parents, had written. "It seems forever since we have heard from you. How have you been?"

Listening intently, I thought for a moment of white sand and bushes of pink hiproses.

"Let your daughter come now," the letter urged. "Summer will soon be gone."

My mother looked up. "Would you like to go?"

Would I? I did not know England — and yet, I did! Ever since Elizabeth Levy had given me her radio, England had been with us night after night. The BBC had become the timetable of our daily lives, our gathering point and our source of hope. It was strictly forbidden to listen to any foreign station, but that only made it the dearer to us. We made sure that no windows were open and that our heavy curtains were pulled. Then we tuned in and sat close together, for the volume had to be low.

It was not so much the news itself which kept us tied to the radio. Listening to the voice of BBC gave us the feeling that we were not alone; and what we heard led us to believe that everybody outside Germany was with us in our opposition to the Hitler regime.

I felt I knew even the Thompsons from our sessions with BBC. "I will go as soon as I get my passport," I said.

I had it in less than a week. I was not Jewish, and apparently I was not on the Gestapo's list. My passport arrived so quickly that it seemed as if people like me were being encouraged to travel abroad. Perhaps they believed it was one way of reassuring the world that life in Germany had not changed. Although we were apprehensive about the ultimate outcome of Germany's dictatorial system, even we could not imagine that war was only ten weeks away.

I had my passport and my luggage was ready. But there was still something I lacked: a ticket. We simply could not afford it. My father at last found the solution:

"Mr. Jenkins . . ." he said.

Had it not been for the letter from England, I never would have met Mr. Jenkins.

He was a shipping agent who supplied freighters bound for England and Scandinavia. My father had met him only once. Mr. Jenkins' daughter had been one of his students before my father lost his position in 1933. At that time my father had been surrounded by a barrier of silence, but Mr. Jenkins had dared to cross it.

"He was the only parent," my father told me, "who came asking if I needed help."

Early next morning I set out to find Mr. Jenkins.

We have periods in our life that, like dreams, leave no trace; and then there are moments or even seconds, when we catch impressions or thoughts which stay with us always. Little did I realize that some of my impressions this day would be like a preview whose meaning I could understand only after having seen the entire movie.

When I left home, I had my passport in my pocket and Mr. Jenkins' address in my hand.

Following my father's directions I searched out Bismarck to find Mr. Jenkins' place. Bismarck, of course, was dead. It was his monument my father had referred to, the landmark of Hamburg's port. It was an oversized statue of Bismarck, standing high on a hill and towering over the harbor.

The former chancellor stood with his hand resting on a huge sword that I was sure was taller than our house. We had studied about the founder of the German "Reich" in school. Long before Hitler, Bismarck had created an empire whose Kaiser had said, "We Germans fear God and nothing else in the world."

Bismarck was the first and last impression of Germany for any incoming or outgoing ship, and when I passed the stern statue, I thought of Mrs. Manning's postcard and the gracious lady with the torch.

Sliding my hand into my pocket, I touched my passport and hurried on to the waterfront. A boat was leaving and the long sound of its horn made me aware of a world outside. The tall, narrow houses along the piers were bent and battered by age. Most of them were more than a century old.

Before I could decide which direction to go I noticed in front of me a modern brick structure. It was shaped like a ship and the mast was a tower with a bell in its steeple. The door stood wide open and in the hall was a steep, narrow staircase leading to the upper floor. Behind one of the windows was a Norwegian flag. A sign on the wall read, "Norwegian Seamen's Church."

I wondered what it was like inside and I wanted to enter. Then I remembered what I had come for.

I found Mr. Jenkins in one of the old houses. His office was on the ground floor. In a big armchair I saw a huge man sitting at a desk which was actually only a wooden table, with a mountain of paper. He had a hat on his head and a pipe in his mouth. He did not get up when I entered, but tipped his hat a little farther back from his forehead in welcome.

"So you are his daughter!" he said stretching out his hand, when he heard who I was.

Looking over the walls I found no picture of Hitler, but there was a map of the world.

He smiled when he heard what I wanted. "Is it one way to England," he asked, "or do you intend to come back?"

I was stunned by his question; it had never occurred to me

that I had an alternative. But I hastily answered: "Round-trip," adding awkwardly, "why do you ask?"

"Don't mind me," Mr. Jenkins said, lighting his pipe again.

He pulled some schedules out of the stacks of paper and reached for the phone. While I was quietly sitting and waiting, my mind was spinning.

Mr. Jenkins was right; I had a choice. I could stay away if I wanted to. I thought of the fears I had. I thought of the sleepless nights, watching the beams of the oncoming cars, always anticipating that the Gestapo might come.

Then I thought of my father. I thought of my home and my family. I had no alternative.

"All clear," I heard Mr. Jenkins say, putting down the phone and turning to me. "I found a boat. Keep yourself ready and I'll call you when it is leaving."

"Thank you," I said, and I asked what I owed.

"Forget it," he answered, shaking my hand. "Tell your father that I am here if he ever should need me again."

I did not tell my parents what Mr. Jenkins had asked. They seemed to know what was on my mind anyway, for a few days later my father summoned me to his bedside.

"Have you considered not coming back from England?" he asked.

I did not answer but continued to look at him, hoping he would make a suggestion. I should have known better. He had never yet made a decision for me.

"How could I stay away?" I asked. "My home is with you."

It was not Germany I thought of but my parents and the world we shared.

"Eventually you must walk on your own wherever you are," my father answered.

I knew he was telling me I would find freedom only if I could free myself from the ties by which I was bound. Tears burned in my eyes, and in that moment I wished we had never got the letter from England.

There was a knock at the door and Willfried stuck his head in. "Hurry up," he said, "Mr. Jenkins is calling. The freighter will leave tonight."

Guenther and Willfried took me to the pier. After the boat horn had blown for the third time, the freighter began to move.

I stood on the bridge. Guenther and Willfried were waving good-by. Mr. Jenkins stood behind. He bade farewell by tipping his hat. The night was too dark for me to see Bismarck up on the hill. As the ship pulled away, I watched Mr. Jenkins towering over my brothers. As he stood there motionless, he, too, looked like a monument, though I could not then know that he would one day become a tower of strength to me, representing a Germany of whom the world would know little.

10

MY SHIP LANDED in Liverpool and I had to take a train going south. Looking out of the window I eagerly searched for the England of my BBC. What a disappointment it was. All I saw was a long stretched-out seaport; it could as well have been Hamburg. Even the sky was as gray as at home.

It was late afternoon when I arrived at Brighton, the English sea resort. The sun was shining and the sounds of vacation filled the air with laughter and hellos between the train and the platform. Waiting for the Thompsons amidst this bubbling life I felt strangely remote.

"Hiltgunt, how are you!" somebody behind me said.

Turning around, I saw a tall young man with a young woman standing beside him. "My parents asked us to pick you up," he said, stretching out his hand.

They are much younger than I, I thought, although I knew our age was the same. John was in slacks and an open shirt, with a navy blue jacket leisurely slung over his shoulder. Doris's light blue dress matched the color of the ribbon tying her long hair. There was something hard to define about them, a casualness I had never known, and a confident ease, which made me feel clumsy and awkward right from the start.

"How was your trip?" John asked, picking up my bags; and Doris added, "Did you have nice weather?"

She smiled, but actually she did not see me at all. Her eyes seemed to wander over the platform, as if she were expecting someone else. Suddenly she grasped John's arm and I heard her excitedly whisper, "Look, there is Allen!"

The young man who passed looked studious and at the same time very much alive. I liked his smile when he waved and called: "Hello!"

It was obvious that Doris was disappointed; he had not stopped. I saw her eyes fill, but only for a moment. She was British enough not to lose her control. To break the silence, John asked me good-naturedly, "Well, how are things in Germany?"

"Bad," I answered, taking his question seriously.

A puzzled, almost embarrassed expression came over his face. "Oh, really?" he murmured and moved on.

I met John's and Doris's parents in their family quarters on the top floor of the hotel. Mr. Thompson was limping; an injury from World War I, I later learned. During our third cup of tea he, too, asked in a pleasant, conversational tone, "Well, how are things in Germany?"

For a fraction of a second I hesitated, realizing that this question meant nothing more than another "How do you do?"

Yet, once again I ventured, "Not so good, I'm afraid."

He responded with the same puzzled expression I had seen before, reminding me of the "curtain," but in a different way.

"More tea?" Mrs. Thompson asked quickly. Turning to me, she said, "We want you to have a vacation. Try to forget what is happening over there."

I took the hint, not mentioning again what was "over there"! But I caught myself looking frequently at the Thompsons, trying to find in their faces a clue to what I was unable to comprehend. They were kind to me. They inquired after my parents and brothers, but why did they show no interest in what was happening outside their world?

One day, when we were listening to the news on the radio, we heard about German troop concentrations at the Polish border. I quickly glanced at Mr. Thompson.

"Damn it!" he said and turned off the radio.

"I hope we won't get involved," Mrs. Thompson commented.

I met their guests, too. Most of them were widows and officers, retired and living on a pension. They were by themselves most of the time, seated in comfortable armchairs. Their rooms were furnished in a Victorian manner. Their curtains were pulled regardless of the time, warding off the sun and — or so it appeared to me — shutting out life itself.

I was introduced to them the very first night, and one of them, a colonel, looked up, when he heard my accent. "Where are you from?" he asked.

Before I could answer, Mrs. Thompson took me away, and seated me next to her at the other end of the table.

We spent our days at the beach. There was no white sand, only stones, and we sat on chairs. Most of the time I kept my eyes closed, letting the bits of conversation flow over me like the waves of the ocean. Secretly I counted the hours.

The nightly supper was the event of the day, with lighted candles, and the different courses served with ritual solemnity. Everyone else was in formal attire, but it was not my casual dress alone that separated me from the group. Listening to the chit-chat around me, I wondered that so little could be said in so many words.

Was this the "normalcy" of the life I had yearned for? I thought of our nightly sessions with the BBC, of how eagerly we had identified BBC's editorials with the intentions and attitudes of the British people, and even of the world. How stubbornly we had ignored the lack of response from abroad which had proven over and again our belief an illusion!

Doris and I were sharing her room and I watched her carefully. It puzzled me how preoccupied she was with herself, how she worried about her appearance. While it took only minutes for me to get ready for bed at night, she would spend hours preparing herself for the day to come, brushing her hair, setting it, and doing it over again. She pulled out drawers, opened and closed closets, as if her life depended on what to wear.

What did she really think and feel? I wondered, but she did not confide in me.

One night, when she assumed I was asleep, I observed her through my half-closed eyes. She sat in front of a mirror and studied her face from all angles. I noticed a frightened expression, as if she were watching a stranger.

Then I remembered the first night at the station and how her eyes had followed the young man who had passed us. On the spur of the moment, I asked, "What is Allen like?"

She turned around. The ice was broken. Her words fell over one another. They had grown up together, she told me, but he had left town and now worked as a journalist for one of the papers in London.

"Was he in love with you?" I asked.

"He used to be," she answered.

The very next day we met him. He was friendly with Doris, I thought, but after only a few words he turned toward me and asked, "How are things in Germany?"

I looked at him and knew instinctively that he wanted to know. For hours we talked together, and even Doris would listen at times. Not only did Allen understand, he cared, and it took only his concern to restore my hope and belief in the England of BBC.

A few nights later something disturbing happened. Immediately after supper the colonel approached me, the same one who had asked me where I was from.

"So you are from Germany?" he started. "I'll say, you have a good man over there."

"Who would that be?" I asked, remembering how Mrs. Thompson had quickly separated us when he had approached me before.

"I admire your Hitler," he said. "Germany needs a strong hand."

I did not answer.

"We, too, have many Jews in this country," he persisted. "I wish Hitler would take care of them."

"There is a good chance, sir, that he will soon take care of you," I retorted, no longer being able to hold back.

The colonel looked up. His face turned purple, and grabbing his cane, he shouted, "What the hell are you implying?"

Silence fell over the room and all eyes were upon us. Mrs. Thompson came over quickly; and raising her teapot she asked, "More tea?"

○

"He is a big bore, and his generation will eventually die off," Allen said, when I told him later what had happened. "But it troubles me that the world is full of Thompsons, of nice people whose sole interest is not to get involved."

○

One night when Allen was visiting he said, "I want to ask you a question."

"I wonder," he began, "whether you have considered staying in England? I could talk with the Department of Immigration. I can help you to find work in London."

I looked up. The room was filled with music from the radio, someone was playing the piano. It was beautiful. While I listened to Allen, I searched my mind: where had I heard that theme before? I had heard it, I knew, somewhere . . .

"I will help you in any way possible," Allen urged.

I glanced over to the Thompsons; they, too, were listening to the music. It is Mozart, I thought, one of his piano concertos . . . D minor . . . there . . . that passage . . . I heard it when . . .

It struck me like lightning. It all came back: the piano in our living room at the window, the hawthorn in front of our house, the undefinable sounds of an early summer day and the voice that had whispered, "Pull the curtains . . ."

There was only one who could play the concerto this way. Could it be? It had to be . . . yes! I was sure now, it *was* Elizabeth.

I grabbed Allen's arm.

"Listen!"

I ran over to the radio, touched it as if it would bring me

closer to her. I held my breath, barely able to wait out the end, hoping to hear her name. Then I heard the announcer. Yes, her first name was Elizabeth; but the surname was different.

"Help me to find her," I begged Allen. "Call BBC."

It was a long wait. But I finally heard her voice on the phone. I was almost too excited to speak.

"I wrote you a letter, Elizabeth."

"Yes, I got it."

"Why then did you not answer?"

"I wanted to forget."

"Let me come to London to see you."

"I'm leaving tomorrow morning."

"Whatever you do," I said, "stay away from Denmark. Hitler is going to start a war and soon he will occupy Scandinavia."

I don't know what made me say this. I knew nothing of Hitler's plans.

"I'm on my way to South America," Elizabeth answered. "But what about you?"

"I'll go back," I said. "My place is over there."

"Good-by, Hiltgunt," Elizabeth said and, after a moment of silence, she added, "Take care of yourself."

The sound of the piano was still in my ears when I went to bed. I spent a restless night. I was happy for what Elizabeth had achieved, but I was unhappy, too, for I sensed that I would not see her again. She could have delayed her departure but it was obvious that she did not want to see me ever again. I felt rejected and very much alone. It did not occur to me that she might have acted in self-defense, deliberately shutting out everybody who had belonged to her past.

She had found her way. I had to find mine. Through the open window I saw the new moon and heard the murmur from the waves of the ocean — like a tune of a bygone past. My thoughts turned to home, and the next morning I placed a call to Liverpool, telling the agent that I was ready to go.

11

IT WAS LATE SUMMER in Germany when I returned, with the chill of autumn at night and warm days. Dr. von Berg was at our home when I arrived. It was not a Tuesday, the time for his regular visit, and I knew at once my father was worse. I could see from the tired expression on my mother's face that I was needed. Several days passed before my luggage was unpacked.

September 1, 1939, started out like any other day. I always awoke early in the morning and, before I was fully awake, I would look for the sun. When its rays reached my bed, I would look for my shadow on the wall. If I moved my head slightly to the side and turned my eyes all the way, I could study my profile.

On this particular day I saw no shadow, since there was no sun. But it was not the overcast sky alone that made me sense that something was different. Straining my ears, I listened intently. Where were all the usual sounds of the morning? I held my breath.

A sudden fear swept over me and I thought of my father, but the deep silence did not come from inside the house alone. I went to the window and looked down the street. It was deserted as far as my eyes could see. Even the birds seemed silent.

I was the only one up. I opened the front door and was surprised to find the front step empty; no paper or milk had been delivered.

I turned on the radio and in seconds a pompous voice told me: Hitler's troops were invading Poland. The war had finally begun.

Although I had anticipated war, now that it was here I was shocked. Stumbling backward for support as if from a blow, I fell against the piano and struck a shrill discord.

My mother was beside me when I looked up. From the radio came the first bars from the National Anthem, and I saw her reach over and turn it off.

We went upstairs to my father. My brothers joined us and

once more we were all together. After the first shock we almost felt relief. We were sure the turning point had come. The world would now know, and rush to our rescue.

As the day progressed, life resumed. The milk and the paper were eventually delivered. As we listened to the radio, the bureaucracy in control gave us our first taste of war. There was a flood of orders, restricting our lives in every possible way.

Although we were asked to believe that Germany's invasion of Poland was spontaneous, everything had been meticulously planned.

Stamps for rationing food and gasoline were issued and a general blackout ordered. I hurried to the store but, when I arrived, all the material for covering windows was gone. As I wondered what to do, it occurred to me that the war had not started that day. It had begun that morning long ago when our windows were first covered with yellow paper and black swastikas.

I thought black paper might do, to begin with at least. During our family discussion we had all agreed the war could not possibly last more than three months, four at the most.

Passing our grocery store, I saw a long line of people waiting outside and others scurrying away bent over with heavy loads of merchandise. There were still unrationed goods left, and I immediately stepped into line. I did not know what to buy but in that moment it did not matter. The mere fact that people were standing in line to get goods which might soon become scarce caused me to join them. It had taken only a few hours of war to induce my greed. It would never leave me. Even today I find it difficult to buy just one of anything.

I was swept by anxiety and panic, but I did not know what I was afraid of. I had never experienced war and did not know what actual destruction meant.

I waited hours for my turn and all that was left was scouring powder. I bought ten pounds of it and was as proud of myself as if I had achieved a major victory. Leaving the store, I held on to my package tightly, thoroughly enjoying the envious stares of the people behind me.

Guenther and Willfried were called up for active duty and their train was to leave around midnight. On this first night of serious blackout the station was dark and crowded; the voices subdued, in sharp contrast to the station in England with its sounds of vacation. The thought of John flashed through my mind, his casual question about "things in Germany" and how he had turned away and quickly moved on at my answer.

I looked at my brothers and wondered what would happen to them. Guenther and Willfried were called up as physicians; it was unlikely that Hans, a professor of mathematics, would have to go, at least not at once, and we all were convinced that the war would be over soon.

°

For our neighborhood the war started the next day. Our bell rang early in the morning and Mr. Braun stood on our doorstep. He wore a helmet, and the pants of his suit were tucked away in a pair of long brown boots. Pointing at the armband around his sleeve he announced, "I am the Warden of your precinct."

He waved us aside and stepped in.

We had never met Mr. Braun but I knew his voice. He was a teacher, close to retirement age, and he lived alone. He was stout, rather short, and his face had an angry red flush. He was at odds with all of his neighbors. The point of contention was the apple tree in his yard.

It was a huge tree with branches embracing heaven and earth, and some of them hung over the fence. Each fall they were bursting with apples, juicy and red, tempting the eyes and the hand, and, looking at them, I understood why an apple had once decided the destiny of humanity.

It was still the same. You were granted only a look. A wrong move with your hand would elicit a growl, and a touch would cause Mr. Braun to raise his voice in a thunder from the depths of his yard. It was rumored that he made daily "rollcalls" of his precious apples, and many an unexplained "absenteeism" had added to his disagreeable manner.

Today, however, he was in high spirits, casting an admiring glance at his helmet as he passed the mirror in our hall. Before we knew it he was taking our living room under inspection.

"You have heavy curtains," he remarked, while his eyes glanced toward our radio.

We appeared calm, silently watching him pace the floor, but my heart was pounding. What did he want?

At last he turned to my mother and said, "I want you to be an air-raid warden!"

I breathed a sigh of relief.

"This neighborhood needs a strong hand," he announced, "and they will get it from now on."

It sounded like another declaration of war.

He beamed. "You will be responsible for the proper blackout in your block, and you will get your own helmet" — for him the ultimate reward.

My mother's response was less than enthusiastic until she learned that, as an air-raid warden, she would have access to every house — day and night.

She broke out in a smile. "That is a wonderful job," she said, accepting.

When Mr. Braun had left, she explained, "We'll have one fear less. No air-raid warden will ever invade our home."

The skies were quiet. There was no air raid; not even an alarm was sounded. But Mr. Braun followed through with his threat. Night after night he patrolled the streets, shouting his orders into the darkness surrounding the homes. He knocked at windows and rang doorbells at the slightest suspicion of a trace of light. He even stopped passers-by with burning cigarettes in their mouths and we heard him yell, "Put it out! Don't you see that you give a light to the enemy in the air?"

One night my mother approached him. "Don't you think it is dangerous talking so loud?" she suggested, pointing at the sky. "Somebody up there might hear you."

At last we got used to his voice as another sound of the night, blending with the bits and fragments of the music from the tavern, where they were still dancing.

During the day the air vibrated with the burring sound of drills. Adjacent to Mrs. Manning's farm, bulldozers were digging into the ground bringing up a mountain of soil, leaving a deep, huge square. Then other machines arrived and poured in concrete. A massive structure emerged like a catacomb, compact, threatening and almost black. It was to be a public shelter, we learned.

o

A few weeks later I was awakened by my mother in the middle of the night. "I have sent for Dr. von Berg," she said.

He came and he stayed with us.

It was all over at dawn. The first pink showed at the horizon when I opened the window. Then I looked at my father. In the gray light of the morning the lines in his face, bearing witness to suffering, had gone. I was sad and at the same time relieved. The complete stillness of the room was reflected in my mother's face, and for a moment I grasped that my father had reached the ultimate goal of life — peace.

But when Dr. von Berg left, I broke down, suddenly understanding what my father's death meant for us. I started to cry. Never again would we sense the hope which had led us from one Tuesday to the next. Never again would I walk with my father. I was on my own.

He was part of us and that part had died. Once more I was looking at him and something came back to me. Each thought, each word, and each action leaves its trace, he had told us. His words had filled me with awe, when he first said them, but now they filled me with joy; for, if they were true, life was eternal. He would continue in us.

We sent for my brothers and we notified our friends.

We wanted my father to rest in a small cemetery above the Elbe river. We did not belong to any particular denomination and I went to a church nearby to ask the minister to perform the service.

51

He was a man in his thirties with part of his face hidden behind a mustache. "I know of him," he said vaguely, when he heard my father's name. "He was not quite in step with the times."

"He was in step with what he believed in," I retorted.

"Why are you so angry?" the minister asked. "I am willing to perform the service, but then let the past rest. You are young; you can bend. Go along — and the future will be yours."

He raised his arm and mumbled, "Heil Hitler!" as I was leaving.

I did not answer, but at the door I turned once more toward him. Taking a deep breath, I said very slowly, "We won't need your help after all."

○

We buried my father from the cemetery's chapel. It was small, but big enough for us and the few friends who had joined us. Dr. von Berg was there, and Mr. Jenkins. My brother Hans read some of my father's favorite psalms. There was no organ, but the walls of the chapel resounded from our voices when we sang the hymns.

PART TWO

12

THE NAZI TROOPS were all over Europe when the hawthorn bloomed again. In spring 1940, Denmark and Norway were invaded; Germany was at war with England and France.

"We will have to replace the black paper with sturdier material," I said, looking at our windows.

We were alone, my mother and I. Hans had been called up as research scientist at a weather station; Guenther was in Holland; and Willfried in Denmark.

One night I awoke to a screaming sound and for a moment I froze. It was the siren with its terrifying seesaw sound. After it faded, I was covered with sweat. I rushed to the window and looked up to the sky. What would an air raid be like? Would it mean fire? What was a bomb? For me it was nothing more than a word.

We did not turn on any lights, but threw on whatever we had near and rushed to the public shelter. Mr. Braun stood at the entrance, and amidst fear and excitement I suddenly laughed. He had pulled his helmet low over his face and tightened his belt. His face was flushed; he stood far back from the entrance, well protected from the outside, and directed the flow of people.

"He is the *maître d'* of the war," I whispered to my mother.

In an hour it was over. Nothing had happened. Mr. Braun stood outside when we left, holding his helmet under his arm.

"I knew they would not dare," he said to my mother, wiping the perspiration from his forehead.

The next night we stayed home, seeking shelter in our own basement. But we felt trapped. It had no door to the outside and its windows were tiny. If anything happened, we would never get out. We heard a silvery buzzing overhead. Reconnaissance planes, we were told when we turned on the radio.

They came night after night, but no bomb was dropped.

We got used to the siren; but the silvery buzzing sound stayed in my ears, coming out of the darkness from somewhere above, steady, persistent, biding its time.

Fall and winter passed by. Our life was centered around the siren. We got little sleep. No longer did I look for the sun. Only overcast skies would promise a night of rest. When the moon was out, we went to bed early, trying to catch some sleep before the siren would sound; but I tossed and turned, waiting, listening, and watching the huge beams of light searching the sky.

13

I WAS WORKING at the Postal Censorship of Hamburg. Since the beginning of the war all mail passing between Germany and abroad had to be censored. Civilians did the work, but the army was in charge, officially at least. My job was to read letters going in and out of Scandinavia. On my first day an officer handed me a manual of rules. It was thicker than any book I had read, written in obsolete language, with instructions obviously carried over from World War I.

But there were supplementary pages, too, stamped "Special Order" with big, red letters. These updated pages were clearly written in Nazi language. They were signed by an unrecognized name, and meekly initialed by an officer of our department.

Consciously I had never met any member of the Gestapo, but I was made aware of their presence one day when I was summoned to the officer in charge.

"You have been given a special assignment," he said.

He was a colonel of the army, a man in his fifties. In civilian life he was an officer at a bank. All that mattered to him was to stay safely tucked away at a desk job, remote from the hazards of war. His "Heil Hitler" was dutiful and without conviction, and his face remained passive when he passed on "Special Orders," regardless of their contents.

On that particular day his desk, usually empty, was

covered with stacks of letters. Handing me the "Special Order," he said curtly, "Read for yourself."

I had hardly begun to study the Gestapo-issued order when he said abruptly, "Get these out of here!" and shoved the letters toward me. They almost fell to the floor. I caught them in my arms.

They were tied together and I glanced at the address on top. Although it was written with a pencil, it was meticulously printed as if the writer wanted to make sure it would not go astray.

I opened the bundle of letters and saw that most of them were written not on stationery but on odds and ends of tissue papers, which the writers had folded and glued together. Many of the edges were torn.

The letters were written by Jews from the ghettos in Poland. I had heard rumors that, ever since the German occupation of Poland, the German Gestapo had driven Polish Jews into the ghetto in Warsaw. Only now did I realize that Warsaw was not the only ghetto in Poland, and that there were others crowded with Jews deported by the Gestapo from other German-occupied countries. The letters were mostly written in German and addressed to relatives and friends in Scandinavia.

The German Gestapo was in control of the ghettos; however, at this point in the war, some of the ghettos were still officially allowed to mail letters and to receive parcels — if they arrived.

But in their "Special Order" the Gestapo had found a way to cut off help. The instruction was to tear up any letter containing a plea for food. A postscript stated, "Destroy any or all of the letters you personally find objectionable."

I signed my name to acknowledge I had read the order. Then I drew a deep breath.

My chance had come. At long last I would be given the opportunity to do whatever I thought was right. But opening the very first letter, fear swept over me. It was so intense, I had to put down the sheet.

57

Why had they given this special assignment to me? Was it a trap? Would they reread my letters to make sure I complied with their order? What would I do with a letter containing a plea for help? Even if I would not destroy it, how could I bypass the mail? How could I get it to Scandinavia? I thought of no answer.

I looked around the room, for the first time really taking it in. Eyes seemed to watch me from every side. More than fifty censors were seated at long wooden tables, two yards apart. It resembled a school classroom . . .

My mind flashed to the moment when as a schoolgirl I had defied the order to say, "Heil Hitler." I remembered the night before when my father had asked me, "Is it worth the consequences you might face?"

I now understood what he meant. At that time my defiance was a childish gesture of youthful rebellion. If I were to rebel today, it would be for a cause. It would be out of deep conviction. I returned to my work with my decision made.

An afternoon stillness fell over the room and clouds of smoke from the homegrown tobacco spread a drowsy curtain over the faces. Nobody appeared to be watching me. Pulling open the drawer of my desk, I looked at my purse. It was a good-sized purse. I looked at the censor in front of me; he was a huge man resembling Mr. Jenkins. His back would shield me, and it gave me an idea: perhaps I had found a way.

That same night I carried my first letters out, and before I went home I hurried down to the port. Mr. Jenkins recognized me at once. "Back again?" he asked, tipping his hat away from his forehead.

"I have to talk with you," I whispered anxiously. "Alone."

He understood.

"You once helped me," I said after everyone had left.

I opened my purse and handed him the letters. "Will you find a boat for these, too?"

From then on I went to Mr. Jenkins week after week; and, as time progressed, I read in the letters from the Polish ghettos that parcels from Scandinavia, containing food and clothing, had reached them.

Each day I carried letters out in my purse, not many of them, only ten or twelve at a time, so they would not show. Soon, I went one step further. If there were not enough letters asking for help, I scribbled at the edge of the sheet, "Send food."

One day I came across a letter addressed to Elizabeth Levy. I was startled. It had been sent to a Denmark address where it would never reach her. I knew she had left, and I looked at the calendar, thinking of the night when I had spoken to her on the phone in England. I was stunned to see that it was exactly two years to the day, I could still hear her last words.

"Take care of yourself," she had said.

When I looked up, it was late and the others had gone. As I left the building, three men stepped in front of me.

"Gestapo. Follow us."

I was terrified. All blood drained from my face. What had happened? Had I been reported? How much did they know? What about Mr. Jenkins? Had he been arrested? All feeling left me; I was numb. Then it struck me like lightning . . . My God . . . the letters . . . my purse! I usually put in the letters before I left. Had I done it today? I could not remember.

They took me back to the office and locked the door. They reached for my purse. I stood motionless staring hard at their faces. I was amazed to discover that all three looked alike. I clutched my hands behind my back and tried to look confident.

I heard my purse click open. They held it upside down and its contents spilled out on the desk and floor. I held my breath. My eyes looked for the letters — they were not there.

My preoccupation with the Levy letter had saved me. Thank you, Elizabeth!

"It was a spot check," they said, while they helped me pick up the pieces. "We are only doing our duty."

"So am I," I replied and managed a smile.

❂

I did not go home at once but aimlessly walked the streets. My feet hurt. Still I walked on . . .

My first encounter with the Gestapo had been a close call, and I had not been prepared. How could I have explained the letters, if they had caught me? I knew of their methods of interrogation. Would I have held out or would I have given Mr. Jenkins away?

I decided to pay heed to the warning. The little I could do was not worth the risk. After all — it was not tons of food and clothing which had arrived — only a parcel here and there. It was less than a drop in an ocean and regardless of what I could do — the Jews were doomed.

I had come to the port and found myself standing in front of the statue of Bismarck. The sun was almost down. The summer clouds, wandering along the sky, were purple, lilac, and gold, but the sword Bismarck held stood firm against them like a huge, black, immovable object.

Abruptly I turned away and continued along the Elbe, looking for the path I used to walk with my father. There it was — I recognized every bush and tree, and suddenly I knew I had to go on, even though fear would always be as close as my shadow. I could not let it stop me now.

For a brief moment I believed I had grasped something of the meaning of life. By rising above my fear, I might touch the world in its course. Having made my choice I felt strangely relieved, exhilarated by a feeling of ultimate freedom.

*

My mother was waiting when I came home.

"Somebody is here to see you," she said.

The living room windows were open to the twilight, letting in the fragrance of roses from the yard. I could see only a tall outline, but I would have known him anywhere.

"Eduard!"

14

"I HAD TO COME BACK," he said, smiling.

"Why?"

"Because of you . . ."

He held out his hand but I did not take it. I was stunned. Eduard had come to me, the schoolgirl, after all! Trying to regain my composure, I moved to the window.

I was both confused and elated. First the close call with the Gestapo, then the searching of my innermost feelings and the decision finally reached that I knew would determine my life. And now before me was Eduard, representing all that I had yearned for, when I once thought life was passing me by.

I turned to Eduard; his eyes were searching mine.

"I need you," he said. "I need someone who understands me, and you accepted me from the very beginning. You understand what my art means to me. One day I want to create a painting that will reflect life as I see it. I need your love to succeed."

I was startled. The thought had never entered my mind that Eduard needed me. I had worshiped him from a distance. He had seemed aloof and strong. This was a different Eduard — or was it I who had changed?

I remembered that summer in Denmark. Eduard had hated the Nazis as much as I did; but he had turned his back, refusing to get involved, and my concern had annoyed him.

"You once told a schoolgirl that she was young and still could adapt." I looked at him across the darkening room. "I want you to know — I never did."

"Is that all you have to say?" There was a hint of anger in his voice. "Why don't you forget what you cannot change? Come with me and let us live in our own world."

For a moment I was tempted to tell Eduard about the letters I read every day — from a world I did not live in but could not shut out. Instead I asked, "Why do you want me?"

"I want you to help me find my way," he answered.

I stood by the window looking into the night. There was lightning on the horizon and the searchlights were probing the sky. I felt they were searching my heart. What was it that still tied me to Eduard? He was the first person I had loved more than myself, and one I could never forget. Yet now he was oddly out of place in my world. I sensed that Eduard had not changed. He was only longing to recapture a schoolgirl's admiration.

Again he held out his hand and again I could not take it. "Will you help me?" he asked.

"You are late, Eduard," I said, "too late. You must find your way for yourself. I have found mine, but I can only share it with someone who believes as I do."

○

I went with him to the station, relieved that he was leaving, but still not wanting to lose him completely. Like a child, clinging to an old toy, I wanted him back in his place, distant, unattainable, and yet present whenever my memory called him.

"You told me," I ventured, "that you dream of creating a painting so beautiful that it will reflect life. But I believe life itself is a painting, where each day is like a stroke of the brush. Whatever we had can never be erased."

I touched his hand and said, "Whatever I once felt for you has left its mark in my painting."

I waited in vain for an answer; and, when he stepped on the train, I asked anxiously, "Will I see you again?"

He turned around and his words fell like a blow. "You are still a schoolgirl," he said. "Don't you understand there is no in-between? Either we'll have it my way, or nothing at all."

I was bursting with anger. A few hours ago I had proudly rejected him and now I had been rejected myself. I felt humiliated and angry.

"I'll have it my way," I shouted, "and don't you ever come back!"

A jolt — and the train started to move. I saw Eduard open the window, and while the train was gaining speed, I heard his parting words, "Maybe one day, many years from now, I will be back to show you my painting!"

There was still some time left before work. I went to a little café near the station. It was empty and I was alone with the sounds of the city, coming to life, the rattle of the milk trucks and the whistle of the boy delivering the paper. I heard the scraping of a broom, and I saw an old woman sweeping the sidewalk, clearing away the debris of the night.

It would be another hot day, but this early the air was still brisk and clear. There was no cloth on the table, and after two years of war the coffee before me was chicory and water. A man entered, quickly moving from one table to the next, searching the ashtrays, hunting for cigarette butts.

Some soldiers took a table nearby. From their words I gathered they were bound for the Russian front. One of them looked at the clock. "Two more hours to go before the train is due." He yawned, stretching his legs.

"Two more hours to live," said another.

"Hell!"

There was silence.

From the harbor came the sound of a boat horn, and I left, arriving much too early at work.

o

I continued reading the letters, carrying them out as before. But one day in the fall my desk was empty. I approached the colonel, the officer-in-charge.

"What about my letters?" I asked.

"Which letters?" he asked, as if they had never existed.

"The ones from the ghettos," I said.

"There are no more letters," he answered. "Resume your regular duties."

"What has happened to the Jews?" I persisted.

He did not look up. "We are not here to ask questions," he said. "We follow orders."

o

When I returned to my desk, there was sadness in my heart

and I felt a deadly silence coming from ghettos I had never seen. Walls seemed to close in on me and my life turned gray. I felt without purpose.

Once more I looked around the room — with the same awareness I had experienced when I started my special assignment. Nothing had changed. I was surrounded by the same censors, and clouds of smoke still spread a drowsy curtain over their faces. But it had changed for me.

There was nothing more I could do here and I decided to leave. At this point anyone capable of working had to participate in war-effort employment. I had to find a valid reason to leave the Postal Censorship.

As the months went by, I was biding my time, waiting, hoping, trusting that I would find a way.

15

IN JUNE 1941, Germany began war with Russia, too, and that fall Hitler struck out against all Jews still living in Germany.

It started with the order that each Jew had to wear a yellow star of David. They had to sew it on all of their clothing, so that any Jew could be singled out.

One day standing in line in front of a store I saw a young Jewish woman with her child, both wearing the yellow star. On the mother it only covered the lapel of her suit, but on the chest of the child the yellow star seemed to be all-encompassing.

Then the final blow came.

An order was issued to all Jews in Hamburg to report early the following morning to the main railroad station.

It was late in the afternoon when our telephone rang. I answered it.

"I am Elizabeth's grandmother," a shaky voice said. "Will you come to us? It is urgent."

It was dark when I arrived. There was no light in the entrance of the building, and fumbling my way up the two flights of steps I passed the other apartments — but I heard no sound behind the closed doors.

The Levys' apartment was unlocked. Through the half-open door I saw the electric bulb still freely dangling from the cord in the hall. There was no luggage.

The Levys were waiting for me in the living room and I noticed, spread over one of the chairs, several suits, altered and pressed, ready to go.

Mr. Levy bent over the table pointing at a piece of paper. I glanced at it. Their name and address were carelessly scribbled down with a pencil, with the date and the time they were to report to the station. Underneath was the official stamp, the German Eagle resting on the Swastika, and an added note: "Five pounds of luggage."

"Thank you for coming," they said; and, looking at the paper, they added, "We wanted you here on our last evening." Their eyes went to the piano. It was closed now but on it was still the smiling girl in the photo. Mr. Levy stepped forward, took it, and laid it face down.

"We won't see her again," he said. "But maybe you will."

They looked at the clock on the wall, excused themselves and went to the kitchen, shutting the door behind them. They were back in less than a minute. Neither of them spoke. Mr. Levy's face was ashen and he bent over the table as if to get hold of himself.

Then he took my hand.

"Remember us to your mother," he said.

He must have noticed my startled expression. Before I could answer he added quietly, "She helped some of our Jewish friends out of the country."

I was stunned.

"You mean to tell me that she has been here?" I was barely able to form the words.

He nodded his head.

"She was," he said. "She offered her help to us, too."

"But why — why then did you not leave?"

"We have been here all our lives. What would we have done anywhere else?"

"But you had no choice!" I shouted on top of my voice.

Mr. Levy, turning away from me, looked at his wife.

"We must go now," he said.

Then I knew. They *had* found a way out. That minute alone in the kitchen — they had taken something.

He took the Gestapo's notice and tore it up. He pulled out a drawer and reached for a yellow envelope. It was stamped and addressed containing several papers.

"Please mail it — afterwards," he said, handing it to me.

I saw that his hands trembled.

"Stay with us a little while longer," he said.

They embraced me; and, when I saw Mrs. Levy's closed eyes I understood it was Elizabeth they were saying good-by to.

They never looked back. After they had entered the bedroom, with their arms linked to each other, they knelt down at the bedside and started to pray. I heard them but I could not understand the words. It must have been in Hebrew.

I was in a turmoil. An ocean of thoughts went tumbling through my head. I felt utterly helpless; for although I knew what was happening, it was beyond my grasp. I could not accept it.

I was near the piano. The window was closed and no sound came from the hall or the staircase. I had to do something and I ran to the window. I opened it and looked down, just searching for help. The street was deserted and I turned back to the room, suddenly remembering the ghettos and the letters which had ceased to come.

The Levys were doomed — one way or the other.

I listened to the mumbling voices from the bedroom. Then I thought of my mother. I felt disappointment and rage. The day flashed through my mind when she had asked me whether I had been back to the Levys'. Why had she not confided in me that she had gone herself? My father must have known, perhaps my brothers, too? Why had I been left out?

In these moments between life and death I was thinking only of myself. The ultimate pain I was witnessing was far in the back of my mind.

I held my breath, listening again. The mumble of the voices was fading away; I was frightened. I wanted to run to the Levys and shake them but my fear kept me back, and what was there left to do now?

Why had I not come before? When Elizabeth had left Germany, I had promised to look after her grandparents; but as soon as she was gone I had forgotten about it. I had helped people in ghettos far away and failed two friends nearby.

I was overcome with remorse. There was no chance left to make up and in my despair I did something I had never done before. I went down on my knees and started to pray. I began to say the Lord's Prayer. The last time I had said it I had been a child, and I stumbled over the lines.

". . . forgive us our trespasses," I mumbled, ". . . as we forgive those . . ."

I don't know how many minutes had passed. I looked up and saw Elizabeth's grandparents slumped over the bed, their arms still linked to each other.

The silence around me was so deep I could hear my own breath. I touched nothing, slipped the letter into my pocket and hastily left, not closing the door behind me.

°

The yellow envelope contained two letters still open, a burial policy, paid up, and a letter to Elizabeth, addressed to South America. Before mailing it I made sure that there was no return address on it, and I did not add any note.

I let one week go by before I dared go to the Jewish Cemetery. From the policy I had memorized their lot. It was way down and I passed several other graves where the soil was still fresh and black and no grass had been sodded.

It was an old cemetery. It must have been there for hundreds of years. The legions of stones, varying in shape and sizes, revealed their different eras.

Near the Levys' plot was a mountain ash tree, and in the gray light of the fall its berries looked brown and wilted. No stone or flowers marked their soil and the recently torn-up grass sods lay scattered about. I looked to all sides before I quickly took white chrysanthemums, the last ones from our yard, from my bag and placed them on the grave.

The daylight had almost faded away when I went back to the gate and found myself face to face with a woman who was about to enter. She was in black.

I recognized her immediately, and, by the expression on her face, I knew she saw me, too. It was Miss Brockdorf, my former teacher from high school. We looked at each other.

Startled, I asked bluntly, "What are you doing here?"

Her hair was white. She had aged in the years since I had seen her.

"Come with me," she answered, reaching out for my arm as if she needed support.

There by another fresh and black soil plot I learned that her roommate had been Jewish. For a lifetime they had lived together; and, when she was summoned by the Gestapo to the station, she took the same way out the Levys had.

"Do you now understand why I had to pretend from the very first day the Nazis came?" Miss Brockdorf asked. "To protect her I had to go along with them."

For a moment the bitter memory of those early days came back. In the end, her "going along" had not saved the life she had wanted to protect; but it had been the example for a class of students to follow.

Under the streetlight I discovered the many lines in her face and I took hold of myself. What right had I to argue with her?

On my way home it began to snow, the first snow of the year, melting as soon as it touched the ground.

But later in the night I awoke and opened the window. It was still snowing and the snow was beginning to pile up on our fence. I could barely see the road.

I was thinking of trains — long, endless freight trains, deporting those Jews, still alive, to the East . . .

I thought back to the summer night when I was standing at the window, listening to the fragments of music. There was no music tonight. I guessed the tavern was closed because of the snowstorm. Tomorrow they would dance again . . . someone would always dance.

But then what did it matter what anyone else might do? What would I do? This decision was mine. Where would I go from here? I did not know.

There was a stillness in the air as if the whole world had come to rest and was trying to forget what was happening. The whiteness of the snow spread a mild light and made the night less dark. I thought of the graves in the cemetery. They would be covered, too, whether they were marked by stones or not. I took a deep breath and felt free again as if I had been given another chance.

16

I WAS STILL WITH THE POSTAL CENSORSHIP when the Christmas mail began passing through. One morning in December I found a letter addressed to Santa Claus. It was in German and the clumsy printing spelled an early attempt at writing. A child had painted a Christmas tree and underneath was printed, "Send Peace!"

We passed it around the office. For a moment the clouds of despair lifted, giving way to a hope almost gone, and the tree in the letter, colored green with bright, red dots on the branches, seemed to spread a fragrance of Christmas. The colonel entered and the letter was handed to him. He glanced at it briefly and said, "I have important news."

"I want your attention." He stood very straight, showing no emotion in his face.

"Germany has declared war on America," he announced.

The smiles on the faces froze. There was deep silence. The only response was the crack of paper, as heads bent down again over letters and hands turned pages.

The colonel was still holding the letter in his hand.

"What about Santa?" I asked him at last.

"Oh, that one," he said. He shrugged his shoulders, handing it to the nearest censor. "Return it! Stamp the envelope: Cannot be forwarded. Moved to unknown address."

＊

That night I was on my way to Mrs. Manning. It had been snowing all day and there were no footprints on the road to the farm. She won't know what has happened yet, I thought, and hurried on.

The gusty winds, stirring up the silence around the shack, rattled through spouts and gutters. The icicles from the roof resembled bars in front of a cell. The mountain of coal usually shielding the north side had diminished to a size barely promising warmth for the worst of the winter.

There was no answer when I knocked at the door. It was unlocked and coming in from the night I saw the room barely lighted by the green hanging lamp which spread only a dim light over the table and chairs. A candle was fastened to a branch of pine on the table but it had not yet been lit. It was chilly and there was no heat from the stove.

"Anybody here?" I called out.

There on the wall was the postcard — the lady with the torch. The room came to life; and before I knew it, I was waving at the picture, hearing myself say, "Hello!"

But where was Mrs. Manning? I turned toward the alcove, where her bed stood. The light from the lamp did not reach there, but, listening closely, I heard harsh, rapid breathing.

I grabbed the candle, impatiently tearing the pine apart. Finding one ember still glowing in the stove, I lit the candle and carried it to the alcove, where Mrs. Manning was sitting bent forward and clasping her chest. Her face was flushed and under the blue scarf her hair seemed whiter than ever. She did not seem to know who I was.

"Is it Christmas?" she asked, staring at the burning candle. But as soon as she talked, her breath gave way. She started to cough, broke out in sweat and gurgled as if she were drowning.

I wanted to run, call for help, but I dared not leave her. All I could think of was putting my arms around her trying to give her support. It was as if she were breaking apart, and under my hands I felt her heart pound away like a racing engine.

"What has happened, Mrs. Manning?" I kept asking.

She did not hear me and I looked for her ear trumpet. It was nowhere in sight. Mrs. Manning followed my eyes. "Outside!" she gasped, "outside . . . on the fort."

I rushed out fumbling my way through the dark, and somewhere near the cabbage I found it. Back at the bedside I held the horn to her ear. She pushed it away. "Not that!" she whispered between two breaths. "The mailbox! Go to the mailbox . . ."

At last I understood. She was expecting a letter from America. Her son wrote only at Christmas, and she had been waiting for days.

I hurried out again, hoping and praying that the letter had arrived; for, if it had not, the declaration of war meant no further mail from America.

There was no letter.

When I came back, her cough had stopped, but she still bent forward. She glanced at my empty hands, leaned back, and turned her head to the wall.

I knew she could not hear me, but nevertheless I made a feeble attempt to console her. "It may come tomorrow or the day after," I said, deciding not to tell her the truth.

She must have sensed something was wrong, for suddenly she turned back, and looked at me sharply. She raised her horn to her ear and asked, "Why did you come here today?"

I kept silent, ran out to the fort, and carried in some coal, then busied myself with the fire. I watched the top of the stove and when it turned red again, I warmed some soup.

But she did not touch it. She kept looking at me and repeated, "Why did you come?"

I avoided her eyes. "I must go," I said. "I must find a doctor for you."

It had stopped snowing but the gusty winds whipped up the flurries, lashing my face. From home I called Dr. von Berg. When at last he arrived, the wind had died down. The skies were clear, the searchlights were on, and on our way to the farm the siren sounded its seesaw scream, following us into the shack. Even Mrs. Manning might have heard it; but she lay back in her bed, barely moving her head.

"Pneumonia," Dr. von Berg said, listening to her chest. "I'll have to take her to the hospital."

Mrs. Manning shook her head. "I must stay here," she whispered.

Dr. von Berg looked over to me and I took him aside. "Her son lives in America," I explained. "He writes once a year at Christmas. She has been waiting for his letter for days."

"But did you not tell her what has happened?" Dr. von Berg interrupted.

"She was too ill to be told."

"Too ill for the truth?" There was disbelief in his voice, and he went back to her.

I stayed behind.

"Your life is at stake," I heard him say.

"I cannot leave," she insisted.

"I think I know why," he answered. "But you are waiting in vain. Germany, today, has declared war on America."

I was startled by his directness. A life was hanging by a thread. Did he not realize, as a physician, that it might be crushed by the news? I bent forward, listening intently for Mrs. Manning's response.

For a moment she was quiet, then she began to cry. "What more is there to live for?" she sobbed. "Why shouldn't I die?"

"You have a life of your own," Dr. von Berg answered curtly.

The alarm was still on, and high above in the sky was a buzzing sound . . . steady and persistent. Although the war was far away, for the first time it became real to me. It was touching this shack and a life close to me. I got up and went to the alcove, anxious to talk to Mrs. Manning.

She ignored me, reaching instead for Dr. von Berg. "I will go," she said to him. "I trust you . . . you told me the truth."

Her words struck as if she had slapped my face. I went

back to my corner and waited out the alarm in silence, pretending to be asleep.

Through my half-closed eyes I watched Dr. von Berg. He had not hesitated to tell the truth. I remembered he had been the same way with my father. From the beginning he had told the facts about my father's illness . . . there was no cure. But at the same time he had never ceased to instill his belief that life, even in the limitations of an illness, was to be lived to the fullest.

I began to understand why Dr. von Berg seemed unmoved by the events of the time. He was devoted to serving life itself, to touching the individual, and to creating a bond that reached far beyond the surface of most human relationships. Tonight I recognized in him an example of what I had strived to achieve all my life.

Suddenly I knew what I wanted to do. It seemed so obvious that I wondered why I had not thought of it before. I wanted to become a physician.

There was the long-drawn sound of the siren, ending the alert. I got up and went to call for an ambulance. Outside dawn had come with the first light at the horizon. The nearest phone was at the Public Shelter, and the last of the people were leaving when I arrived. Among them was Mr. Braun. He wore ear muffs under his helmet. In the icy coldness of the morning his words came like steam from his mouth.

"Another long night," he said, "and again nothing has happened."

A great deal had happened to me.

❋

A few days later I got my release from the Postal Censorship. Medical training was considered a higher priority in the interest of warfare. Dr. von Berg had written a letter of recommendation and the University of Hamburg had accepted me for the premedical course.

I registered one day near the end of January and, when I

came home from the University, there were two letters in the mail, one from the District Attorney of Hamburg, asking me to appear. Probably some translations, I thought, putting the letter aside.

The other had no return address, but I recognized the shaky handwriting. There was a note in the envelope — and something more!

"I am back home," Mrs. Manning had written. "Here is your Christmas present. It comes late, but then, haven't we learned to wait?"

It was the postcard with the Statue of Liberty and her son's address. On the other side she had scribbled, "Maybe you will see her one day!"

For the longest while I looked at the face of the lady with the torch. I thought I detected a smile.

17

JUST A WEEK LATER I started my premedical studies. The first day I found myself in an auditorium with more than a hundred students. The building was not much more than a barrack, hurriedly put together for the added needs of the war.

A hum of anticipation was in the air. We sat on long wooden benches; and, turning my head back and forth, I studied the faces around me. I did not know any of them. They seemed much younger than I, and many of them were soldiers. The wooden planks of the floor sounded hollow under the nervous rap of their heavy boots. Their eyes had a look of determination — it was either this bench or the front lines.

It was my one chance, too. I could hardly wait for the lecture to begin. When I opened my purse to pull out my notebook, the letter from the District Attorney's office fell to the floor. I had made an appointment to meet him after today's session. I stuffed it back into my purse; and, opening my notebook, I eagerly scribbled the date at the top of the first page: January 30, 1942.

Through the window of the barrack I saw a piece of the gray wintry sky. Although it was covered by clouds, I envisioned new horizons — six years from now, I would be a physician!

One lecture later I was not quite so sure. My confidence changed to doubt, when I realized I had forgotten even the most simple fundamentals of chemistry. Was it only eight years ago that I had graduated from high school? I barely remembered the chemical symbol for water. How could I ever catch up?

There was only one way out — I would have to start from scratch, going back to my high school chemistry book. One class later I was regressing to junior high physics; the law of gravity had escaped me.

Again I looked around, hoping for any signs of frustration on the faces of the other students. While the lecture rolled over me like a wave, they appeared to understand what was being said. My eyes got heavier, and at last I felt as if I were adrift in an ocean with no more land in sight.

❋

On my way to the District Attorney I made up my mind. I would give him notice that I would no longer work for the Court. To catch up I would need every moment to study.

He was an elderly man, pale, with deep shadows under his eyes. He sat in a chair with a very high back, but it was not quite high enough to cover Hitler's picture on the wall behind him. There was an unwritten law that Hitler's picture had to be on each and every wall. By its size you could almost tell the degree of Hitler's presence. This picture was small.

The District Attorney did not salute with "Heil Hitler" but only nodded his head, and kept his hands tightly pressed together.

"I have an assignment for you," he said.

"I cannot accept it," I replied quickly. "I only came here to tell you . . ."

He did not hear me out. "This is a *special* assignment," he said.

His words startled me. I had heard them before, and I glanced at his desk. It was empty.

"Several hundred prisoners have been sent to Hamburg's prison," the District Attorney said. "They are political prisoners from Norway, civilians arrested by the Gestapo for resisting the German occupation. We need you to censor their mail."

Stacks of letters flashed through my mind . . . letters I had read for months . . . letters no longer permitted, and perhaps even the people who had written them no longer alive. Had I ever really helped them? This question haunted me constantly. Despite my efforts their future was destined.

If I were to try again, would not the result be the same? If I had been unsuccessful before, why would my help be more useful now? But then if I did not try, how could I ever know? After all, this job offered to another might only be a position.

Yet, if I wanted to be a physician, I would need every minute for my studies. I hesitated.

"You have the necessary qualifications," the District Attorney insisted; "and, besides," he added, "you have been recommended to us. We trust you!"

I looked up quickly. His words came as a surprise. Who could have recommended me for this job? I was not a Party member. I did not know anybody in the penal system. Who could it possibly have been?

His fingers drummed on the desk. He was waiting, while I looked around trying to find an answer. At last my eyes stopped at the calendar on the wall: January 30, 1942.

Here in this room I remembered what had escaped me earlier this morning, when I had written the date in my notebook. It was exactly nine years ago that I had awakened to a window covered with yellow paper and black swastikas. I had had to scratch for the light.

"I will accept the assignment," I said quietly.

°

I continued my premedical studies, going back to my books from high school and stubbornly calling back facts which had slipped from my mind. But late at night I was again reading letters, stacks of them.

They were sent to me daily from Hamburg's prison. Thick letters from Norway and thin, single-page ones, written by the prisoners themselves. Each time a list was enclosed stating crimes and sentences of the prisoners whose letters I was to censor. It was the same crime over and over again: "Resistance against the Third Reich," and, for most of them, "Solitary confinement for life."

The prisoners could write only once every six weeks, fifteen lines in all. Their letters were strangely anonymous in content, and not even the strictest censor would have found anything objectionable. As hard as I tried I found no clue to the kind of persons they were. Only occasionally did I catch a glimpse of their inner selves — a handwriting, a sentence, or maybe only a word.

I noticed one letter whose writer had to be very young. His name was Bjoern Simoness. Though he expressed himself in an awkward way, his handwriting showed a rare beauty. He might be an artist one day — if he survived.

Another prisoner wrote to his wife, closing his letter with "Your happy and free Frederik." What man was he to be happy and free in the confinement of a prison?

Why were these prisoners placed under the jurisdiction of the Department of Justice, when other members from the Norwegian Underground Movement were sent by the Gestapo without trial to German concentration camps? Would my prisoners eventually be transferred, too?

I remembered the letters from the Polish ghettos. Their names and addresses had faded from my mind, as if they had never existed. I could not let that happen again. Whatever the outcome might be, I would not let go of the Scandinavian prisoners' existence.

From the very first day I started a file, printing a card for each prisoner with his name and home address, his serial number at the prison, and adding any piece of information I could pick out from the letters written to him.

In the daytime I continued attending my classes at the

University. At night I read letters. I barely listened anymore to the siren. Sometimes I heard in the distance a detonation and the fire of an antiaircraft gun. It seemed far away. More Norwegian prisoners were arriving every day. One year went by and I had over a thousand cards in my file.

It was spring again when one night I read a letter containing only a single sentence.

"*I AM ALIVE.*"

The words did not even touch the printed line of the sheet, as if the man who had written them needed no support.

His name was Gunnar Dal.

18

APRIL 1943. Easter was late that year. Not that it mattered. One day was now like all the others. We did not expect any of my brothers to come home for the holiday. Hans was still at the weather station, Guenther was in Holland, and Willfried was three hundred miles away in a rural area in Germany. Though the war had not touched my family with bullets or bombs, it was in and around us; and I could no longer remember what peace was like.

The day before Easter I stood in front of our house, looking at the hawthorn. We had been short of fuel this past winter and one cold night both my mother and I had been tempted; but the hawthorn was still there, and it was now covered with tiny buds. Even in the dusk of the evening it had a rosy shine.

From down the road I heard the sound of a helpless bleating. A man in uniform was walking toward me with something white and wiggly under his arm. When he came close, I recognized Willfried. He was holding a lamb.

"A farmer gave it to me," he said.

It was only a few days old, and touching it I felt its heart racing. But suddenly it stopped bleating and began to sniff at one of the hawthorn branches.

"I got my orders for Russia," Willfried said in a matter-of-fact tone. "I have to leave early tomorrow morning."

It was almost dark now and we took the lamb to Mrs. Manning's. She was still in the field putting in seedlings. A good strong smell came from the freshly plowed soil. The lamb had quieted down and was asleep in Willfried's arms.

"Will you keep it for us?" we asked.

She nodded her head and silently put the lamb into the basket which had held her seedlings. Then she turned to Willfried. Lifting her horn to her ear, she spoke loudly, "When will this war end?"

Willfried shook his head and smiled wanly. As if he could know.

She walked behind us down the road, carrying the basket. We did not speak; but, when we parted, the lamb awoke and started to bleat again.

The night was clear and huge floodlights searched the sky. Soon the siren would go. We would stay up all night, anyway, just to be with Willfried in the short time he had left.

The next morning, when we returned from the railroad station, the house seemed quieter than ever.

°

The following day I got a call from the Warden of Hamburg's prison.

"The District Attorney has another assignment for you," he said. "The Department of Justice has granted the political prisoners the same rights as the criminal ones. They may now get a visit every four months. We want you to be in charge."

Here was the opportunity I had been waiting for! It no longer crossed my mind that I would have still less time for my medical studies. I smiled — I would finally meet the prisoners — my friends as I secretly called them. But I gave my voice a disapproving tone when I asked, "Who here in Germany would want to visit a Norwegian prisoner?"

"The Norwegian Seamen's Pastor has applied," the Warden answered. "He usually takes care of Scandinavian sailors. His church is somewhere near the docks."

However, the Warden hastened to add that the Pastor would not be allowed to come in his capacity of minister. He would be admitted only as a representative of the families in Norway.

"You will be responsible for every word and action during the visits," the Warden said, launching on a lengthy explanation of rules and regulations governing the prison.

I had stopped listening. My mind flashed to the day when I had set out to find Mr. Jenkins . . . the monument of Bismarck . . . the hundred steps down to the port. Amidst the row of old houses on the pier I had seen the modern brick structure, built like a ship with a mast-like steeple.

"Look up the minister," the Warden finished his instructions. "Make it clear to him that we don't want any sermons or prayers."

I did not waste any time and went the same afternoon. There was spring in the air and hope in my heart when I arrived at the Norwegian Seamen's Church.

I crossed the doorstep and found myself standing at the foot of a steep staircase. I looked up. At the top of the stairs stood a tall young man, motionless, making no effort to greet me.

Eagerly I went up with my hand stretched out.

Ignoring my hand he spoke without warmth: "So you are the one who will be in charge of my visits?"

"Yes, but . . ."

He cut me off. "There is nothing to say! I'm Reverend Svendsen — I'll abide by your German rules, and you let me know when we can begin."

o

I had to wait for my official appointment to come through; and when I was summoned again to the District Attorney's office, the Prison Warden was present. He was a small, bald-headed man.

"Heil Hitler!" he said measuring me coldly through his narrow eyes and apparently disapproving of what he saw.

"Heil Hitler!" I replied, trying to sound pleasant.

"You are now a member of the Department of Justice," the

District Attorney said, shaking hands with me. "Here is your credential."

It was a small green card, smooth as wax. I quickly signed my name.

"She is much younger than you told me," I heard the Warden say. His voice sounded angry. I glanced at my photo on the card. He was right — that girl looked rather serious and older than her years. I thought of Eduard. "Much too preoccupied!" he had said.

Then my eyes caught a line in bolder print at the bottom, "The owner of this card may carry a gun."

"I am short of guards," the Warden said. "I can spare none of my men to sit in on your visits."

I would be on my own!

"You will not only be in charge of their visits," the Warden continued. "These political prisoners are the worst enemies of the Third Reich. Since you understand their language, we want you to report whatever might sound suspicious to you. We want you to keep an eye on the minister, too, and remember: no prayers or sermons."

That night when I was in my room I studied my green card closely. It would not give me access to concentration camps. They were sealed off by the Gestapo. But it was my key to any penal institution, run — at least officially — by the German Department of Justice. I would be in charge of men who had been sent there for the sole reason that they had resisted a political system imposed on their country — as it had been on mine.

I was on their side, but the Norwegian minister had let me know that for him a German and a Nazi were one and the same thing. I wondered how I could ever get them to trust me . . . and if I did, how could I actually help them? All afternoon I had been indoctrinated with the prison's rules and regulations and additional "Special Orders." They would be walls blocking my way.

Sleep would not come. I tossed and turned. I remembered something more. At the end of the session the Warden had asked, "Do you realize what will happen to you if you break any rules?"

○

We started the very next day. It was the first warm day of May, and our hawthorn was almost in bloom. I met the Norwegian minister at the prison gate. He was as aloof as before. Without any comment he handed me the list of prisoners he wanted to see. There were about twenty names. He must have got hold of them through their families in Norway.

Two of them caught my eye. They were no strangers to me. I remembered the handwriting of Bjoern Simoness, awkward in its youth but of a promising beauty. Neither had I forgotten the line, "Your happy and free Frederik."

I could not resist. Pointing at their names, I eagerly asked Reverend Svendsen, "Do you know them?"

"Do you?" was his curt reply, cutting me off.

I turned to ring the bell and thought to myself, "Perhaps I know them better than you do." Waiting, I looked around. I had passed by here before, but the prison wall was even higher than I had remembered.

An elderly guard let us in. He seemed puzzled as he took a second look at my credential and shook his head: "You are the first woman official we have ever had — you are just a young girl!" and he added with an almost fatherly concern, "Are you not afraid . . . ?"

Yes, I *was* afraid.

He led us through three different courtyards, down halls and narrow passageways with bars in front and behind us. There was a key for each door. Each time it was locked, hope seemed further away; and within the gloom of these walls I forgot that I was still free to come and to go.

The small visiting room was located at the end of a long corridor. The only furnishings were a wooden table and benches. The guard took the list and counted the names.

"Twenty pieces," he said.

We waited. The sounds of life I was used to had ceased.

The world outside no longer existed. All I could hear was my own breath. The air was stale. I felt chilly in my summer dress. Where had the light and the warmth of the May day gone? I looked up to the bars at the window but could only see a tiny piece of the sky — and another wall full of barred windows — black holes, devoid of life.

I walked to the window and stood on tiptoe. Down in the courtyard I spotted some motion. Prisoners in black uniforms with yellow stripes. They walked in a circle. It took them the longest time to finish one round — as if each step was an effort.

There was something peculiar in their walk. It was mechanical, as if their steps were directed by some central force. They walked with their heads bent down, never looking up, yet each of them kept the same distance . . .

A guard was sitting nearby. A gun dangled from his shoulder; and, as he stretched his legs, he yawned.

There was something more in the courtyard. Hidden away in the corner stood a chestnut tree. Though its branches were bent and crooked, arrested in their growth by the wall, it was in bloom. The blossoms resembled candles, upright and proudly insistent in their claim to life.

Turning back to the room, I saw on the wall a row of posted rules and regulations, and Hitler's picture. I felt the white of his eyes with their button-like stare directed at me.

"Did you bring your Bible?" I asked Reverend Svendsen.

Before he could answer we heard a commotion in the hall. The door was flung open.

"They are here!" the guard shouted. "Help yourself!"

Then he left.

As soon as the sound of his boots had died down, I stepped out. There they were, ten on each side, two yards apart. They had to stand with their faces toward the wall. Through their wornout uniforms I could see every bone in their bodies. Only their legs and feet were heavy.

As I looked at their feet, I saw myself as a child standing at the station at the end of World War I . . . looking at the soldiers, or had they been prisoners of war? . . . staring at their foot wrappings, following their slow, halting steps, listening to the click of their wooden shoes.

○

We saw the prisoners, two at a time. No guard was in the room. Still, there was one person too many. There was a smile of surprise when Reverend Svendsen addressed them in Norwegian, but one glance at me and their faces closed up. Each word was carefully weighed and very little was said.

I caught Bjoern Simoness' eyes when he sat opposite me and I could read his mind, "Why would a woman take on the job of spying on us?"

I found out that he had been arrested while still in high school. He had to be as young as I had guessed from his letters; but his face looked flushed, and I noticed his dry cough.

"How are you, Bjoern?" the minister asked.

"I am in solitary confinement," he answered. The words came slowly, "I have been there for quite some time."

Then we met Frederik Ramm. It was hard to tell his age, but I guessed him to be about sixty. He was not only the editor of a newspaper in Norway, he had also participated in one of the expeditions to the North Pole. He had written several books, but mostly he was known for his work in trying to further understanding between nations.

Of course, at that time I did not know who he was. Still, there was something which set him apart from the others, something difficult to define in words. I sensed his strength, tempered by kindness, his scholarly wisdom, and a timeless innocence, which defied both his surroundings and the emaciated state of his body.

He shook hands with the minister; but, after exchanging a few words, he turned toward me. He looked as if he wanted to ask a question; then, as if reaching his conclusion without it, he smiled and stretched out his hand.

We talked freely about the war, about Norway, and his years of solitary confinement.

"Life has to be lived at its fullest, even now in its limitations," he said.

Frederik reminded me of my father. Before he left, something happened.

"Let us pray," he said, folding his hands.

It came so unexpectedly that I was startled. Not being used to praying in the presence of others, I was embarrassed, but I folded my hands. I was so overwhelmed that I did not even realize it was the first prison rule I would break!

Frederik prayed in his own words and, coming to a close, I heard him pray for me. "Protect her in the work she has taken upon her," he said.

It was a moment I would not forget. The gloom in and around me lifted. One prisoner had given me trust, had prayed for me. Why, I don't know. The heart has its own reason. But it took only one man to tear down a wall!

"I think I have my Bible with me," Reverend Svendsen said before I called in the next prisoner.

"I thought so all along," I answered.

Our work had begun.

19

"HEIL HITLER!"

The heavy prison gate was closed behind us. We were out.

"It was a good day," the minister said before we took off in different directions.

But my moment of elation had passed. Words are stones, when you need bread, I thought, feeling tired. A truck passed by, packed with soldiers, some children were playing in the courtyards, and a boy was throwing a ball against the prison wall. He kept on throwing it higher . . .

"Watch out!" his mother called from behind the fence.

"Don't worry, the wall is high!" the boy shouted back cheerfully.

I looked up to the sky. Another day had gone by and the sun was ready to set. It was warm, unusually warm for this time of the year, and I noticed some clouds turning fiery red — they said that meant rain. I hoped it held true. I needed a long night of rest.

At home I went up to my room. I would have a test the next morning and had not yet studied for it. I pulled the shades and turned on the lamp on my desk; but, instead of opening my books, I began to pace the floor restlessly.

At last I sat down and started to read prisoners' letters. They had come alive today. I thought of Bjoern's flushed face, heard again his dry cough and saw the prisoners walking in the circle. I had wondered why they walked slowly. Now I knew. "Edema" was the medical term for their swollen ankles.

I pushed my medical books aside. How could I study, settle for shallow words when life was calling on me? Yet what really could I do? All I could give was words, and words are stones when you are hungry.

I went down to my mother. Could she read my mind? She asked no questions, yet she always seemed to know.

"You must have faith!" she urged.

She had said it before when I doubted, but I was not as trusting.

She led me outside. "Look at the hawthorn!"

Its buds, dormant for so many months, had opened, and the tree was covered with blossoms. The moon was up. The beams of the searchlights were creeping over the sky and I suddenly remembered. I said, "I must go to see Mrs. Manning."

०

She was still in the field pulling weeds. I had not seen her since we had brought her the lamb, and I signaled to her that I wanted to talk. She went up to the shack to fetch her ear trumpet and I sat down on the ground to wait. The soft light of the moon was over the field and I ran my fingers over the soil. It was dry; the plants needed rain. The strawberries were late blooming, and the cabbage and potatoes had a long way to go.

"Today I met people who are on the edge of starvation," I told Mrs. Manning when she returned. "They have no way of helping themselves. May I come back one day and ask you . . ."

I broke off, feeling foolish. What was I talking about? Even if I had all the food in the world, it would not help . . . there were walls, there was a gate to pass . . .

Without answering Mrs. Manning dropped her horn into the basket and knelt again, silently working the ground. Soon her ear trumpet was covered by weeds, and only when the basket was filled did she get up.

"I will help you," she said. "But it takes time for the seed to grow."

She wiped her hands in the apron, straightened her blue scarf and repeated, "Yes, it takes time."

It was dark now. There was thunder in the distance.

"It is going to rain," she said, stretching out her hand as if she wanted to catch the very first drops.

She led me to the shack, leaving the basket behind; and as we came nearer, I saw our lamb. It was tied to one of the apple trees but was tearing at its rope, bleating and pacing back and forth.

"It is scared," Mrs. Manning said. "It senses the storm."

She bade me wait; and, while she went up to the shack, the lamb came close to sniff at my shoes, rubbing its head against my knee. It felt good and warm.

Mrs. Manning returned with a bar of chocolate in her hand. "I got it from somebody in exchange for potatoes," she said. "I want you to have it."

It was wrapped in silver paper. Real chocolate — I had almost forgotten the smell. It smelled like birthday and Christmas; it smelled like peace . . .

I put it into my purse. "It was a good day, after all!" I exclaimed and on the spur of the moment I gave Mrs. Manning a hug.

It took her by surprise and she smiled — the biggest smile ever.

Then I was on my way. I could no longer see her, and I

knew she would not hear me; but I waved and called into the dark, "Good-by, Mrs. Manning . . . Good-by!"

◦

Later that night I awoke. The storm was over us and lightning and thunder came so close together that I could barely count them apart. The lightning flared into my eyes, even when they were shut. Suddenly I heard a sizzling sound in the air, like a whistle, then a crash and a detonation. The house rocked and for a moment I froze — it sounded like a bomb. But I had heard no alarm; and, as nothing more happened, I settled down, convinced that the turmoil of the storm had tricked my mind.

I was dozing off, not really asleep, but far enough away to lose track of time . . .

I heard the siren and wondered why it came after the crash, but I was too exhausted to move and its seesaw scream was drowned by the thunder. Then came the first drops of rain, soft taps to begin with and later hammering and pouring as if the sky were to empty itself. I heard the siren again. This time it was a long, monotonous sound — end of the alarm. Soon I was falling off into deep sleep.

It was dawn when I awoke. I could hear peculiar noises and suddenly I was wide awake. I sat up and listened . . . the wretched sounds were cutting through the stillness with the sharpness of a knife. I leaped out of my bed, pushing the table aside to get to the window. But the sounds did not come from the yard and I ran to the front . . .

There it was — our lamb!

It was standing under the hawthorn bleating into the dawn — sounding like a trumpet. I opened the window, and, as soon as it heard me, it looked up. Its wool was streaked by the rain.

I threw on a coat and ran out.

The ground was red with blossoms from the hawthorn and several of its branches were slashed down by the storm. The lamb clumsily stepped over them to get closer to me. A piece of rope was still hanging from its neck.

"So you tore yourself loose," I said, petting its head and trying to calm it down.

"How in the world did you make it all the way here?" I asked. "Well, after all, it was your first storm — next time you won't be afraid."

But the lamb was trembling all over and continued its wretched bleating.

"Come on, let's go home," I suggested, taking the rope.

I felt the first rays of the sun on my face when we set out. The raindrops on trees and lawns glittered like thousands of diamonds, and the air was pure. I took a deep breath, and, coaxing and pulling the lamb along, I set off for Mrs. Manning's farm.

As I came near her fields I saw several men and women gathered together. I recognized Mr. Braun. His helmet was still on his head, but his tie was loose.

"They only got by because of the storm," I heard him say. "But just wait — one of these days we'll pay them back!"

I let go of the lamb and grabbed his arm, "What happened?"

"What happened?" he repeated. "Don't you know?"

He pulled his tie tight and pompously announced, "The Americans have dropped their first bomb on my precinct!"

"Never mind your precinct!" I cried. "What happened to Mrs. Manning?"

"She is dead," he said. "It was a direct hit."

I pushed him aside and ran up to the shack . . .

Nothing was left but rubble, half-burned wood and ashes.

I stood still, unable to move, until I heard the lamb behind me. It was back under its apple tree and sniffed at the loose end of the rope which was still hanging from the stem.

Our hawthorn was old, but this apple tree was young and had weathered the storm without losing as much as a twig. The fresh green of its leaves and its veil of pinkish blossoms had defied death.

"Wait here!" I said to the lamb, tying together the loose

ends of the rope. It had stopped bleating; but its eyes seemed to ask, "Where are you going to send me?"

I quickly turned away.

○

"Did you know Mrs. Manning?" a young woman questioned me when I was back on the road.

"She was old, all by herself," she told Mr. Braun. "She had nothing to live for . . ."

They were about to go but they still lingered on, standing near the strawberry field where Mrs. Manning had been working only the night before. Just a few yards away I spotted her basket. I went over and knelt down on the ground. It was soaked and the weeds in the basket were dripping wet, but her ear trumpet was still down at the bottom. I took it, hiding it under my coat.

I could have left then but I stayed, waiting for Mr. Braun and his people to go. I did not want them to see me cry.

○

The postcard of the lady with the torch still hung on the wall in my room. I addressed her in English to make sure that she would understand.

"I would have liked you to meet her," I said. "She was a fine woman, like you, but she did not quite make it . . ."

Maybe her ear trumpet would. It looked old and battered, but I carefully wrapped it and locked it away in my desk.

Some time later that day I took a farmer to Mrs. Manning's place to pick up the lamb. I left before he loaded it on his truck.

20

I WAS EXHAUSTED, but I tried to shut what had happened out of my mind, attended classes, studied and took tests. At home late in the evenings I read letters.

Through the open window came the fragments of music from the tavern . . . stomping . . . they were still dancing. I tried not to listen.

After midnight the siren began screaming. Now it filled me with terror and we decided to go to the shelter.

Mr. Braun stood in the entrance. "Standing room only!" he proudly announced.

"At last they realize that they have to depend on us," he said turning to my mother, generously sharing with her what he considered a victory of his own.

No seats on the benches were left. We stood shoulder to shoulder — one big mass of people. We were talking loudly, as if to deafen our fears, but as time passed and the air remained quiet, we toned down.

We got drowsy, one after the other sagging down to the floor, arranging and rearranging ourselves to find room for our legs, and the silence was only interrupted by an occasional mumble or the sudden outcry of a child.

Nothing happened, but after last night's surprise attack everyone had become cautious. The alarm lasted longer than ever. Beside me an infant was sleeping in a carriage. His mother was also asleep, but her foot kept rocking the carriage . . .

My eyes were burning and I buried my face in my hands. I thought of Mrs. Manning, trying to undo what had happened in my mind and to force her back to life. I envisioned her in the field; I saw her kneel on the ground and watched her working the soil. Her face was hidden from me; still the blue scarf she wore summer and winter signaled her silent presence. But then she faded away . . .

All that was left was rubble and wood and ashes.

I clasped my hands. She did not die. She was killed. Her life was cut off like a rope, with its ends hanging loose . . .

I looked toward my mother. How could I have "faith" in life when I had seen it so senselessly destroyed?

❉

Only a few days later, we were visiting a Norwegian prisoner in one of Hamburg prison's outposts, a camp where they were cutting peat. It was far out in the country and we could find it only by following elaborate directions.

There was no station where we got off the train, just a sign near the tracks. It was a one-way sign with the name of the camp pointing down a dirt road. Here in the middle of nowhere, I remembered that I had heard of this place before — long before I had started my prison work. I wondered from whom . . .

It was a long walk on the dirt road. The clouds were hanging deep over this flattened brown earth, and before and behind us was nothing but the dust raised by our steps. The road came to an end at a gate.

The barracks behind the barbed wire were like clusters of gray spots, lost incidentals in this vastness of peat bogs where the only sign of life was the humming of flies, and some bluebells, hiding away in the weeds.

I rang the bell, and the air was pierced by a maddening howl. German shepherd dogs, a whole pack of them, fell over each other as they rushed toward the gate.

"Shall I let them loose?" the guard said, barely attempting to make it sound like a joke.

I held up my green card and he stood at attention.

He took us to the Commander and in the deserted barrack our steps sounded hollow. The prisoners were out cutting peat. They were cutting seven days a week.

"Visit?" the Commander grinned. "We don't have a visiting room. Nobody ever bothered to visit when we had only the Germans."

Now they had political prisoners from thirteen nations.

"I don't understand their language but they all understand mine," the Commander said, swinging his club — a solid shaft covered with rubber.

Then I remembered.

This was the place where they had taken Mrs. Manning's husband. One day she had told me, "It was the kind of camp where you either survived or died."

Her husband had died.

o

A guard took us out to the peat bog. We stood waiting, while he walked on to the edge of the pits and shouted the name of the prisoner we had come to see down into the black silence.

Although hundreds of men were working in the pits we could see no one. It took a long time for our man to appear; and in this wide empty space it looked as if he were climbing from his grave.

He walked slowly, driven toward us by the guard's shouts. We greeted him in Norwegian but he did not respond. I looked at his hands. They were a bruised mass of flesh, bloody and torn.

"I have a letter with me — from your wife," Reverend Svendsen said and began reading it aloud.

The prisoner barely seemed to be listening. His face was unmoved as if her words did not reach him. His hands fumbled in his pockets looking for something he could not find. At last he brought it out — a wedding band.

"It does not fit anymore," he said.

There was the humming of the flies, and from the distance came an occasional howl of the dogs. Time was running out.

How could I break this death spell, if only for a short moment?

I thought of Mr. Manning and I felt helpless. From the bog came the shouts of the guard. He stood with his back to us; and while I watched him closely, I opened my purse. I still had Mrs. Manning's chocolate and with trembling fingers I tore off the silver paper. Then — inch by inch — I shoved it over into the prisoner's hand.

A sweet taste in the mouth, a moment of kindness — it would pass, not changing the outcome of whatever might happen. Maybe he would die as Mr. Manning had done.

None of us knew what was ahead; death was a part of our way of life. Mrs. Manning had died, but in this moment she lived.

The minister opened his Bible. "The Lord is my shepherd . . ." he read.

I had heard the words before, but for the first time I

93

understood what they meant. As I listened, I forgot where I was, not even aware that the guard was looking in our direction.

❂

I was back in class the next morning. The wooden benches of the auditorium were tightly packed. We were sitting side by side, soldiers in their uniforms, officers with shoulder pieces and decorations, war widows, and young girls.

"Ladies and gentlemen," the professor started, "today I want to talk about fat . . ."

I heard the rattle of the paper. Hundreds of copybooks were opened and pens were ready to write.

"Last winter you had your first course in the dissecting room," the professor continued. "You worked on corpses, studied the skin, muscles, and organs. But one thing you missed out on, and for this I want you to accept my apologies . . ."

For a fraction of a second he paused.

"You missed out on fat!" he resumed. "We had no way of letting you dissect fatty tissue. Sorry, but those corpses were poor material — they were prisoners who had either perished or were executed in camps."

Hundreds of students were listening, but their faces stayed blank and their hands did not move. Nothing had been said worth putting on paper.

The professor stepped over to the blackboard and took up the chalk. The audience came to life, and brains and pens went to work. With their heads bent over their notebooks, they were eagerly drawing the big grapelike structures of fat cells.

I did not begin. I had pushed my notebook aside and looked at my purse. It was the same large-sized purse I had used for carrying out the letters from the ghettos. Impatiently, I followed the hand of my watch, barely able to wait till the end of the class. At the first sound of the bell I left.

I headed for the port. I ran as if every minute counted, passing Bismarck's monument without as much as a glance at

94

it, hurrying down the steps, not stopping until I reached one of the old battered houses on the dock.

I had not been there for some time, but nothing had changed. It was a warm day and the tiny windows on the ground floor were open. There were the sounds of the ships' bells, and Mr. Jenkins sat in his huge armchair in front of the wooden table which made do as his desk.

"I knew you would be back," he said and pushed his hat away from his forehead, not looking the least surprised.

His words startled me. How could he have known? He gave me no time to think.

"What do you have in your purse today?" he inquired.

"Nothing, Mr. Jenkins," I replied. "This time there is nothing to be taken out of the country. But I need your help in getting something in."

I wanted vitamin tablets. Lots of them — as many as my purse could hold without showing when I passed through the prison gate. Vitamins had become scarce in Germany and were only given out on special prescription.

"I'll try to get one of the ships to bring some from Sweden," Mr. Jenkins said without asking any questions.

It would take weeks; and, in the meantime, any amount, even a small one, would do. I went to Dr. von Berg.

"Are they for yourself?" he inquired, looking sharply at me.

"No, they are not," I quietly replied.

He did not demand an explanation. But, as he was writing out the prescription, he shook his head.

"Why don't you concentrate on your medical studies?" he asked. "The help you can give some day as a physician will be much more important than what you do now — at so great a risk."

I thanked Dr. von Berg and stubbornly asked, "Does it really matter how important my work is? Isn't it the effort that counts?"

◦

95

"The Warden wants to see you," the guard at the gate said when we were back at the prison.

I had with me my first batch of vitamins.

"You have been reported," the Warden said with tight lips and an icy stare in his eyes. "Did you allow the minister to read from the Bible?"

Chills went up my spine but I thought hard and fast, instantly realizing where the report came from. The guard at the peat bog! Even from the distance he must have picked up what went on. I had made a mistake.

"Didn't I tell you what will happen to those who are helping the enemy?" the Warden asked.

I pressed my purse closer to me but outwardly I was calm, calmer than ever before. From now on I would play it their way. I had observed for years, and now it was time to apply it. Threat I would counteract by threat, intimidation by intimidating. By using their methods I might lose or wind up despising myself, but whatever the outcome I had no more choice.

"I suggest you be more careful with your wording," I coldly encountered. "Who do you think I am?"

The Warden seemed startled and I could almost read his mind. He knew I was a member of the Department of Justice, but was I a member of the Gestapo, too?

I took one more chance. It was nothing but a wild guess. "In fact," I added, trying to give my voice a secretive sound, "I am considering a report on something I have observed in your camp."

Was it really I who was speaking? I listened to my voice as if it came from a stranger.

It worked. The Warden got up from his seat like a shot.

"Never mind!" he shouted. "Let's forget it all. But from now on remember — God is not in charge here. The Fuehrer is!"

o

Was he really?

As summer 1943 went on, thousands of vitamin tablets

passed through the prison's gate — my purse was bulging at times.

I had resumed my visits to Mr. Jenkins, picking up the "deliveries" brought in by Swedish boats. Carrying home the parcels I wondered who in Sweden would give so generously, not knowing where the help would go. Not even Mr. Jenkins knew — at least I thought not.

One day I attempted to tell him about the Scandinavian prisoners, but he cut me off. Turning away, his eyes went over the port. Did he debate with himself whether he should hear me out or did he not want to know? For a moment I wondered, but then he turned back. He smiled; and, pushing away his hat from his forehead, he said, "Didn't your father ever teach you that the right hand must never know what the left one is doing?"

21

WE HAD A DRY SUMMER in 1943. The ground was hard as stone and the leaves on our mountain ash tree were turning brown. Since the storm in May we had not had any rain. They cut our rations. Potatoes were already getting scarce and with the turnips far behind we worried about the harvest.

Night after night we could hear the silvery buzz in the sky. The alarms were lasting forever, sometimes all night; but, as nothing happened, people became careless again. I still went to the shelter. Ever since Mrs. Manning's death I had gone, freezing at the first sound of the siren.

I had no time to waste and took the prisoners' letters along. In the bleak, half-empty shelter I would sit on a bench, scanning the pages with the aid of a flashlight.

My eyes were heavy in the morning and in class I often lost what was said. I began to fear for the outcome of my premedical finals. They were due in July, and July was here.

Only four more days to go. I had to concentrate on my studies and put all other work aside. The day had been hot and at dusk there was still no letup. I stayed in the yard. My books were stacked up on the small garden table in front of me and I was mumbling chemical formulas. But my eyes wandered over to the roses in the bed near the fence. They were in bloom, defying the drought as if they were nurtured by some secret well in the ground.

I turned back and opened my botany book; yet no matter how hard I tried, I could not shut out summer. It was in the air, in the trees, in the sky — it was in my blood.

I heard the music from the tavern and the pounding of feet — they were still dancing. I listened to the crickets' chirp; it was loud and persistent.

At last I went up to my room, pulled down the shades and turned on my desk lamp. Time was running out and this morning an older student had told me: "In zoology they'll ask you how many legs the spider has. If you don't know the answer, you'll flunk."

I did not know and nervously leafed through my book, trying to find out. But the more I studied the more restless I got and the less I seemed to know. Questions leaped up like hostile troops from the trench, closing in on me . . . and I lacked the answers.

I paced the floor. I sat down again and reached for my textbook in physics, opening it at random.

"SPECTRUM" was the title of the chapter. "Light," I read, "is only visible since its wave length is visible to the eye. There are other rays, X-rays, ultraviolet, and infrared rays, which the eye cannot see. Still they are there . . ."

I studied for the rest of the night, not going to the shelter when I heard the siren.

o

Only three more days to go, but again I put my books aside. We were to visit a Norwegian in the detention prison. We were needed there more than anywhere else. My studies would have to wait.

The detention prison held prisoners who had not yet been

tried. Political prisoners would sometimes be kept there for years, waiting for their trial. Or they might be kept there only for days, never getting a trial, just being transferred to a concentration camp. It was a place where the only certainty was uncertainty, where a man was not yet damned but knew he was doomed: it was like the Third Reich itself.

Outside the prison it took courage to stand up to the system. Inside it was nothing but a question of endurance, of waiting and holding out for a day of trial which might never come.

The Norwegian prisoner we were to see had been in detention for almost two years. He was an attorney and we had not seen him for several months. I noticed the deterioration of his body and the flickering unrest in his eyes. He had presented his case to us before and he did it again, as if its outcome depended on us. We listened quietly.

Near the end of the visit the minister reached for his Bible.

"No, don't!" the prisoner cried out, lifting his hand in protest. "Outside I never prayed. I will not ask for God's help now. That would mean accepting defeat."

There was pride in his voice, but the intense fear I had seen in his eyes haunted me on my way home, and I was overcome by doubt. What would I do if I were arrested and sent to prison? Would I have the strength to endure? Would my faith in God be strong enough to sustain me?

I remembered another visit, another prisoner — Frederik, who had openly prayed in our presence. One man had rejected God's word as decisively as the other had accepted it.

○

I was supposed to do some last-minute studying with a fellow student but I did not yet go home. I walked over to the Elbe river, looking for the path I used to walk with my father.

I thought of the day when he had said to me, "Eventually you must walk on your own wherever you are." I had been taking dangerous steps and, indeed, I was alone.

My friend was waiting for me when I got home.

"What kept you so long?" she asked angrily.

"Something of importance to me."

"What could be more important than your finals?" she argued.

We studied till dawn. Half-heartedly I was mumbling and reiterating facts I knew my mind would drop as quickly as I had picked them up. But outside my room was a reality I could not forget; and the siren at night sounded to me like the outcry of a man, screaming his despair into the darkness.

○

At last I went to sleep. I awoke to a room filled with summer and light. It was late. My books were scattered about on my desk and floor, some of them still open from the night before. I picked up the one nearest to me and wearily started again, mumbling to myself line after line, while my mind kept repeating, "Only two more days to go!"

By afternoon I got a call from Hamburg's prison: "We need you at once!" the Warden said.

"I can't make it today."

"You must — it is a special assignment!"

I pushed my books aside and hurried to the prison, going straight to the Warden's office.

"A Swedish captain is here to see one of your Norwegian prisoners," he said.

"Is that your special assignment?" I asked, frustrated at having missed out in my studies.

"I have my orders to grant this man special permission," the Warden said curtly. "After all, Sweden is neutral and we haven't many friends left."

"But remember," he pointed to a file on his desk, "*this* one is an enemy of the Reich!" He read aloud from the prisoner's record, "Gunnar Dal, age 30, Norwegian, married, author and journalist, sentenced to death, commuted to life . . ."

Gunnar Dal. I had never met him but at the sound of his name I remembered a letter I had censored several months ago. On the entire allotted page had been only three words, written in a bold, strong hand: *"I AM ALIVE!"*

I wondered what kind of urgent business had brought a Swedish captain to see this man. It seemed a long time since I had met a man whose country was still free. But the Swede was a stranger and not to be trusted. I was determined to keep my purse tightly shut. I would not give out any vitamin tablets today.

The captain was a stout man with a ruddy face and eyes blue as the ocean. At the sight of his dark uniform, the guard stood at attention, addressing him with "Sir"; but the prisoner was pushed into the visiting room with a loud curse.

When the door had closed behind the guard, there was a moment of silence. The prisoner stood before me, a tall man, not much older than I. The smile in his eyes made me forget the emaciated state of his body. Then he glanced at the captain; and the guarded expression on his face told me they had never met.

I stepped forward. "Sit down, Gunnar Dal," I motioned him to the bench.

"After you," he replied, bowing slightly. "You are the guest. I'm at home here."

We laughed. The ice was broken and I suddenly realized it was the first time I had heard a prisoner laugh.

"I think I owe you an explanation," the captain began. "I don't know Gunnar Dal, but somebody in Sweden sent me."

I did not understand what he meant; but what would have puzzled me on another occasion, now did not matter. I was strangely indifferent to the captain's presence or his reasons for being here.

"I am happy to meet you at last," Gunnar said turning to me. "I have heard about you through the other prisoners." And then he added, "I feel I have known you for a long time."

"I remember a letter," I responded, "containing only one line. Why was it written that way?"

He smiled again, remembering. "Never was I more intensely alive than the day I was sentenced to death," he said.

"With nothing left but the present, I became aware of the fact that life has its purpose now."

I was struck by his words. Had I not always thought of yesterday or tomorrow instead of living today?

"I still have my moments of fear just as you do," Gunnar continued as if he were reading my mind. "At times I get impatient and angry. I miss what I love. I think of music I no longer hear and of books I once read; but then I know that they are only a reality as long as they stay alive in my mind and heart . . ."

Time came to a standstill, and I forgot my surroundings. Only when it was time to part did we remember the captain.

"When will you be back in Sweden?" I asked.

"My boat leaves tonight."

Gunnar looked at me and for a long moment our eyes met again.

✿

The captain walked with me to the railroad station. I listened absent-mindedly to his rambling comments; I was wrapped in my own thoughts. At the station the captain looked carefully in every direction as if to make sure that we were not being observed.

Then he asked, "Didn't you wonder why I came at all?" From his pocket he pulled a credential and held it under my eyes.

I stared, stunned and confused. The card said plainly: "Swedish Red Cross."

I clutched the purse tightly under my arm. It was filled with vitamin tablets. "But why didn't you say so at once?" I almost shouted. "At least you could have told Gunnar Dal!"

"The true purpose of my visit was you. We had to find out who you are."

"And what is the verdict?" I asked with a hint of sarcasm.

"We trust you."

My mind was spinning. The deliveries from Sweden, the vitamins — it suddenly made sense. Still, how did the

Swedish Red Cross know that I was supplying the prisoners when I had not even told Mr. Jenkins?

But why ask questions when a hand in the dark was reaching out to steady mine. My eyes were burning as I mumbled, "Thank you for what you have done already."

"Let us know what more medications you need," he replied. "We'll keep in touch through your contact."

Then he was gone, lost in the crowd at the station, and it occurred to me that I had not found out his name. But — I was no longer alone.

○

I walked toward home. It was late afternoon, the sun was still high, casting its gold over the earth. To me the leaves on the trees no longer seemed wilted and the grass seemed greener than ever.

I passed Mr. Braun's place. The apples were turning red; one of them was within reach and I wanted to touch it, but warned by a shadow on the pavement and a motion behind the fence I restrained myself and walked on.

22

IT WAS SATURDAY NIGHT, but I spent the evening at my desk in a last-minute effort to study. Before me was the textbook in physics, but under my eyes the words faded away. Dusk fell, the moon came up and the lightbeams began their search of the sky, while my thoughts went back to the man in prison who today had entered my life.

I winced at the sound of the siren which cut through the night like a knife. My mother and I decided to go to the shelter. I brought along a stack of prisoners' letters. Mr. Braun stood by the door, holding his helmet under his arm and counting the few who entered.

"Who do they think they are that they don't come anymore?" he remarked sullenly to my mother. His face looked flushed and he loosened his tie.

I had a whole bench for myself and settled down to my work. A few feet away, near the wall, I noticed the young woman, her foot rocking the baby asleep in the carriage.

"Don't you ever get tired of reading all those letters?" my mother asked with eyes heavy from lack of sleep.

I barely looked up. The ink had run on the first envelope and in the beam of my flashlight I recognized Bjoern's awkward handwriting: "Mother, don't worry about me . . ."

A sudden blast shook the shelter. Was it inside or out? My flashlight dropped to the floor. The baby carriage was rolling with the vibrations. I jumped up. The light flickered — then another blast — followed by total darkness. I fell down on my knees, covering my head with my hands.

The bunker shook to its foundations. The lid over the air vents burst open and the iron doors groaned under the pressure. I was terrified, too frightened to move.

The roaring outside continued. From somewhere in the darkness I heard the infant, but the thunder above seemed to choke the sound of his cries. Blast followed blast. There was a frantic hammering at the door of the shelter. Wild screams pierced the night.

Someone opened the door, and a wave of yelling and panting bodies burst in on us. The concrete walls echoed with the wailing of children and frantic women. Mr. Braun's voice boomed, "Take it easy. There's room for everyone!"

The blasts continued, each one exploding, it seemed, in the very center of ourselves! I had stopped thinking. I did not pray — I was numbed, and I don't know how long it went on . . . Hours? Minutes? Seconds? In the darkness we huddled close to each other, body jostled against body, while the explosions continued to shake the bunker.

My mother and I clung to each other, closing our eyes against the blasts we could not keep from our ears, wondering when it would end.

Then it was over — silence. Deep silence. No more whining bombs streaking out of the sky. No more blasts outside. All that remained was silence. A flashlight lit up, shining for an instant over the young mother. She was clutching her child. I was still holding on to my letter and the ray of light fell over the childlike writing: "Mother, don't worry about me . . ."

Mr. Braun appeared. He had lit a carbide lamp, and in its yellow light I could see the waxen faces staring at him. His helmet was pulled down all the way to the eyes.

"So you finally came," he addressed the stupefied crowd. "You could not make it on your own, after all!" His voice shook with triumph and he petted the concrete. "These walls are strong," he said, "strong as the Fuehrer."

They listened with empty eyes, not talking back. Abruptly I got to my feet and opened the heavy iron door. Mr. Braun did not attempt to stop me. Blinded by a sudden glare of light, I staggered backwards — the sky was alight with raging flames.

It flickered in the windows across the street — no, it was just the reflection in the glass panes of the raging furnace downtown.

"The bombs must have hit the inner city," I said to a man who was leaning against the shelter. He coughed, struggling for breath, and the shadows around his eyes looked dark blue in the reddish glare.

"Bombs? That wasn't bombs," he coughed again. "Fire rained from the sky."

The earth shook under our feet and a deafening blast made us crouch against the wall. There was no letup. The air was full of the sound of crackling flames and explosions.

The way home seemed longer than ever, but when we arrived the house was safe. Not even a broken pane of glass; we had left all the windows open.

I rushed into the living room, pulled the curtains and turned on the radio. But it was dead; the electricity had gone, and in the darkened room I fell against the piano. My hands hit the keys, striking a shrill discord.

From the road came the sound of shuffling feet and the mumbling of voices. The procession began. Hour after hour they went by in nightgowns and pajamas, with coats hung loosely over their shoulders, heading toward the city, eager to witness the inferno between Heaven and earth.

The night air was stifling and the earth rumbled with thundering detonations. The sound of the fire engines had long since ceased. All we now heard was the crackle of the fire and the crash of collapsing houses.

I could no longer catch my breath in the sweltering heat. The first wave of smoke was rolling over us, filling every room; and we sought relief in the yard.

Under my window I stumbled over something: white pages, moving with the breeze — my physics textbook! In the light from the fires I could make out the paragraph: "Visible and invisible rays . . ."

The wind was increasing, whipping the leaves of the book and bending the trees and bushes. Within minutes we were caught in the storm and still the fury of the wind was rising, reaching hurricane strength, lashing the flames. The tongues of fire leaped furiously up as if to devour the smoke-blackened sky. The wind whistled and howled, and the mountain ash tree in our yard swayed dizzily. Its leaves were carried away by the hot, swirling air and the petals from the rose bushes fell to the ground.

The storm and the distant rumblings of detonations had drowned the sound of the shuffling feet. My mind was blank, and my exhaustion faded into apathy. Only toward dawn did I fall into a short, fitful sleep.

°

I awoke and found my room in a dim, sulfur-like light. Was it night or day? It was hard to tell. What had been a deep blue summer sky had darkened to a solemn gray. The sun, which had always painted a bright path of light across my bed, had turned into a murky, yellow blotch in the smoky sky.

The events of the preceding night rushed back into my mind, and I felt myself bathed in perspiration. The horrid stench in my room was that of burnt flesh, bodies cremated in the burning ruins of the city.

I buried my head in the pillow. If I could only shut out the sight of the black sky, the sound of shuffling feet and the horror of the procession drawn to the spectacle of death and destruction.

But something was different this morning. I lifted my head to listen more closely. The shuffling feet were still there; but they were moving more slowly, dragging over the road. I could hear no voices, only a hushed silence that made me run to the window to look. During the night the human tide had turned. They were walking away from the city, with smoke-blackened faces marked by the terror of the night. Some women wore fur coats rescued from the flames. They were coughing in the sweltering heat. Others wore thin summer dresses over mismatched stockings. Shaken from their sleep by the falling bombs, they had dressed in panic, grabbing whatever they could as they ran from the burning buildings.

Children were being pulled along, tripping and stumbling over their own short legs, trying to keep pace with the grown-ups. The men carried bulging suitcases held together with paper string. Some sat on the curb to pull the shoes off swollen, aching feet. Others simply lay down in the middle of the road, staring vacantly up into the smoke-filled sky. No one cried or complained. The faces were dark and empty, as if life had gone out.

The procession seemed endless; legs moved mechanically; hands held tightly the last of their belongings until numbed fingers gave up. For a while they rested, bundles and suitcases stacked up on the sidewalk. Then they hurried on — out of the city, death at their heels, abandoning whatever they could no longer carry.

Then night came again — another night of bombs and detonations, of sweltering heat and a storm. We got no sleep, and in the first gray of morning I suddenly remembered. My premedical finals. They were to begin today. The thought was absurd. For weeks and months the exams had been threatening me, and now I might never have the chance to take them. I was desperate. The University was in a different part of the city, a part which might have been spared. Impossible as it seemed even to get there, I was determined to try.

All traffic was paralyzed. The tram rails were buckled by the heat or torn up by bombs. I set out to cross the city on foot. There was only a trickle of people going toward the inner city, pressed over to the side of the street by the outgoing crowd.

The first few hundred feet looked unchanged, but smoke burned my eyes and blurred my vision. As we reached the first pile of rubble and collapsed houses, our pace was slowed. Ruins blocked the street, but the tight mass of people moved on, climbing over the piles of rubble and soot-black timber like a column of ants. Automatically, hands were extended to steady the next person in line.

A few feet ahead of me the wall of a house tumbled into the street. In back of me a sudden explosion went off — time bombs!

"Look out!" a voice yelled from behind a pile of rubble. "Unexploded bombs are all around!"

In stupefied indifference the column dragged on. It would be of no use trying to avoid the danger areas. The bombs were everywhere. One step in any direction might be as fatal as the next.

Furniture was piled in stacks in the streets. Overstuffed chairs and mattresses were singed by fire and mahogany was scratched and blotched. The owners sat nearby, as if waiting for a moving van. In the torn-up streets no vehicle could possibly get through. Some streets were still passable, and here cars and trucks sped by. With each new explosion the ground shook and the walls of bombed-out houses swayed dangerously. Many of them collapsed, blocking off still another street.

Telephone lines were down, electricity gone, and there was no more water in the pipes. The last trickle had been poured over the raging flames.

I watched a woman dig out the remains of a chair, a table, and a buffet in front of her burned-out house. In helpless anger she stamped her foot, crying, "Damn it, damn it!" An elderly man sat forlornly on the housesteps. She began pounding him furiously with tight fists, "You blasted fool!

Why did you throw the furniture out the window instead of carrying it down the stairs!"

I walked on, my shoes covered by a heavy layer of red dust. My throat was burning and it hurt to swallow. The smoke was getting thicker, and tears ran down my cheeks. I tried to take a shortcut down a sidestreet but heard someone yell, "The street is afire!"

Quickly I jumped aside into a doorway. A few feet away a small blue flame skipped along the asphalt. It moved rapidly, then exploded. Phosphorus.

A woman hurled herself into the moving mass of people. "My shoes! My shoes are burning!" she cried hysterically. Small blue flames were licking the soles of her shoes. She disappeared among the crowd as they moved along. Everyone was on the run.

Something hard and smooth was hidden in the dirt beneath my right foot. Suddenly curious, I kicked the dust and sand away. It was a picture of an angel holding a palm leaf and bending over a soldier. One of its corners was torn. The angel's right wing was missing and the tear had marred her face. Big, bold letters underneath read, "No one can do a greater deed than to die for his country." Then someone had carefully written the name of a soldier, a city, and a date. I brushed away the sand to read more clearly: "Fallen near Verdun, August 1, 1916."

The paper was yellowed. For more than twenty years it must have hung in the place of honor — over a sofa in a parlor.

I dropped the angel back into the dirt and moved on.

But once more I stopped. A boy sat on a broken stairway. He looked to be no more than four years old. His hands were folded, as in prayer, and his eyes seemed unnaturally large in his pale face. He stared at the leaping blue tongues of fire, then at the ruins, and finally fastened his gaze on the empty, burned-out windows, where singed curtains moved in the breeze. His fragile body was that of a child's, but his silent wounded eyes resembled those of an old, helpless man.

I walked on. The march through the ruins lasted for over

109

an hour. Landmarks I had known were gone, and without street signs I could barely tell where I was.

Then I reached the "border." No more ruins, no more empty burned-out shells of houses. Only a few broken windows, and here and there a patch over a hole in a roof.

◦

The University Institute of Physics was on the other side of the "border," next to the detention prison. The large clock on the wall looked unharmed, but its hands had stopped moving.

The professor was standing by the entrance, looking out searchingly. We were to be examined in groups of four. One of the students was missing — the girl I had studied with. She lived in an area that had been covered with phosphorus.

The professor led the way up the steep stairway to the third floor. "We'll have to meet in my study," he said.

On the way we waded through broken glass. Doors had been ripped off their hinges. Instruments and equipment were strewn around.

"The pressure was too strong," the professor said, waving his hand over the chaos. "Everything is destroyed." He looked shaken and bewildered.

The three of us sat facing him, and in a weary voice he started the oral exam, "What is the definition of heat?"

The other two were asked first and I sat looking around. The equipment had been destroyed in this room as well. Pendulums were bent, large pieces of plaster had fallen from the walls, and pictures were thrown on the floor. I recognized the portrait of the man with the small mustache, button-hole eyes, and open coat. The Fuehrer was on the ground.

The room suddenly seemed brighter. I looked out the window — in the distance was an ocean of ruins, but nearby the massive red-brick detention prison still stood. From here I could see that not one brick had been moved by the bombs. No one could have escaped during the turmoil of destruction. Even now, as I looked toward the gate, a new truckload of prisoners was arriving.

I felt burned out, with no hope left, and suddenly the

words rang in my ears: "God is not in charge here. The Fuehrer is!"

The professor's voice startled me. He was directing a question my way. I read the sympathy in his eyes. "Were you bombed out, too?" he asked. His eyes went past the massive brick prison building, to the smoldering ruins beyond.

It was my turn to be examined. The professor asked: "Can you tell me about visible and invisible rays?"

Something happened inside me. It could not be accidental that I was asked this particular question.

I heard my own voice answering, strong again and without hesitation, "Only the rays with wave length visible to the eye can be seen."

My doubt and despair were gone. The ruins were only visible expressions of fear, of hate and doubt, of human minds gone astray. I looked past the professor and my fellow students, past tall brick walls and paved enclosed yards to the barred prison windows. I could see no movement behind them, but I knew my challenge was *there*.

°

A little past 10 A.M. we heard a distant humming in the sky. It came closer and grew to a menacing roar. The sirens were no longer functioning. The ominous sound in the sky was alarm enough.

In the basement of the Institute we crowded together, professors, students, women, and children, men in work clothes, dirty from cleaning up after last night's attack. There were no windows. All electricity was gone and we stood packed shoulder to shoulder in the darkness, listening to the thunder rolling outside. It sounded like hits near the harbor. Then came a shattering blast nearby and we stiffened in silence. Even the children were hushed.

In the quiet we could hear rumbling in the distance and from the far corner of the dark shelter a man's voice reported, "London has been under bombardment for the last nineteen hours."

"How do you know?"

"Loudspeakers carried the news through the street this morning."

"We are getting revenge!" the voice rang with hollow enthusiasm; but the crowd in the basement remained silent, weary of the drums of propaganda.

"Churchill has given Hitler an ultimatum," somebody suggested. "Hamburg will be bombed until he capitulates."

The crowd made no response. The rumbling outside came closer again, and in the darkness a voice whispered, "He'll never capitulate — even if we all perish!"

"Who said that?" A flashlight shone.

The door burst open and a man in green uniform called out, "He has resigned!"

A sudden hope soared, "Who?"

"Mussolini."

The door banged shut again and we settled into silence.

◦

The humming in the sky had ceased and the streets came to life again. We students walked to the Botany Institute for the next exam.

An eerie silence filled the building. We waded through glass. At last we heard the sounds of steps in the basement and called down, "Anybody there?" No answer, just a door slamming shut. We called again.

Then came the sound of slow steps up the basement stairs. An elderly lab assistant in a white coat stared at us.

"How can you still be thinking of exams. Don't you see the broken glass?"

I kicked the tinkling bits. "So what? It is just glass. The building still stands."

The old man stared at me. He was shaking and began to laugh hysterically. Then came a flood of tears. "Only glass!" he moaned. "For thirty years I have worked with these preparations. A lifetime of work!"

We heard other steps coming up the basement stairs. They belonged to our professor, who walked carefully over the heaps of broken glass as if they were still intact. He stared at us in a daze.

He conducted the exam with an almost automatic precision. We listened to his questions and gave the answers, but in the back of our minds we all felt that by tomorrow perhaps we would all be gone.

The clocks of the city had stopped. My wristwatch showed 2 P.M.

We were outside the closed door of our zoology professor's study. I knocked. There was no answer and I carefully opened the door. The professor looked up quickly, obviously embarrassed, "I didn't tell you to come in!"

One glance was enough. He was crouched over a small battery-operated radio; and, before the door closed, I heard the distant signal: three short, one long beep. The professor was listening to the BBC.

Exactly fifteen minutes later he called us in.

०

I returned home late in the afternoon and found the house packed with strangers, people off the street, overcome by exhaustion. My mother was cutting bread. A fire had been kindled over four bricks in the yard; and paper trash was burning under a large, rusted pot filled with water.

The air was heavy with a sickeningly sweet odor. The city was sweltering in the steaming smell of burned and rotting corpses. I had put on a light-colored windbreaker that morning. Now it was black with soot and smelled of smoke and death.

I took it off, but the smell stayed with me and I went upstairs to my room. I wanted to sleep but tossed and turned instead, as the chattering voices below were blended with my thoughts and associations.

The dim, sulfur-like light in my room — it had been the same that morning in 1933 when it all had begun. The smell of fire — I remembered the stacks of books, tossed into huge bonfires and reduced to ashes. The shuffling feet, today's silent procession, clutching their bundles — that is how the Jews were driven on their death march toward the East. Now it was their captors who were driven.

My mother woke me at dusk. The only hope for space in the shelter during the nightly bombings was to arrive early. The bunker was packed and we were among the last people Mr. Braun let in. Then he locked the door.

We stood near the entrance, crowded into the stale stinking darkness, a mass of bodies pressed together, breathing the foul air. Hours passed . . . then the roaring resumed outside, blast after blast. The shelter rocked; and we swayed with it, grabbing each other's shoulders, fighting to stay up — for if anyone fell, he might be trampled to death.

There were screams outside and hammering on the door. Words were yelled in a foreign language.

"Oh, it's one of them," Mr. Braun said with disgust.

Nearby was a barrack housing men deported for forced labor from the occupied countries. They were without a bunker and one of them must have run to our shelter in panic. He screamed again, this time in broken German, "Help! Please open up."

"For God's sake let him in!" somebody said in the darkness.

But Mr. Braun did not move. "I have my orders!" he shouted. "The shelters are for us Germans."

A blast rocked the walls. We clutched each other's shoulders . . .

It was a hit immediately outside the shelter but the walls of concrete had held.

When we got out, we saw that the road had been torn open. A man lay in the gutter. His right arm had been severed. He was dead; and, in the glare from the sky, I could see the asphalt around him dark red with blood.

o

For seven days the sky was black with smoke and for seven nights it was red with fire. Hamburg lay stretched out underneath, like a military map. Methodically, block by block the bombers covered their target, continuing wherever they had left off before.

All communication was gone. No telephone, no mail, no papers. With no electricity the oven in the bakery stood cold. Meat rotted in the cold-storage plants and had to be released at last to the markets. Warehouses and pantries were thrown open. The howling mob grasped for the loot, carrying away armloads of meat, butter, eggs, chocolate, and coffee. In the stampede some were crushed and lost. Yellow blotches of eggs and butter swam in the brown dirt.

The exodus continued. One night beyond the hedge I heard the sound of marching boots. The oncoming crowd gave way to columns of men carrying shovels over their shoulders like guns. Were they soldiers or prisoners? I could not tell in the dark. Their shovel blades glimmered with the reflections of the flames. Their masklike faces caught the red glare. They were gravediggers marching toward the city. The shovels were their tools.

For days they kept trying to dig their way through the rubble. Faint cries could still be heard from buried basements. Then they ceased and only the sound of muffled knocking remained. The gravediggers gave up. They joined the firemen who had stopped their futile attempts at salvaging and sat idly along the curbs of the street.

Shortly after, I saw them dig up the ground in the cemetery. They were digging mass graves. A city official and a man in a brown uniform with shiny silver ribbons measured off the space.

Mountains of dirt were piling up.

"Dig deeper!" the city official shouted.

"Hurry up! There are more holes to dig," the man in the brown uniform yelled.

The first truck rolled up. Soldiers opened the tailgate. I watched corpses and bones tumble into the black earth.

○

One day at noon we heard a light, silvery buzz in the air. It sounded like an enemy plane gone astray. Only one bomb was dropped.

It tore up the asphalt near Mr. Braun's place and it felled his tree. The massive tree was split open, blocking the road, and the smashed apples on one of its branches resembled a big bloody mass.

At night we saw Mr. Braun at the shelter. His eyes were red and his face was ashen.

I stood near the door and later, when the shelter was rocking again from the turmoil in the air, I heard a voice mumble, "Oh, God, help me!"

Was it Mr. Braun? I thought so — but then I forgot, numbed by the thunder outside.

After the air had quieted down, we waited in vain to be let out. A flashlight shone, and by the door a man had sagged to the floor. His hand was clutching the bolt as if he had attempted to open the latch. It was Mr. Braun.

They carried him outside and put him on the ground. White froth stood on his lips. The motionless stare of his eyes was directed toward the sky.

A medic bent down and examined him briefly.

"Dead," he stated. "His heart must have given out."

"He *is* dead," one said in disbelief to the next, as they were filing by.

Then they stumbled into the night, each to his own.

◦

The air remained swelteringly hot and the stench of death was around us, but on the seventh day of the bombing I remembered a man and his letter. *"I am alive!"* I repeated to myself; and, amidst the aura of gloom, hope came to my heart.

23

RAIN CAME TO THE CITY, not a cleansing, torrential downpour, but an incessant weary flow from a sad, gray sky. It drenched the smoke-blackened houses and soaked the furniture piled high in the streets. Little rivulets of pink water flowed from the red plush sofas and chairs, and joined the streams gushing through the gutters.

During the day our street reverberated with the sounds of pounding hammers. The bomb which felled Mr. Braun's tree had smashed our windows. Now they were covered with paper or boarded up. At night there was deadly silence. Gone were the shuffling of the feet and the steady hum of voices.

August had not yet come to an end; but the leaves on our hawthorn tree hung lifeless and brown. The city lay prostrate after days of terror and tension. The work battalions had left, carrying their shovels with them, heading for the next bombed-out city.

Days blended into weeks, but somehow life resumed.

The thin trickle from the faucet grew to a steady stream. Electricity was restored to the part of the city not yet destroyed by the bombs. The gas was turned on; and one night, in the tavern nearby, the music struck up and feet began pounding and stomping. They were dancing again.

And, as the city awoke from its stupor, the Third Reich tightened its grasp. More rules and orders were issued. Food rations were cut, electricity and gas were restricted, and housing officials went from door to door.

A woman appeared at our front door one morning and stepped in with a brisk "Heil Hitler!" She had short, straight hair and wore hornrimmed glasses. She wasted no time, walking through our house as if it belonged to her. With machine-like precision she measured every room, mumbled figures, and noted them down.

From now on we would be allowed to use only a limited space, she explained.

"We will dispose of the remainder," she said cheerfully. "From now on it is one for all, and all for one." She rolled up her tape measure like a rope and departed with another "Heil Hitler!"

Later that day an elderly couple arrived. The woman carried a small bundle and the man leaned on a shovel.

"Heil Hitler!" they said and held up a slip of paper. Their names, Mr. and Mrs. Decker, and our address were carelessly scribbled down with a pencil; underneath was the official stamp, the German Eagle resting on the Swastika. They had been assigned to the rooms of Guenther and Hans, and they would share our kitchen and bath.

The door to our living room stood open, and they glanced at one of the armchairs.

"We have nothing left," they said and their eyes filled.

I felt guilty, sensing their unasked question, "Why we, when you have been spared?"

With their arrival, we, too, in a way, had lost our home, the island we had so carefully guarded. Hitler at last had gained entrance. We did not know the Deckers. Could they be trusted?

They seemed to be good people; but they greeted us with the raised arm and "Heil Hitler!" whenever we met in the hall. Was it done out of habit? Were they pretending or was it true conviction, not even shaken by a bomb? We dared not take chances. We began to talk only behind closed doors, and the voice of BBC was turned down to a whisper.

But something else happened the day the Deckers moved in.

At night there was a timid knock on the front door. I opened it and saw a man standing on the steps. In his hand was a slip of paper. Maybe another boarder, I thought.

He asked my name, then handed me the paper and quickly slipped away into the dark before I had time to take another look at his face.

But I recognized the handwriting on the paper at once. The strong, slanted letters, not even touching the printed lines on the sheet, as if to demonstrate the writer's independent spirit.

The message must have slipped through the walls during the turmoil of the air raids. It was unsigned.

"They are sending us away," it read. "We don't know where. Do follow us!"

Early next morning I was on my way to Hamburg's prison.

"Oh, it's you!" said the guard at the gate. "Don't you know that most of your Norwegians have been shipped away?"

"Where?"

His face turned blank.

I went straight to the Warden's office, this time indirectly inquiring, "What about my job?"

"We still need you," he said. "There are a few Norwegian prisoners left."

"What about the others?" I ventured.

He looked up. "Why do you ask?" he inquired coldly. "We got rid of them. That's all we care about, don't we?"

I went to the District Attorney. "We are not supposed to concern ourselves with those who are gone," he said cautiously. But, as I left he shook hands with me and with a weary smile suggested, "Why don't you try the prison in Rendsburg?"

✲

I would have liked to go at once, but I had to wait. Rendsburg was a small town in the country, a hundred miles north of Hamburg, and trains were not yet running.

I had finished my premedical exams. Still, when word came that I had passed, I was almost disappointed. What before had meant so much, now seemed only another delay. To continue my studies I would have to go on dividing the time I needed so desperately for the prison work.

When the trains began to roll, I was on one of the first heading north to Rendsburg.

As soon as the train left the ruins of Hamburg, I realized that the war was still going on as much as before. In the midst of the burning inferno I had felt so sure that the end must be near. But now, on a train, traveling across a seemingly untouched landscape, I thought I could hear the wheels singing against the rails, "Months — it will take months."

The train picked up speed and I looked out over lush green fields and trees. Every so often my view was cut by a southbound train on the other tracks, painted camouflage green-brown-gray, carrying ammunition. The sounds of the wheels changed their tune, harsher, quicker, "It will last for years — years!"

Soon the train thundered over the concrete and steel bridge crossing the Kiel Canal, the water shone in the soft light, the surface shattered into myriads of tiny circles by the raindrops.

In the distance I could see the massive walls of the prison in Rendsburg. In the inner courtyard the prisoners were marching in a circle. The concrete wall surrounding them was painted yellow, like the yellow stripes of their prison uniforms.

A quick glimpse — then the train had passed and the prison yard was no longer in view. The elevated trainbridge wound through the city like a ribbon.

At the prison gate I pulled the bellstring, and the little window in the wall opened.

"What do you want?"

"I'm the interpreter for the Norwegian prisoners."

"No one has notified us of your arrival."

"I must speak with the Administrator."

"He isn't here."

As the window was pulled shut, I quickly put my hand in the opening.

"I've come all the way from Hamburg; you must let me in," I demanded.

"Calm down! We can't let anybody in unless we've been notified of their arrival."

Getting into a prison was proving to be as difficult as getting out.

"Then let me speak to whoever is in charge."

At last the guard led me down a long corridor where a runner softened the sound of our steps. It seemed unusually quiet for a prison, no harsh shouts of commands or stamping boots.

A door opened, and a large dog came out. Instead of barking he wagged his tail and sniffed at my feet. A slightly stooping older man peeked out from the doorway.

"The interpreter?"

"Yes, this is the lady."

I glanced down at myself. Lady! I did not look like one. The last days in Hamburg had left their mark. In Rendsburg my smoke-blackened windbreaker seemed suddenly less than proper. The distance between the two cities was a mere hundred miles; now they seemed worlds apart.

A cloud of pleasant tobacco smoke hung in the room, no doubt the home-grown variety. The Warden waved toward an old green overstuffed sofa. "Won't you sit down?"

Over the sofa hung a large portrait. A broad face under a steel helmet and a uniform cloak. Hindenburg, the general from World War I. I breathed a sigh of relief. Much later I discovered the picture of Hitler, half hidden behind stacks of documents and the size of a postcard.

"You are a guard in Hamburg?" said the Warden without further preliminaries.

"Guard?" I tried to hide my surprise. "No, I'm just the interpreter."

The old man ignored my remark.

"As a guard you've already given the oath and are familiar with all regulations. If it suits you, you may take over the censoring of letters and the guard duty during visits . . ."

"Yes, but . . ."

The dog stirred in his basket under the desk and began to bark.

"Easy, Greif!" The Warden turned to me again, "You were saying?"

The good old dog had given me the few seconds I needed to collect my thoughts. Of course I was not an official guard, I had never given the oath, but the misunderstanding could be a useful aid in my work. The Warden was watching me.

"I just wanted to say, sir, that I am willing to take over the censoring of letters and guard duty during visits in the same manner as . . ."

"As in Hamburg," the Warden finished my sentence.

It turned out to be a good day. The prisons in Hamburg and Rendsburg were in the same district and governed by the same regulations. But one institution knew little of what was going on in the other. Distrust served as an efficient shield between them. No public institution ever wanted to admit that it did not know what was going on in another sector.

A mere hint on my part about what was standard practice in Hamburg was enough to open wide the doors for our work in Rendsburg.

"Just make the arrangements here as you did in Hamburg," was the usual response.

Within an hour I had made it clear that prisoners were to receive their letters from home as soon as they arrived — not one every six weeks. They would receive *all* letters. Photographs would no longer be confiscated, but given to the prisoners. The Warden agreed that the prisoners should be allowed to request permission to write extra letters — and the decision to grant or refuse such a request would be made by me.

"What about visits?"

"In Hamburg the minister and I came as often as my time allowed it."

○

On my third visit to Rendsburg I finally met the Administrator. His office was in direct contrast to the Warden's. A quick glance revealed a neat, shining, glass-top desk; and over the comfortable sofa a large portrait: the staring eyes, the brown coat collar turned up, arms folded, and the mustache. I had seen a copy of the same picture on the floor amidst broken glass in the University Institute of Physics a few weeks earlier. But here the Fuehrer still hung in place.

A fine aroma of cigar filled the room.

"Heil Hitler, Herr Chief Administrator!"

"Not 'Chief,'" he said with a dissatisfied smile. "Not yet, but perhaps soon, if the war will only last a little longer."

He sat in a deep leather chair, his short, stodgy legs crossed.

I looked at the lapel of his dark suitcoat. It was empty, but sometimes an empty lapel could mean greater danger than one graced with the Party emblem.

"As you've already observed, my duties take me' on extensive journeys." He snickered and rubbed his fat hands. "I'm actually more of a weapon manufacturer than a prison head."

The oily voice was silken smooth, "I can get more work out of prisoners than any other administrator of a prison command. I expect your cooperation." He smiled. "During the visits you are to make the prisoners understand that laziness will not be tolerated. My prison, down to the last solitary-confinement cell, is a munition factory. Well, you're already familiar with the work in Hamburg and have been given the oath."

I smiled and he accepted that as a sign of agreement and continued, "So there's no need for me to instruct you further. Just bear in mind that our common cause is at stake."

"You mean the promotion to Chief Administrator," I thought to myself. Aloud I said, "Yes, a good cause is at stake."

"What is the Norwegian minister like?" His voice was as silken as ever, but his eyes stared coldly.

"The authorities in Hamburg had no reservations." I tried to sound noncommittal.

"I detest ministers!" The pudgy hand struck at the air as if hitting a fly. He moved his chair closer to mine and lowered his voice, "Confidentially — doesn't he attempt to give the prisoners spiritual counseling?"

I smiled carefully. "That is precisely why I'm present during the visits — to prevent any such communication."

The immediate attack was averted, but the oily voice continued to probe. The technique was too familiar. I thought: Gestapo!

At last he handed me the green police pass. "Just sign here, please."

He stamped it, then glanced at my signature.

"Hiltgunt! What an unusual given name," he said casually.

°

The woman with the hornrimmed glasses sent another boarder who moved into Willfried's room. Mr. Mangold was in his early twenties. A man his age not in uniform was a rare sight. He came with nothing, not so much as a bundle. But his shirt, although smoke-blackened and in need of washing, was of silk, and the material of his suit was of such a fine quality that one would have liked to touch it.

On the evening of his arrival we had our pot of potato soup on the stove in the kitchen, and the Deckers were warming some oatmeal. But Mr. Mangold pulled from his pocket a small package with coffee — real coffee, and soon the house was filled with its aroma.

The Deckers whispered together and the old man at last inquired, "Have you, too, lost everything?"

"Yes and no," Mr. Mangold replied vaguely. "I was bombed out, but whatever I've lost, I'll soon get back."

"You have made a good start," I remarked as he was gulping down his coffee.

"Everything has its price." He smiled and carefully put away what was left of his coffee. He was using only his left hand, and I noticed that his right one was crippled. A couple of fingers were missing.

That night, while listening to BBC, we heard a noise in the hall. I got up quickly, and, opening the door, I almost collided with our new boarder. The blood drained from my face. Could he possibly have heard BBC's voice? I searched for a clue in his face, but it was blank. Mumbling an apology, he explained that he wanted to use our phone.

We did not trust him and decided to give up our sessions with BBC. Still, the next night we were tuning in again — so intense was our need to hear a voice from outside those walls which now were closing in on us, even at home.

As the days passed, I began to sense that the three parties, accidentally herded together under one roof, were leading lives of deception — each in his own special way.

Mr. Mangold often stayed out for days. When he returned, he carried large parcels and quickly headed for his room, locking the door behind him. Then, leaving again after a while, he carried a shopping bag with the contents carefully hidden under old scraps of paper. He frequently used our phone, making sure that nobody was around when he talked.

He avoided us in the kitchen and prepared his meals during the off hours of the day. But he could hardly conceal the contents of his pots and pans. A smell of food would spread through the house, food we had almost forgotten existed.

One night, sitting in our living room, I could almost see the steak sizzling in the kitchen. My own reaction was an unpleasant mixture of mouth-watering hunger and fierce resentment.

Not that we ourselves were starving. At this point we still had enough to see us through the day and we did not yet awake with hunger pains during the night. The fourth year of the war had gone, and we were still allowed an occasional ration of meat, but the main fare was turnips. We made desperate efforts to break this monotony by inventing recipes never heard of before and — hopefully — never to be repeated.

One of them was the special treat Mrs. Decker prepared on Sundays. She baked a pie — with oatmeal crust and a filling made from chicory grounds saved from the pot through the week.

The Deckers, who were retired, left our house each morning. As the old man walked away leaning on his shovel with the woman walking three steps behind him, they resembled pilgrims whose destination we could only guess.

One morning I overheard Mr. Decker say to his wife, "Come on, let's go home."

They could not give up searching the rubble for what might be left. One night they returned with a vase; and, although a piece of the edge was broken, they carried it upstairs as if it were the most precious treasure. The following day, perhaps encouraged by the recapture of one of their possessions, Mr. Decker built a wagon from an old wooden box.

From a distance, the squeak of its wheels announced their

return each evening at dusk, and their sad faces mirrored the reluctance of aliens forced to come back for shelter under the roof of strangers.

The alarms had resumed. Nothing happened. The humming in the air was loud and persistent, but we were passed by like a dead spot on the map. September had come, and, though I no longer went to the shelter, I left home each night. I, too, took a shovel along.

The Third Reich had made a no man's land of Mrs. Manning's farm. Big machines had moved in. They bit their teeth in the rubble and ashes of her shack, spat it out and then dug a huge hole. Trucks were unloaded and lumber piled up beside mountains of sand and cement. They were building an additional bunker.

The fields were overrun with weeds. People had dug up the ground, taking what was left of her harvest. But I knew of a patch, hidden away in the bushes, where she used to grow potatoes for her own supply. After the rain the soil was loose and easy to work; and, as I reaped what she had sown, I remembered her saying, "It takes time for the seed to grow."

°

The Administrator of the Rendsburg prison was gone on official business a great deal of the time, and our visits began and ended in the Warden's office.

We were such regular visitors that Greif gave us only a sleepy glance of approval from his basket under the desk.

"Would you consider letting the Norwegian Seamen's Mission deliver cod-liver oil to the prisoners?" the minister asked one day.

"Cod-liver oil?" The Warden looked perplexed. "We're no sanatorium, Herr Pastor."

"Exactly," said Reverend Svendsen.

"In Hamburg . . ." I said with an air of confidence.

The Warden also gave his consent to a Norwegian library and I was to censor the books. We began to carry heavy suitcases every time we arrived at Rendsburg. We brought stacks of books with us, not only German books, but English,

French, and Scandinavian books as well. Books had become scarce in Germany, and, after combing Hamburg's bookstores, we traveled to other cities, going from one store to the next, always keeping our eyes open for books of art, dictionaries, encyclopedias, and good quality fiction. After our own book collections at home were thinned out, I turned to my friends.

Visiting the prisoners left in the Hamburg prison, we were still subject to the old, rigid regulations. I could carry only my purse, bulging with vitamin tablets and medications; but the guards in Rendsburg had become used to seeing our heavy suitcases, and what had started with books, soon turned into an assortment of goods.

The suitcase was our most necessary tool, and I was determined to make it a permanent one. People taking their air-raid luggage with them had become a common sight everywhere; and, if a guard at the gate looked the least suspicious, I mentioned casually in passing, "If they bomb my home in Hamburg, all I'll have left is what I carry with me."

I smuggled in medicines and suitcase loads of vitamins. Prisoners with heart ailments needed medications; others needed pain-killing drugs. There were sores in need of bandaging. The medicine cabinet in the prison lacked nothing, but it was not for the prisoners.

I went back to Dr. von Berg. No longer did he reprimand me. "Do what you must," he said, aiding me with whatever was in his power.

I resumed my visits to Mr. Jenkins. The old house on the dock had been badly battered during the air raids, but he was still sitting in his armchair, buried in paper, never talking much, quietly responding in deed. With the windows of his office boarded up, the only light now came from the lamp on his desk; and in its rays the huge man reminded me of a lighthouse in the dark.

I had never mentioned to him my encounter with the Swedish captain, having at last understood that silence was our protection.

Aside from the medicines, I carried something else into the

prison: bread. Not fancy sandwiches, just dry bread saved from our rations. That was how it began, but more bread was needed and I found a way . . .

Night after night I went over to Mrs. Manning's, and the mountains of potatoes which once were stacked alongside her shack now lay hidden in our basement.

The aroma of coffee which filled our home whenever Mr. Mangold was present gave me a clue to his trade; and one day I asked him for flour, offering the potatoes in exchange.

"I don't deal with those petty things," was his overbearing answer.

But the following night he appeared in our living room. "Maybe we can get together after all," he suggested as his eyes wandered over our paintings, the china, and the radio.

We started with the potatoes.

We got the flour; and, as we were baking the bread, I smiled, thinking of Mr. Mangold's words, "I don't deal with those petty things."

There was something sacrosanct about bread. Words were stones when you were hungry, and to offer bread was saying what could not be put into words — its language was universal.

The minister carried in chewing tobacco rather than smoking tobacco. The guards could smell smoke, but the chewing tobacco could be kept hidden behind the teeth day and night.

We did our work without discussing it with each other; we did not meet in town unless an emergency arose. On the way to the prison we hardly talked, aware that looming over and around us was the ever present shadow of the Gestapo. When we arrived, loaded down with our heavy suitcases, neither knew the contents of the other's until we saw them disappear into the pockets of the dark prison uniforms.

I knew little about the minister's help on the outside, he knew nothing about mine. Behind him was his country. He represented his people. Behind me were my family and a few trustworthy friends.

In time we acquired some mutual friends. They were a few

German laborers who had worked side by side with the Norwegian prisoners whom the prison lent out to munition factories. Soon I was corresponding with them. They offered to help and became our lookouts. Whenever they observed special needs among prisoners we had not been able to visit for a while, they reported to us. We sent packages or money to buy the supplies, and they smuggled the goods to the prisoners on the job.

Knowing of their existence restored my faith in a Germany I had lost sight of. Yes, in spite of the Third Reich, there *was* a hidden Germany, not just behind the prison walls but outside, too. They were a silent troop, scattered about — without a leader. They were marching without guns or boots, and their only weapon was the deed done in secret. All odds were against them. They were few in number — but then how many volunteer to go through a mine field if they can find a safer way out?

At the other end of the spectrum were the Germans who actively participated in the evil. Their number was relatively small, too, compared with the vast passive and indifferent majority who pretended not to hear or see what they chose not to know, those who refused to get involved unless their own lives or interests were at stake.

◦

During our visits to the prison I kept a small notebook open on the table before me. I named it the "order book," because I recorded the prisoners' most pressing needs in it.

On one of our first visits to Rendsburg I again met Gunnar Dal. The minister and other prisoners were present, and only my eyes could thank him for the message he had sent me during the air raids. Mindful that he was an author, I jotted down in my order book, "Note paper, pens, ink, pencils."

Several other prisoners had been professional writers and journalists in their homeland, and on my next trip to Rendsburg I brought a suitcase of writing material. Papers and pens disappeared in shoes and sleeves.

"Maybe you will write your thoughts behind these walls," I suggested.

Gunnar was there, and although I dared not look at him, I felt certain he knew my words were directed at him.

о

Yet, there was something no suitcase could hold. It was intangible and the prisoners hungered for it. Only our minds and hearts could give truth and hope.

Rumors would grow like cancers in the prisoners' minds. Uncertainty put them in a state of despair. They longed to know even the bitterest truth about the course of the war.

At first we could only confirm the news of the Nazi victories. Then came the retreats. The German Propaganda Office responded promptly with rumors about secret Nazi weapons and planned superoffensives — we nipped them in the bud; for wherever we came, BBC's bulletins went along.

Yet I was constantly aware of the risk. Fear was always with me. There were traitors in the prison. Some wore the green uniform of the guards, others the black uniform of the prisoners. They were Germans and foreigners. Each nation had its own. There seemed only four walls without ears: the visiting room where we sat.

With the increased volume of mail, my desk at home was covered by stacks of letters. I worked far into the night. I knew the prisoners were waiting for mail, and waiting for us.

At night I tossed and turned. Sleep would not come. We were playing a dangerous game. It *had* to work, it *would* work. But what if it did not?

I did not carry dynamite into the prison. I tried only to help those in need. Still, at times, I thought of the District Attorney and the Warden in Rendsburg. They were showing me trust — and I was continuously deceiving them.

But in those moments of depression, my father's words flashed back into my memory, "he who knows the good and refrains from doing it, commits a sin."

Then all doubts were lifted from me; and, as our work

grew and the challenges became harder, I was increasingly aware of a persistent turn of events that I at first took to be luck. It was as if we were guided and carried forward by invisible hands.

Whenever we helped, help was given to us.

24

THE SKY, black from the bomb smoke and storm in July, had turned into a deep, clear blue — without so much as a touch of a cloud. Summer lingered through September. The air sparkled in the golden sunlight and made the rubble of a destroyed city more bleak than it had been in the drenching rains.

The berries of our mountain ash tree had wilted, and the roses had succumbed to the smoke from the fires. The asters, however, were blooming — the blue ones, a variety sturdy enough to survive even an occasional frost.

The siren had not sounded for one whole week. There was no humming in the air, not even the silvery buzz of a single reconnaissance plane. When the music from the tavern died down, the night turned quiet — too quiet. Its very stillness kept us awake. Having lived so long with the sounds of war, we listened in apprehension — but only the occasional bark of a dog or the cry of a child, awakening from a nightmare, interrupted the calmness.

We had adjusted to sharing our home with strangers and had learned to keep our doors closed, carefully weighing every word and action. A single slip could be fatal. Yet, even though caution dictated that we keep to ourselves, I became aware that all of us shared a common bond: the struggle for survival.

One night, after retiring, we heard footsteps on the stairs. I thought it was Mr. Mangold; but after the front door had opened and closed, we heard the unmistakable squeaking of wagon wheels. The Deckers were leaving. In the silence of the night the noise seemed louder and more persistent. At dawn the sound of the wagon woke me again. They had returned, and I listened to them huffing and puffing as they climbed the stairs.

From then on they spent the days quietly at home, but each night they left on their expedition. I watched them from my window, the old man leading, supporting himself on his shovel, and the woman, three steps behind, pulling the wagon.

We wondered where they went. Still, we pretended not to notice, always avoiding them, lest we should be forced to answer their "Heil Hitler!" Since the onset of their nightly outings, however, they seemed to have changed. When we did meet in the hall, they sometimes neglected to raise their arms and offered a friendly "Hello!" instead.

One day in the kitchen they told us that they had a son. He was fighting in Russia, they explained and added with a secretive smile, "But when he returns, he will have a home after all."

That was all they would say. Their faces closed as if they were guarding a secret they had no intention of sharing. We could not even guess what they meant. Everybody knew it was impossible to get supplies to rebuild one's home. In Hitler's Germany all lumber and cement went into constructing bunkers and trenches at the front lines.

Still, it was apparent that their despair had lifted and some spark of hope had ignited their hearts.

Not so Mr. Mangold. He behaved like a haunted man. He held a job. Everybody in wartime Germany had to work. But his job was obviously a mere camouflage for his dealings on the black market. He was always on the run, arriving and departing with parcels. His life at home centered around our phone. Shielding the mouthpiece with his hand, he whispered orders or moved his black-market goods while his flickering eyes kept the room under constant surveillance against listeners.

His trade was visibly prosperous. The day he first came to our house he had nothing but the smoke-blackened attire he wore. Now he owned two suits of the finest material. He was well-fed and seemed wanting for nothing.

One day he came into the kitchen while I was baking bread. Ever since my trips to the Rendsburg prison many more loaves of bread were baked than we needed at home.

"You must be very hungry," he said.

I looked up quickly. Was he trying to pry?

"Indeed, I am," I cautiously replied.

"So am I," he said, "but not for bread . . ."

I wondered what he was talking about and did not answer. Still, he lingered on, and after a long silence he mumbled, "I want to live."

I sensed the strangeness of the moment — not so much because of what he said, but because there was an undertone of despair in his voice.

I glanced at his crippled hand. It was his right hand. Two fingers were missing. He had once mentioned that he had never been in the war. Was the injury of his hand accidental or could he possibly have . . . ?

I stopped, not wanting to complete the thought. Looking at him, I said quietly, "But you *are* alive, aren't you?"

"Not really," he answered, his face a blank.

°

At the University classes had resumed. On my first day back in the auditorium I found some of the familiar faces missing and wondered what had happened to them. Had they been weeded out in the premedical exams and been sent back to the war in Russia; or had they perished in the ruins of Hamburg? No one knew for sure — perhaps no one really wanted to know. Death was so close in those days that we tried to shut it out of our minds.

But the faces of those who had been spared showed a sullen determination, and I remembered the day we had begun our premedical studies. I remembered the stamping boots on the wooden planks and the hum of eager anticipation. Now nothing of that was left.

Sheets were distributed, outlining the courses for the coming semester, and the heads bent down. Silently they studied the paper, accepting their timetable like a tour of duty.

My head was bent, too; but my thoughts were wandering off. The prisoners were on my mind, and all I could think of was how to coordinate my classes with the timetable of trains bound for Rendsburg.

✻

Traveling to Rendsburg I seldom took the time to look up from the stack of prisoners' letters on my lap. Each minute would count until I'd hear the minister say, "It's ten o'clock."

It was his signal for me to stop reading and get to the window to wait for the one sight we never missed: the Norwegian prisoners, walking in the prison courtyard.

When the train slowed down after crossing the Kiel Canal, the Rendsburg prison would come into view and we could see the black-uniformed prisoners walking in a circle behind the winding yellow wall. We could catch only a glimpse of them as we flashed by. But it was always reassuring, for we would know they were still alive.

We never went directly to the prison, but stopped for a cup of coffee first; the lukewarm chicory would turn cold on the table between us.

"How is your list for today?" I would ask.

The minister would look at his papers, leafing through letters he had received from Norway with anxious inquiries from prisoners' families. Name was added to name.

"What about your list?" he would say.

New prisoners had to be seen first; each meant a family waiting for the first sign of life.

". . . and now for the special ones."

They were prisoners who had asked for a visit from the minister in Hamburg in their letters to Norway. It was our secret "code." The prisoners knew I would read their letters, and we had a tacit agreement that they would use the code only when they had something urgent to see us about.

"Now for the combinations," Reverend Svendsen would continue.

Since we always saw two or three prisoners at a time in the visiting room, we could arrange for a father to visit with a son; brothers could meet, or old friends get together. How did we know who were old friends among hundreds of prisoners? Careful study of their letters revealed all that there was to know.

"It's twenty after ten," said the minister. We were expected at the prison at half past ten, and we would be at the gate at the strike of the clock. But this time, instead of rising from the table, Reverend Svendsen opened his brief-case once more.

"I almost forgot the most important item," he said. "We must visit Frederik Ramm."

I looked up in surprise. Frederik Ramm in need of us — the man who used to sign his letters with "Your happy and free Frederik"?

"Is he ill?" I anxiously asked.

"No, it is good news." The minister handed me a letter.

"I hereby inform you," wrote the Warden in his stilted, bureaucratic language, "that in response to your request concerning the Norwegian prisoner Frederik Ramm, we consent to placing him in charge of the Norwegian library . . ."

Frederik, the author and journalist, would be given a new life. He would still be a prisoner but he would be among books and through their pages he would transcend every prison wall.

"What kind of strange man did you recommend as a librarian?" the Warden asked as soon as we arrived at the prison.

"A well-known Norwegian journalist — you wrote your approval."

"I did, yes, but he refuses."

Then Frederik Ramm stood before us, his body shaking from head to toe; I hardly recognized him. Was this the man we had visited only a few months ago in Hamburg? The one who had instilled strength in us by his invincible faith in life?

Today he was stooped, a broken old man.

I could not suppress my concern, stepped forward and took his hand, "Is this *you*, Frederik?" I had never before called a prisoner by his first name, but it was not the time to be conventional. I simply expressed what was in my heart. "Frederik, you are ill — we must get help!"

Frederik's cough was dry. He was hoarse and could barely talk. "I cannot take the job as a librarian," he said. "I would have to walk up and down two flights of stairs a day. I am too weak." Again he coughed. "Just let me stay where I am."

It was obvious that he was seriously ill, and, on a sudden impulse, I decided to send for the Warden.

When he arrived, I saw Frederik leap from the bench to stand at rigid attention; and, as the Warden sat down, the sick man remained standing, motionless — as if frozen.

Watching him in all his helplessness, I disregarded any caution, jumped from my chair and offered it to Frederik Ramm. He did not respond with even the slightest movement, and the Warden stared at me incredulously.

"Herr Warden, this man is ill," I said. "He must see a doctor."

The Warden got up slowly, still staring at me. But at last he smiled, turned to Frederik, and patted him on the shoulder.

"Now, now!" he said soothingly, as if talking to a child. "I know what's wrong with you. Look at your uniform! The sleeves are too short and your hem is torn. We'll issue another coat."

✹

But on our next trip to Rendsburg the Warden met us in the entrance, "You were right with Ramm. It wasn't the coat after all. We had to send him to the infirmary." He shrugged his shoulders. "Tuberculosis."

"We will go and see him," I said.

The Warden shook his head. "You can't. Prisoners in the infirmary have no visiting privileges."

"But in Hamburg's prison . . ."

"All right, all right!"

We were on our way but the old man held me back. "Another of your Norwegian prisoners was taken ill, too — Bjoern Simoness — do you know him?"

Bjoern's tuberculosis was in the beginning stage but Frederik's was far gone. I knew of an ordinance from the Department of Justice stating that a prisoner suffering from tuberculosis might have his sentence suspended. We filed an application at once; but, looking at Frederik and knowing the sluggishness of bureaucracy, I knew that the odds were against us in this race with time.

I put all precautions aside. On each trip our first visit was to the infirmary. I brought in all the food I possibly could, pulling my heavy suitcase up the stairs and gangways.

One day the Warden met me in the hall. "Why don't you leave your luggage in the visiting room?" he suggested.

Clutching my suitcase tightly I stubbornly answered, "It's all I have in the event of an air raid, and I'll keep it with me wherever I am."

The old man kept looking at me. "You are leading a dangerous life," he finally remarked.

I gave him a quick glance. Was this a hint that he suspected the true contents of my luggage or did he refer to the constant threat of air raids? I decided to ignore his words. I had to go on.

One week later the Warden asked me into his office. He made sure that the door was closed and invited me to sit down. His fingers tapped nervously on the desk.

"I still wonder about the day when you called me in to see Frederik Ramm," he cautiously started. "Why did you get up and offer him your seat?"

"Herr Warden, I offered my seat to a dying man."

"You offered it to a prisoner. You must never ever get up for a prisoner!"

I did not answer but continued to look out the window, trying to see beyond the prison wall that was staring me in the face.

There was a long silence. At last the old man, clearing his throat, said, "You are still very young; I don't want you to get hurt."

"Is that a warning?"

"Rules are rules, whether we agree or not."

Then something unexpected happened. He went over to the closet in the corner, where the postcard-size picture of Hitler hung on the wall. Behind some files, he had carefully hidden a basket. He brought it to the desk. From under the cover came a fine fragrance of apples, and in a gap at the edge I saw a glimpse of red.

"Something from my yard," the old man said almost apologetically, and, barely audible, he added, "For you — and your friends."

Did he know that I was bound for the infirmary? I did not ask but shook his hand after tucking the apples away in my luggage. The medic who let me into the hospital cell shook his head and wondered, "How can anybody nowadays look as happy as you do?"

○

While Reverend Svendsen talked with Bjoern, I remained beside Frederik's bed. For the first time I was witnessing at close hand a man's struggle between life and death. I felt a pang of guilt. In spite of the signs of death all around — or perhaps even because of them — I felt more alive than ever.

It seemed as if Frederik were reading my thoughts. "So you don't believe I'll ever return to Norway?" he asked.

I hesitated. I thought of Dr. von Berg and tried to be truthful. "I want to believe it," I said, "you must!" and in a sudden burst of confidence I added, "What will happen to us after the war? Hatred may be all that is left, and we will need men like you."

I wondered whether he had understood me, for his eyes stared off into the distance as if he had forgotten my presence. Outside the bars of the prison window I could see thick fog. Fall had come.

"When will I get home?" Frederik muttered. He coughed,

and when he removed the handkerchief from his mouth, I saw dark spots of blood.

I suddenly felt alone — as alone in life as this man was in approaching death, and I looked around the cell. On top of the cupboard was Frederik's bowl. It was untouched. The spoon was stuck in a stiffened gray substance — oatmeal.

The cell held four iron bunks, two fastened to each opposite wall. There had been a third patient, a German prisoner. We had not paid much attention to him, only exchanging a word now and then. But his eyes had followed our every move as we had talked with Frederik and Bjoern.

Now his bunk was an abandoned island against the steel-gray wall. The blanket with the pattern of blue cubes had been removed and a few blades of straw stuck out of the sack-covered mattress. Two thin blankets were folded neatly over the end of the bunk.

Frederik had fallen silent beside me. His eyes followed my glance.

"Dead?"

He nodded.

❖

The days and weeks went by without a decision. We were well into October. The appeals for postponement of sentence were caught under dust and stacks of other papers — or they ended up in the wrong office. It took time and prodding to move them back into the proper channels.

We got the Warden's permission to take passport photos of Frederik and Bjoern, so we would not have any further delay if the decision came. Each day counted. Frederik had to be helped up and supported when his picture was taken.

I brought a special gift that day, something I had never carried into a prison before. Flowers! After almost four years of solitary confinement, they were the first flowers Frederik Ramm had seen. He touched them as if they were the very promise of life. "Blue asters," he whispered. "Do they grow in your yard?"

Then his thoughts wandered off. "We have them in Norway, too."

"Yes," I said, "it is a variety sturdy enough even to survive an occasional frost."

I saw Bjoern looking at us. He must have heard my words; he smiled.

○

November — I received a letter postmarked Berlin, sent from the Bristol Hotel, but unsigned. It was written in Danish. "Do all you can for Frederik. Be patient for just a few more days. Tell him that Danish friends have gone to the highest authorities."

The next day we headed for Rendsburg.

Frederik smiled faintly. "Highest authorities . . ." He seemed to brighten a little but the cough and hoarseness were getting worse. He made a sign as if there were something he wanted to say.

Then he began to talk, haltingly, "I've thought of what you told me. You were afraid of what will happen to Germany once the war is over. But I am concerned not only for your country. The survival of mankind will depend on peace."

Frederik's voice grew stronger. "Perhaps the only way to it is that we find peace within ourselves." He turned away from me as if he spoke to himself. "Peace! We must have the courage to do what is necessary and to accept what cannot be changed."

The bells in the tower struck the hour. It was time to leave. Once more I looked at Frederik. "Don't destroy yourself with hate. Go on serving life," he whispered.

From the expression on his face I could tell that his days were numbered. I felt no peace, just a blinding hate against those forces of destruction which seemed to win out.

○

At seven o'clock our day in the prison ended. Lights went off in the cells and keys rattled in the locks. It was time for the changing of the guards.

The Warden walked with us across the courtyard. Once more I looked back toward the barred windows. The glass reflected a faint shimmer of light. Beyond the dark bulk of the prison the moon was rising, but we still stumbled in the pitch black of the shadows.

We knew the prisoners could hear our steps across the cobblestones to the gate — the dividing line between their confinement and our "freedom."

The small window at the gate went down. The Warden gave the password and the gate opened.

"Such a long day," he said, "and you still have a long way to go."

He followed us down the road and stopped in front of a low wrought-iron gate in the fence. He stooped down, patting the head of his dog, and said, "Come, Greif, we're home."

Half-embarrassed, he lifted his hand. It could be taken as a "Heil Hitler," or merely the touching of his fingers to the brim of his hat.

"Good night."

✿

I glanced quickly out the window as the train thundered over the Kiel Canal. There stood the prison. The moonlight softened the harsh outline of its forbidding walls.

The train wheels rolled on, toward home. Opposite me were seated two soldiers; one of them started to hum.

"Shut up," said the other. They suppressed a laugh.

I knew the tune, an army march. New words had been added with a refrain everybody knew, yet no one dared sing it out loud:

> *Soldier, if you hate to fight,*
> *It only takes a knife*
> *And guts to cut your fingers off,*
> *At least you'll stay alive . . .*

I closed my eyes, remembering a crippled right hand with two fingers missing. Mr. Mangold, well-dressed, well-fed, and alive but haunted by his obsession to live. Then I thought of the Deckers, the squeak of their wagon wheels on their nightly expeditions to the ruins of their home.

The train slowed down. We were approaching the suburbs of Hamburg. The moon was high and its light more intense. Searchlights probed the sky, forming parallels and crosses. We passed the first ruins. The moonlight flowed ghostlike over the empty house shells and the train moved slowly, like a hearse. We were back in the city.

Suddenly my eyes caught a startling sight. I pressed my face against the window. I saw a chestnut tree in full bloom. It was November, but the heat from the burning city forced the tree to bloom out of season.

I was oblivious to the dark railroad station and the loudspeakers blaring an air-raid warning. Hoarse commands drove us to the bunker, moving us down a staircase through a tunnel which led us to a catacomb under the station. We stood shoulder to shoulder, packed together under the bleak light of some bulbs in the ceiling which flickered at times, as we heard the rumbling in the distance.

The alarm lasted for hours, and deep below the ground the air grew staler, as stale as in a grave . . .

But I was aware only of the day gone by, of the signs of life stronger than death and destruction, of the peace a man in a prison cell had found within himself.

✣

Yet the closeness of death became more obvious to me than ever when I went to the dissecting room early the next morning. The long, wooden barrack was damp and unheated. The windows in the ceiling were frosted, filtering the already gray light.

I had to catch up on my studies; and, feeling cold and worn out from lack of sleep, I turned up the collar of my white coat, as if that would warm me.

At this hour of the day I was all alone with the corpses. They were lying on stretchers and the heavy odor of formaldehyde filled my nostrils. The corpse I was going to dissect was toward the back of the room, and the bare walls of the barrack echoed the sounds of my steps. Unconsciously, I stamped my feet a little harder as if reassuring myself that there was still life left in this room.

They were lying in long rows, yellow emaciated bodies, the corpses of prisoners, many of them executed, put at the disposal of the Department of Anatomy by "courtesy" of the Gestapo.

I propped open my book and began to dissect the thorax, but today the silence was distracting me. The corpse on the stretcher did not look young or old. Its skin was stretched across the knuckles like shrunken leather. The blank face looked upward to the frosted glass in the ceiling and the closed mouth was like a narrow strip of blue. There was no pain left.

I stared at the eyes. They were without expression; they asked no question and gave no answer.

One corpse looked like the other. Still, at one time these corpses had been alive like Frederik, like Bjoern, like me. They had been waiting, with despair in their hearts, and hope, that spark of hope, always present till the last breath of life.

I winced at the hollow sound of my book falling to the floor; and, picking it up quickly, I shut out all thoughts and started to work.

A few minutes later the door opened. Students in uniforms. Heavy boots stamped through the room — the steps of our time. Once the corpses had heard them, too, anxiously listening as the boots marched over stones, over gangways and stairs, approaching those waiting to be executed. Men in uniform had stood beside them, watching them die.

Now marching boots were approaching them again. But the bodies did not stir. Their fear had gone with their pain, extinguished with that last spark of hope.

The silence of the early morning hour was gone and the room resounded with voices. The students flocked around the stretchers, their uniforms covered with white coats.

The women sat with their anatomy books open, cutting daintily with small, sharp knives. They chatted with the men. Words were thrown from one end of the room to the other.

One of the girls suddenly giggled, "Look what they did to my buddy — extra ration for him!"

Shrieks of delight . . . women in high heels standing on tiptoe . . . loud guffaws from the men: someone had put a lit cigarette between the blue lips of the corpse.

There were six at our corpse. The student working on the head started to curse. He had to hold it up or it would slip to the side. Others came to his aid. One of them felt the upper vertebrae. "Broken, he was hanged! That's why," he stated matter-of-factly.

They kept on working, dissecting, leafing through the pages of the anatomy book, whistling, and chatting.

I left, though I had not yet finished.

On my way out a hand touched my arm. It was the lab assistant. Summer and winter he wore a red fez which made him look like a Turk. A few days ago I asked him for a brain to dissect at home in my spare time. Tweezers and knives were sticking out of his pockets, and he was carrying a saw.

"You can have a brain — bring ten cigarettes tomorrow."

He tipped my shoulder with the saw and added good-humoredly, "In two weeks the professor is going to lecture about the heart. I've got only one left, but I put it into your package. No charge for that."

°

At home my mother was waiting. "You are early. Did you already hear?"

"A message from Rendsburg?" I held my breath.

"Yes, the Warden called. Frederik's sentence has been suspended."

Now every minute would count. I had to get word to the

144

Norwegian Seamen's Church. But the port had been bombed. The telephone lines were destroyed.

I ran.

I ran past Bismarck who stood with his sword high up on the hill. I sent him a glance of triumph, as if by carrying the news of one prisoner's release I had broken his sword.

One hour later a telegram was on its way to the Danish Red Cross, "Tomorrow."

○

Frederik Ramm did not survive the transport home to Norway. He died among friends in Denmark, but a few days after his death the BBC reported that his funeral had been turned into a national demonstration.

"Let's be glad that he's resting in peace," the Warden in Rendsburg said when we told him about Frederik's death. "What would have happened had he lived? The day after his release the Gestapo called. He was too well-known a man to be set free, they said. They ordered me to hold him back."

Reverend Svendsen glanced at me sideways. If the kind old man behind the Warden's desk had not let us get the passport pictures early . . .

Again I heard the Warden's quiet voice, "Just a few minutes ago I was informed that the other Norwegian, the one who shared Frederik Ramm's hospital cell, has been given a suspension of his sentence, too."

The minister held out his hand. "On behalf of Norway, I thank you, sir."

The Warden, clearing his throat, cast a quick glance at me. Then he bent down to pat Greif and spoke to the dog as if the two were all alone in the world.

"We both have been in the prison for a long time, Greif," he said, "and what's happening now we don't understand anymore. But see, once in a while we still have a happy moment."

I sat rigidly on the sofa pretending not to hear. I looked at the portrait of Hindenburg, the old general from World War

I. It was over the Warden's desk; Hitler's postcard-size picture was not even in view from where I sat. Never before had I given Hindenburg such a friendly look. Today I understood what it would have been like had Hitler hung in the place of honor on that wall.

25

BJOERN MADE IT all the way home. The Danish Red Cross took him to Norway where he was admitted to a tuberculosis sanatorium for treatment. I wondered whether I would ever see him again. For Frederik Ramm, the move had come too late; Bjoern at least had been given a chance for survival.

In the fall of 1943, there was another cut in rations. The drenching rains of August had not made up for the dry spring and summer, and the harvest was poor. The war seemed to drag on endlessly, and rumors indicating that things were not well at the Russian front increased. The rumors were most emphatically denied by the German Propaganda Office. But the people, weary of war and lied to too often, paid no attention, believing only what they saw for themselves. Russia was far away, and the success of Hitler's armies was measured by reduced rations and grams of rye. "One slice of bread less a day!" was all they could think about.

The sirens screamed every night. The American bombers were so regimented we could almost set our clocks by the moment they caused the sirens to send out the alarm. They were now aiming at other cities and dropped only an occasional bomb over Hamburg on their way back home.

The lamp on my desk burned late every night. I continued reading prisoners' mail, but between letters I sometimes stopped to look up at the picture above my desk. It seemed so long ago that I had watched Eduard paint the notes in the vague blue sky over the white, straw-thatched farmhouse. With my eyes I followed the sandy road going up the hill, remembering the schoolgirl who once had wondered where the road would lead.

By the end of November a gusty wind had torn the last leaves from the trees; and, as the first frost set in, the leaves in the gutters turned to iced lumps which stuck to the asphalt.

But the onset of winter did not stop the Deckers from their nightly expeditions, and the loud squeak of their wagon wheels seemed to defy the numbing cold of the dark.

One night, early in December, I was still at my desk when I heard them leave. I turned off my lamp and peeped through the window, only to see what I had seen so often before: Mr. Decker, supporting himself on his shovel, led the little procession, with Mrs. Decker, pulling the wagon, walking a few steps behind.

Several hours later I woke up to hear them huffing and puffing up the steps. I drifted back into listless half sleep and, toward dawn, somewhere between dreams and reality, a persistent ominous sound pierced my consciousness. Once, twice, three times — the shrill, monotonous sound ripped the veil of my half sleep. I was wide awake and drenched in a cold sweat.

Our doorbell was ringing.

I rushed to my mother's room. She stood at the window. Outside by the curb was an unmarked car with the lights on and the motor still running.

We threw our coats over our nightgowns and hurried downstairs to the front door.

Two men stood before me, holding up their credentials. "Gestapo!"

They shoved us aside, passed through the hall and headed for the kitchen where they went straight to the window overlooking our yard.

"There it is!" They seemed to have found what they wanted.

Still completely ignoring our presence, they unlatched the back door and stepped out. We heard the faint crackle of the thin sheet of ice under their shoes, and watched from the kitchen window as they passed through the yard and stopped near the back gate. There, hidden from the road by the

147

hedge, stood Mr. Decker's wagon. They inspected it from all sides, conferred a few moments, and at last gave the wagon a kick, sending it rolling toward our mountain ash tree.

I looked at my mother. We did not speak, but her eyes reflected the puzzlement and the faint hope I felt. Could it be that they had not come for us, after all?

The Gestapo officers came back to the kitchen.

"Where were you last night?" they inquired.

But before we could answer, Mr. Decker's hoarse voice called plaintively from the hall, "What do they want with my wagon?"

The men turned around quickly. "So *you* are the owner?"

The old man stood at the bottom of the staircase holding onto the rail. He was barefoot in his nightshirt, but he raised his right arm and said, "Heil Hitler!"

The Gestapo ignored his greeting. "We have come for you," they said.

Mr. Decker began to shake. "Let me go!" he pleaded, not even asking why they wanted him. "Let me go! I only did what many others do also."

"Maybe so, but you got caught."

The old man started to sob. "I have a son fighting in Russia! I did it for him."

The Gestapo looked at the clock in the hall. "We'll give you five minutes to dress."

While they were waiting, my mother and I went back into the kitchen. I had to sit down. All I could think was that *we* had been spared.

Mr. Decker came back downstairs leaning on his shovel. His wife was with him and they were both fully dressed, wearing the clothes they had worn the day I first saw them on our doorstep.

"We've never been apart," Mrs. Decker said. "I'll go with him."

"You can't." They turned to the old man, ordering him to let go of the shovel.

"He uses it as his cane," I tried to explain.

They were unmoved; and, as they left, one of them turned

to us and remarked, "Where he's going, he can't take anything with him."

Mrs. Decker stood as if she had turned into stone. At last she let us lead her back to the kitchen, but she refused to take off her coat and hat.

"Where will they take him?" she asked and suddenly started to tremble.

We had no answer. The Gestapo might send him to the detention prison or into the next concentration camp; but, in an effort to console her, we said that perhaps they would let him go, after all. She gave no signs of having heard our words and asked no more questions, but stared at us with empty eyes.

It was still before sunrise and very cold, but instead of getting back into the warmth of our beds, we stayed together. I busied myself with lighting the stove and my mother prepared breakfast.

Mr. Mangold finally appeared. His hair was unkempt, and I could tell from his face that he had followed events from the safe distance of his room upstairs. He surprised us by offering a cup of coffee. Real coffee! In return we put a plate of our oatmeal in front of him, and for the very first time, since our house became a shelter for "strangers," all the occupants shared a meal.

As the kitchen was warming up, Mrs. Decker started to talk. She and Mr. Decker had made their nightly forays to Mrs. Manning's place, where the new bunker was under construction. Night after night they had carted away pieces of lumber and bags of cement with which to rebuild their home, hiding the material in the rubble of their place. Somebody must have seen them and reported them to the Gestapo. Perhaps the squeaking wagon had given them away.

"We've always been honest," she sobbed. "But there was no other way to get the supplies. Why do they punish us small people?"

"That's what war is all about," Mr. Mangold said and got up, pulling his tie tight and combing his hair. "You can get away with murder, but you'll get caught for petty things."

From then on Mrs. Decker stayed at home, barely touching the food we brought her. Always her eyes sought ours with a silent question, but nothing was heard from her husband. His wagon stood near the mountain ash tree, looking somewhat lost, where it had been kicked away from its old spot near the fence. Days turned into weeks. Snow began falling.

The nightly alarms continued; and, although the skies were overcast, the sirens frequently pierced the daylight, too.

One morning I was getting ready to leave for the prison in Rendsburg. I rushed through breakfast, anxiously listening to the martial music blaring from the radio. If the music was interrupted by a beeping sound, it meant an air-raid alarm was coming. I was less concerned with the danger of falling bombs than with the fact that all traffic would stop, making it impossible to get to the railroad station. As I put on my hat and coat, I stared at the radio as if, by holding it within my gaze, I could keep it playing.

My mother came into the hallway to follow me to the door.

"Don't wait up. It will be late tonight," I said, and just then something rustled at our feet. A letter fell through the mail slot in the door, a blue envelope without stamp — official mail — and the sender? Slowly, my heart pounding, I bent to pick it up. Then tearing up the envelope I quickly glanced at the contents.

"I've been called in to the Gestapo," I told my mother, attempting to steady my voice.

I scanned the lines once more, "You are hereby requested to appear . . ." The letter was postmarked two days ago. The summons was for today.

My turn had come. My first thought was Mr. Decker. Had he talked? But then — what did he know? We had been cautious at all times, only listening to the BBC late at night behind locked doors, muffling the sound from the radio with a blanket. And Mr. Mangold? The loaves of bread he continuously saw us baking? I was sure he would never report us. He had too much to hide himself. Perhaps it was only a routine investigation, or — could it possibly be related to my work? Mr. Jenkins? The Norwegian minister? One of the prison guards? My mind raced for a possible connection, but my thinking was blurred by fear and suspicion. Had any of the prisoners reported me, or perhaps a student from the University?

The radio blared on. I looked again at the letter. I knew of people who had been summoned and had never returned. For a moment I thought of running, but where would I go?

My summons was for today, but with sudden determination I put the letter aside. I would go to the Gestapo tomorrow. Today I had someone more important to see. It had been a long while since we had been together.

We were never alone at our visits. The minister and other prisoners were always present, but it did not matter. To me everybody and the world itself was left behind when I saw Gunnar Dal. I could not define it, but there was a secret bond, a silent understanding and accepting of each other without any demands.

That day we spoke about freedom. Often, on earlier visits, we had spoken about the day of liberation, trying to keep the prisoners' hopes alive. Gunnar usually listened in silence. Today he said, "Don't *hope* to be free; *be* free!"

"Behind these walls?" one of the prisoners retorted.

Gunnar smiled. "Wherever you are, you will only be as free as you can free your mind of fear."

Our eyes met. His words are spoken for me, I thought and was tempted to tell him about the letter. Instead I said, "I cannnot think of freedom as only a state of mind."

"Not yet," Gunnar said, "but maybe one day you will."

Time was up — they had to leave. Gunnar stood near me, and suddenly I felt his hand around mine; as our eyes met, neither of us looked away. For a brief moment we looked at each other, trying to say what we felt but could not speak aloud. Then he turned away quickly and left without looking back.

I stood staring at the door that had closed behind him. But

I knew no door stood between us, no wall could keep us apart. We were one in mind.

My hand still felt the warmth of his touch as I headed home. Sitting with my eyes closed to shut out my surroundings, I heard the wheels of the train singing his name, "Gunnar — Gunnar — Gunnar," while my heart talked to him. For once there was no yesterday or tomorrow, only today. I was free of all fear.

❖

Cold fear was back with me when I stood the next morning in front of the stone mansion located near the University. The house looked deserted, hidden from the street by shrubs and trees. I had taken some bread along, just in case they might keep me. Terrified, but with an air of apparent assurance, I walked up the empty driveway.

I had barely touched the iron handle on the massive door, when a buzzer rang and the door swung open. Invisible eyes must have watched me. The empty hall was silent, but on the hardwood floor were the marks of many shoes. All doors were closed, no voices, no sound of typewriters.

I coughed — the sound echoed through the deserted hall. Yet, no one came, no other door was opened. I pulled out the blue envelope and looked at the address again. Yes, this was the house. On the walls hung old copper engravings — left over from the days when this mansion had belonged to one of Hamburg's distinguished families.

I walked past the first door. It had no number, no sign. Carefully I knocked at the next one. No answer. I turned the knob and the door swung open on soundless hinges, revealing another door. It was padded and covered with brown leather, muffling the sound of my knock when I tried again. At last I cautiously turned the handle, opening the door so it was just slightly ajar.

"You may enter," I heard a voice from inside.

I stood in a large room with high ceilings. Behind a huge desk a man was waiting. He was neither young nor old, perhaps between thirty and forty, neatly dressed in civilian

152

clothes. The color of his suit was gray and his face was like a blank sheet of paper. The Gestapo wore no uniforms, yet to me they all looked alike.

He cast a short glance at me. His face was noncommittal and he did not raise his arm to say, "Heil Hitler!"

"You are one day late," he stated, as I showed him my summons, and, staring at me, he asked, "Can you afford it?" He reached for a thick file on his desk.

I turned cold as I faced him while he silently studied page after page.

I started looking around and found myself noticing little inconsequential details. The windows were shining and clean, without curtains, and the house across the street was an empty, bombed-out shell. My eyes caught sight of a door behind the man at the desk. It was painted glossy white and I wondered what was behind it. Did it lead into the deep recesses of the Gestapo chambers? Cold fear cramped my stomach. Would I be allowed to walk back out the way I had come, or would I be led in there?

At last the man broke the silence, "You are aware why you are summoned?"

The game had begun . . . and I had played it before. It was as if a button in my brain had been pushed "on." I was alert, careful, and in control of every word I was about to speak. I felt almost like a distant observer as I smiled and asked, "What exactly do you mean?"

"Your occupation?" he inquired.

"Medical student."

"Oh?" His pencil danced over the paper.

Obviously the Gestapo knew that I was not just a student. How much did they know of my prison work?

"On the side I work as an interpreter," I volunteered before he had time to pose another question. My answers were as smooth as the high gloss on the white door I faced.

"What does your work consist of?" he began again.

"I censor the mail in Hamburg's prison."

"Is that all?"

The Gestapo was well informed!

"No, I act as a guard during the visits."

The man fired questions. I answered them. He knew that the Norwegian minister visited the prisoners. He knew his name. He knew how often we went to Hamburg's prison. He knew that I was not a member of the Nazi Party.

But he did not seem to know anything about our trips to the Rendsburg prison and the heavy suitcases I carried along.

"How is the minister? What do they talk about during the visits?"

The answers came mechanically. My mind worked with precision.

"Why haven't you been sending any secret reports about the prisoners to us?"

"I have been appointed by the Department of Justice and work only for them!"

The man leaned over the desk. "We're not only interested in reports about prisoners. We also want reports on the prison's personnel!"

". . . and who will report on the interpreter?" I asked with a friendly, accommodating smile.

"Don't worry your head with that," he said. "We know all about you."

I hid my smile. My face remained blank. Then he bent forward and asked abruptly, "Why didn't you tell me about your work in Rendsburg?"

So that was it! I thought hard and fast. My summons had to do with my work at the Rendsburg prison. But in what way? I was walking on thin ice and paused for a moment before I answered, "My work is of a confidential nature . . ."

"Where do you think you are? This is the Gestapo!" The man actually chuckled. "But you have potential. From now on we want you to deliver reports to us about the penal institutions."

He got up. "You may leave now," he said. "But we'll meet again."

I mumbled something like "Heil Hitler!" as I walked quickly toward the leather-padded door. The interrogation had left me stunned and bewildered; and, out in the empty hall, I had a sense of unreality. Nobody was at the front door to let me out. It opened again with a buzz, directed by invisible eyes and hands.

I took a deep breath. They had let me go, at least for today. Slowly I walked toward the railway station, not aware of my surroundings, trying to decide in my mind what the Gestapo had really wanted from me. I still did not know.

Once more I turned back to see a last glimpse of the mansion with its imposing façade and shiny windows, revealing nothing of leather-padded and white painted doors.

I was free. They had let me go. At least for today. A glimmer of light hit my eyes; the winter sun reflected in the shining, green cupola of the University building across the street. "From now on I'll study," I thought, "give up my prison work, attend my classes, and bury myself in books at home." Today the Gestapo had let me go, but the implication was clear. They would call me in again — tomorrow, next week, any day. Some day they would come for me.

Again I thought of Gunnar, of the strength I had felt in his presence. It was only twenty-four hours ago, but it seemed a long time. All I felt now was defeat. All I wanted was to end this continuous living in fear, jumping from my light sleep every time the headlights of a car flashed by my window, listening for the car to stop and the sound of our doorbell in the night.

I started across the street. There was the sound of screeching brakes and a hand pulled me back.

"You're as careless as ever!"

A heavy truck passed directly in front of me. A girl held my arm. She wore a black tie and her dark blue coat had a silver stripe.

"Don't you remember me?" she asked.

She was an old classmate of mine.

"I'm a district leader now," she said, "and you?" She did not wait for my answer, but rattled on about woman's draft . . . training camps . . . indoctrination . . . joint war effort. She would have liked to go to college, she said, but she had decided to devote her life to the Party. Dedication shone from her eyes.

At the railroad station she asked me again, "What are you doing now?"

"Studying medicine."

"Then your life is dull compared to mine."

Our trains rolled in and we separated, going in opposite directions. As our trains began moving simultaneously, she lifted her right arm, "Heil Hitler!"

I kept thinking of her while I stood in the overcrowded compartment. She would continue to serve her cause. Was I going to abandon my work and let there be one less on our side?

Arriving at home I found a letter with a foreign stamp inside the door. It was from Norway and had no return address, but I recognized the awkward handwriting at once.

"I am alive," Bjoern wrote. "Thank you . . ."

○

I sent word to the Norwegian minister that we had to go to Rendsburg the following day, and I spent a sleepless night, trying to recall every little detail of the past months that might have prompted someone to inform the Gestapo. I had to find out, and the prisoners had to be warned of the informer.

Next morning at exactly ten o'clock our train was crossing the Kiel Canal and only a few seconds later the massive yellow prison came in view. As always, we stood by the window, watching for our first glimpse of the prisoners, as they were walking in the circle. There was the courtyard, but . . . where were the prisoners? I looked at the minister, and my concern was mirrored in his face. Life in the prison ran by the second hand on the clock. If the prisoners were not in the yard, something had to be wrong. I felt the chill of apprehension. Was it connected with my summons?

The guard at the gate seemed unusually grumpy, ushering us in without his friendly nod. By now I had become so suspicious that I connected anything unusual with what had happened to me.

We were shown into the Warden's office. "He is with the Administrator," the guard stated. "But he wants you to wait for him."

The minister and I exchanged glances again. All the events appeared to be pointing in the same direction: they must have heard something.

The large clock in the watchtower rang out — eleven ominous strokes. The room seemed unusually warm, but the chill stayed with me. Greif was in his basket; his breathing was heavy and labored. At the last stroke of the clock he got up, and, after several heaves, he vomited up a green substance on the gray carpet.

It came so unexpectedly that I suddenly felt more at ease, as if Greif's relief was somehow connected with my own state of mind.

The door opened and the Warden entered. His friendly face looked unusually solemn. *This* was not my imagination.

"I'm glad you're here," he said. "We've been waiting for you."

So it was true. The Gestapo had taken action. The surface calm I had felt the day before in the mansion disappeared, perhaps because this time I was face to face with the Warden whom I had begun to think of as a friend.

"You've waited for me?" I stammered.

"Yes, we've got an empty cell. We'll put you in there."

Any other day I would have laughed about the joke, but now the Warden's words struck me as deadly serious. My hand grasped the arm of the sofa and the old man stepped closer. "What's the matter? Are you ill?" Then he noticed the green spot on the carpet and shook his head. "I wish we could be like Greif — just spit out our discomfort when we feel like doing it." With a sigh he added, "You've probably heard at the gate what's been going on here today?"

Breathlessly I waited for him to continue.

"Inspection."

"Inspection? By whom?"

"Whom? But naturally the Attorney General."

Before I could get hold of myself I burst out, "Thank God!"

"What do you mean 'Thank God!'?" grumbled the Warden. "You can't imagine how it turns this place upside down."

There was a knock at the door. A guard announced that the Administrator wanted to see me.

He rubbed his soft, pudgy hands when I entered his office and said, "I must tell you that the Attorney General expressed satisfaction about your work."

I was not sure I had heard correctly. On a sudden impulse I answered, "I wonder whether that opinion is held by all." I told him about the Gestapo.

He did not seem surprised. "Guess who told them to call you in?" he asked, looking at me expectantly. "I did! and do you know why? Because of your first name: 'Hiltgunt' sounded peculiar to me — a very unusual name, indeed. I know nobody else by that name, and we should always suspect whatever is out of the ordinary. For all I know, you might even have been a foreigner." He rubbed his hands again. He was in excellent spirits. "They called me today — I no longer have to keep an eye on you."

I smiled suavely as if I appreciated the good news; but I clenched my fists, hidden by his desk. I was very calm now and recognized that the time had come to intimidate him once and for all. "Don't be too certain," I said in a smooth voice. "You are only doing your duty when you watch me, just as I will be doing mine."

I stopped. The fat man looked uneasy. "What do you mean?"

I deliberately delayed my answer. From the distance came the sound of wooden shoes against the concrete. The polished desk top shone in the sunshine.

"I wasn't only asked questions. I was also urged to report on the activities of the prison's personnel."

"And what was your answer?"

"Aren't we both equally interested in cooperation with the Gestapo?"

"Cooperation?" He cleared his throat, took a cigar from his drawer and cut off the tip with his knife. "Why would the Gestapo watch me?" he exclaimed. Still, he seemed less sure of himself, and his stodgy fingers turned the lapel of his coat as if he wore secret insignia which only he himself knew about. "I belong to the Gestapo myself," he stated angrily. "I am an officer in their security division."

But obviously he had become aware that even membership in the Gestapo was not enough life insurance in the Third Reich. Small pearls of sweat appeared on his forehead and he got on his feet. "All right! In the future — no reports from either of us?"

"We'll see . . ." I replied vaguely, pretending not to notice his outstretched hand.

The clock in the tower struck again — twelve noon. What a strange hour the eleventh had been. I had been a prisoner of my own fear. I wanted to see Gunnar to tell him that I now understood what he meant. I could not — it would take months before it would be his turn again. But I repeated to myself his words, "Wherever you are, you will only be as free as you can free your mind of fear."

I still had a long way to go.

❖

Shortly before Christmas another official letter arrived. The blue envelope without a stamp was addressed to Mrs. Decker and informed her that her husband was dead.

The letter was a preprinted form with a space left open, where they had inserted his name.

Mrs. Decker had been ailing ever since her husband's arrest, and the morning after the letter arrived, we found her dead in bed. We called Dr. von Berg.

"What was the cause of her death?" I asked when he signed her death certificate.

He shrugged his shoulders. "I could not find any particular reason. Probably her heart gave out."

159

I thought I knew better. She had actually died the day her husband was arrested, but that last spark of hope had kept her breathing until word of his death arrived.

Their room was not vacant for long. Two other strangers came to our house with a slip of paper, authorizing them to occupy a room. Two elderly sisters. The one said when she entered, "We've lost everything twice. It seems that, wherever we go, the house is bombed out."

I resented her words. They stuck in my mind, as if with them death and destruction had knocked at our door. And I wanted to live. But sometimes at night, half awake, I thought I heard again the huffing and puffing as the Deckers had struggled up the stairs. Yet all that was left of them was the wagon, buried under the snow near our mountain ash tree.

26

IT WAS THE FIFTH CHRISTMAS since the war began. None of my brothers had come home. Only Hans, still assigned to the weather station, was in Germany. Guenther was with the German Luftwaffe in Holland, and Willfried was somewhere deep in Russia. In his letters he had mentioned locations we could not even find on the map, let alone pronounce.

For the first time we were without a Christmas tree. It snowed hard when I went to Mrs. Manning's old place and I found only a branch of pine. I placed it on our piano and fastened to it the Christmas angel, which used to sway in the top of our tree.

By evening the wind had whipped drifts of snow against our windows and frost had penetrated the cardboard which replaced our broken panes. We were short of fuel.

We lit a candle, and I read the Christmas story to my mother. But no one was there to play the piano and neither of us felt like singing.

Just after New Year's I fell ill. Dr. von Berg said I had infectious hepatitis and told me to stay home for at least six weeks. But after three weeks I received a call from the Rendsburg prison. "Three hundred Danish political prisoners have been transferred to us by the Gestapo," the Warden said. "We need you."

"I can't," I interrupted, still feeling ill. "Three hundred more prisoners! I can't," I repeated, and felt the perspiration breaking out all over my body.

"You must," the old man persisted. "The war cannot last much longer, perhaps only a few more months."

Only a few more months. How many times I had heard that line, from the very first day of the war, and from the day Hitler had come to power more than ten years ago. I remembered the schoolgirl who once, in her search for freedom, had crossed the border into Denmark. I saw myself standing under the huge oak tree and again relived the moment when a car had stopped and I had been offered shelter.

That day marked the beginning of the road which had led to my present work. How could I refuse this assignment?

o

The Port of Hamburg also had a Danish Seamen's Church, and its minister had obtained permission to visit the Danish prisoners in Rendsburg.

For our first trip, we were to meet at Hamburg's railroad station, and since he had never seen me before, I told him I would carry a tan suitcase. "I always carry my air-raid luggage," I added cautiously.

I had to keep up appearances — the guards in Rendsburg had become used to seeing me with my "belongings," but the suitcase was empty on that particular day. Since I did not yet know the Danish minister, I did not even bring vitamins in my purse.

The pastor was a young man, only recently arrived from Denmark, and very new on the job. I noticed that he carried a bulky package, and when we stopped at the restaurant to make up our prisoners' list, he placed the package in front of me reluctantly, almost with embarrassment.

"For you," he muttered.

I opened it and could not believe my eyes. Danish

sandwiches. At least a dozen of them. Open slices, heavily covered with cold cuts, garnished with parsley, bright green parsley in the middle of winter, pimento, anchovies, and other small extras I had forgotten existed. Staring at their colorful abundance, I was suddenly reminded of the grayness of our existence.

He had asked the Norwegian minister about me and had been told, "You'll have to find out for yourself." And, aware that Denmark was the only country in Nazi-occupied Europe not yet starving, Reverend Svendsen had added, "Take along a big package of tasty sandwiches. She's always hungry."

It struck me that the sandwiches had been provided when I needed them most. Even today I would not come to the prisoners empty handed. "Thank you for being so thoughtful," I exclaimed, quickly rewrapping them.

"But they are for you!" The Danish minister was perplexed.

I laughed and did not answer.

°

With the Norwegian and Danish ministers taking turns, I traveled more often to Rendsburg. As I censored the mail and visited the newly arrived Danish prisoners, their names and whereabouts were added to my growing secret file. The number of Scandinavian political prisoners in my "charge" had swelled to more than twelve hundred.

Before each prison journey my mother and I stayed up late baking bread. Mr. Mangold still provided the flour, but Mrs. Manning's potatoes were gone; and, whenever we needed more flour, he walked through our living room, cheerfully pointing out what he wanted in trade.

My mother was just as cheerful in giving. "How wonderful that what could have been destroyed by a bomb now will serve a good purpose," she would remark happily.

No china of worth was left, and now she had come to the silverware which we used only on special occasions. It had been her wedding present, and she had kept it in a special box in the cupboard of our dining room which previously had held the china, too.

I was with her when she opened the box. She had twelve place settings and each piece was carefully wrapped in tissue paper. She took out one of the spoons and I saw her hold and weigh it in her hand apparently far away in thought.

"Wouldn't you rather keep it?" I asked and anxiously waited for her reply.

"Keep it?" she repeated after a long silence.

The spoon was engraved with her initials. She looked at them and suddenly smiled as if something had occurred to her. Putting the spoon down, she turned to me and took my hand.

"Nothing in life is forever," she said.

She looked intently at me and continued, "You must learn to understand that only what you give, you'll have."

I was startled by her words and wondered what she meant. All I knew was that I felt quite attached to many of my belongings and often secretly worried about having to part with them, especially the things associated with my past.

Once Mr. Mangold light-heartedly touched our piano and suggested, "This piece would easily bring you a whole year's supply of flour."

"I'd die before I'd let you have it," I retorted.

Another time he tapped his finger on the Levys' radio but noticing the look on my face he passed quickly on.

I went to the harbor often to see Mr. Jenkins. He was like a massive rock in the ocean, never demanding an explanation and quietly responding to my pleas for help. I had long since ceased to wonder whether or not he knew the nature of my work.

○

January and February of 1944 seemed endless. It snowed for days at a time; paths had to be dug and snow and ice piled high along sidewalks and streets. Since I had ignored Dr. von Berg's advice, my hepatitis lingered on. I was fatigued and lost weight, but I was determined to go on.

I lived one day at a time, dividing myself between my prison work and my studies. But, more frequently than before, I was skipping classes, trying to make up by studying at night.

No longer did I count the alarms and I barely paid attention to the sound of the siren. The buzzing of the planes in the skies had ceased to frighten me.

Yet I was filled with as much fear as ever. I had become afraid of people. From the very beginning of the Nazi regime I had known their apathy, had observed how they closed their eyes and ears to the obvious, always shying away from getting involved. But after my interview with the Gestapo, I had a glimpse of the deliberate and unpredictable viciousness of the human mind. No siren would warn against its plotting and scheming; it was to be feared more than any haphazard bomb.

The Gestapo had asked me to furnish reports. Since I had ignored their request, I expected to be summoned again at any time. The dread of it faced me as I awoke every morning, and stayed with me at night, when sleep did not come. I lay staring up at the black skies and scattered lightbombs, waiting, watching for a car to stop, and a knock at our door.

Still, in spite of my fears I had moments of freedom, when I forgot about myself, moments when I accepted what I could not change and concentrated only on doing what was in my power each day, carrying bread and medicines to people in need. And truth. We continued passing on the news we heard on the BBC, often turning the prison visiting room into an island of hope, where we trusted and understood one another.

◦

I had not seen Gunnar for several months; then, one day in March, it was at last his turn. I put his name on the list; and as we stood outside the gate of the Rendsburg prison, I felt the first touch of spring in the air — the smell of freshly turned soil, the transparent blue of the morning.

But, as we crossed the courtyard, we saw no prisoners

walking the circle; and, arriving at the front door, we spotted unusual movement inside.

A guard let us in, and as I stepped through the gate I stood still, totally unprepared for what I saw: hall, stairs, and gangways full of men whose faces were familiar to me, yet they looked like strangers. They were our prisoners; but, instead of their uniforms, they were in civilian clothes. It seemed unreal.

My eyes began searching anxiously for Gunnar. I did not find him.

No guards were around. No one seemed to care what the prisoners were doing. They stood and chatted with each other, smoking stale cigarettes which they must have found in their civilian coats.

"We are being transferred!" they called out as they spotted us.

"Where?" We all asked the same question.

The air was tinged with excitement. I was bewildered. How different they looked without their uniforms. Their shaved heads were the only reminders that they were still prisoners. I suddenly saw them in a new light. They had become part of my life. We were like one huge family; and, although I knew from their letters that they had other families and had led other lives, it was not until I saw them in civilian clothes that I understood something I had not realized before: they each had a world of his own — a world I would never share. I felt left out, hurt, bitter.

I turned to the prisoner next to me. "Have you seen Gunnar Dal?" But no sooner had I asked than something struck me — something I had known all the time and yet had never fully understood: Gunnar, too, had a family of his own, a wife and a child.

How could I have forgotten for one moment that all I could hope and work for was to return each of them one day to that world of his own!

The prisoner, apparently not having heard my question, anxiously inquired, "Will you follow us?"

I hurried to the Warden's office. The German authorities

were expecting an invasion from England, he explained. All foreign prisoners were to be removed from areas as exposed as ours.

"But where will they be sent?"

"To many different places. You couldn't possibly follow."

"I will. Tell me where."

"I can't."

"You must."

He shook his head.

But I was not yet ready to give the battle up as lost. I stood at the door and looked at him intently until at last he reluctantly picked up a paper from his desk; and, coming over to me, he asked with a weary smile, "Don't you remember that I once told you a rule is a rule?"

I slipped the paper into my purse and did not look at it until we had left the prison. It was the list of all the camps and prisons to which the prisoners would be sent, and the old man had painstakingly marked how many would go to each particular place.

⚹

I learned Germany's geography all over again. Most of the locations on the list were unknown to me. The prisoners in my charge would be scattered all over the country, but I was grateful for one important fact: they all would remain under the jurisdiction of the Department of Justice.

I put my studies aside and got busy on the phone. I wrote letters to the administrators of more than twenty camps and prisons as far as five hundred miles apart. Eagerly I waited for responses and did not get discouraged when some of the replies were guarded, "Who are you?" "Why would you want to come all the way here?" and "We prefer a man for this job."

I smiled. I was a woman, but I was probably the only person in Germany holding the necessary degree in Scandinavian languages. I continued writing, phoning, and waiting.

One response surprised me. It came from Dreibergen, the prison where most of the Scandinavians had been sent. It was somewhere in East Germany, and, before my letter could have reached them, I received a cable. "You have been recommended to us. Can you come?"

I did not take time to wonder who could have spoken for me. I sent word to the Norwegian minister and we set out the very next day.

°

It was several hours by train. All signs of spring had disappeared when we approached Dreibergen. East Germany was still buried under snow. The town was more than a mile away from the tracks. Some sleighs were waiting at the railroad station, but they were not for us.

As usual we were carrying suitcases. Not that we carried bread and medications on this trip. We would not have dared. But we had made them heavy with personal belongings, trying to impress on the prison's administration at once that we always would have our air-raid luggage with us. We walked past open fields on a dirt road, not yet cleared of snow; and, as we reached Dreibergen's outskirts, I stopped, still weakened from my attack of hepatitis.

Up on a hill stood a castle, ancient and beautiful, and this monument of the past was in peculiar contrast to the shabby cottages around us, huddled close to the frozen ground.

An old woman was sweeping the snow from the sidewalk.

"What is the name of the castle?" I pointed up to the hill.

She looked up with a toothless smile. "Prison," she said and continued to sweep.

At close sight the castle was not beautiful at all. It was a fortress and its threatening gloom bore silent witness to people who centuries ago had given their sweat and blood to build these walls. The Nazis had merely added window bars to convert it to their own special needs.

There was no bell and we knocked, but the iron gate was so thick that we had to use our fists.

"What do you want?" a gruff voice finally inquired.

We were let in; and, as we were led through the courtyard, we saw prisoners walking in the circle. We recognized our friends and slowed our steps. My eyes raced over the faces, searching. He was not there.

Still, what a moment it was. Their faces lit up and they waved their arms as if to keep warm. We knew their language — they were bidding us welcome. My fatigue was gone and my suitcase seemed lighter.

But the walls of this fortress were built to last. The deathlike silence inside was interrupted only by short shouts of commands and the click-clack of wooden shoes on the stone floors. And its smell was familiar — all prisons smelled alike: burned oatmeal.

I was led to the Warden's office alone. The Administrator was also present. His exuberantly red nose shone with perspiration; and, for no apparent reason, he kept saying, "Heil Hitler!" eagerly fingering the Party emblem in his lapel, as if to convince me that he was a devoted Nazi.

The Warden wore skintight brown pants, and, during our session, he continuously exchanged meaningful glances with his superior; they were clearly saying, "Caution!"

They did not inquire about my credentials and told me it would be solely up to me how often the prisoners could write or receive mail and be visited. I was handed a list of the Scandinavian prisoners. "Why don't you tell us how best to place and use them?" they said.

I was stunned. They had met me only today. Why did they so willingly ask my advice? Who could have spoken for me?

I glanced over the list in my hand. But the name I was searching for was not there. I had to get hold of myself.

"What workshops do you have?" I began.

Here was my chance. Prisoners who for years had been in solitary confinement I now placed together in the same cell. Fathers and sons, or brothers, would meet again. I got them assigned to jobs which would at least remotely remind them of their lives outside. Soon journalists and authors were assigned to the prison's printing shop, farmers to the dairy, and physicians and paramedical personnel to the infirmary. Prisoners, blown up by the edema of starvation, I praised as especially capable of working in the kitchen. As our session progressed, my elation was growing about such an unexpected outcome of my first visit in this fortress of gloom.

Before we ended our first meeting, the Administrator asked a question I was not prepared for at all.

"Are you going to see your friend?"

I immediately grew tense. I automatically suspected all strangers, and I recoiled at the thought of an unknown friend. Reverting to the "game," I smiled and asked, "Where would I go?"

"Oh, naturally to the Women's prison," he stated and raised his arm to another "Heil Hitler!"

I was confused, not knowing what to think or expect. Yet I thought the safest move would be to find out at once. More running than walking I covered the half mile to the Women's prison without even putting my suitcase down once.

I was led straight to the Director's office. In a huge armchair behind a desk covered with papers and files sat a woman who seemed vaguely familiar, but I felt certain we had never met. Where had I seen that almost majestic posture, the quiet strength in the eyes?

"I've waited a long time to meet you," she said and the moment she smiled, I knew.

"I know your father!" I exclaimed.

"I used to know yours."

She was Mr. Jenkins' daughter; and, as we sat down and talked, all the pieces at last fell in place.

Before her assignment in Dreibergen, Anna had been employed in the prison system of Hamburg. "I learned about you·when you worked for the Postal Censorship and brought my father certain letters," she said and smiled again.

She was the one who had recommended me to the District Attorney for my initial assignment at Hamburg's prison. "The D.A. is on your side," she added quietly. "He recommended you in Rendsburg, and he again came to your aid here."

I also learned why Dreibergen's Warden and Administrator had acted as if they were almost afraid of me.

"This was my doing," Anna revealed. "I had to lay the ground for your work." She had told them I was in charge of all Scandinavian prisoners in Germany, and had hinted that I had special connections with the Gestapo, since, wherever I worked, they no longer interfered.

◦

It was late when the minister and I arrived at the "German House," the town's only hotel. It was old and decayed. "The kitchen is closed," the innkeeper said. We would have to go to bed without food.

The washbasin in my room had a crack. Plaster rustled from the ceiling, and over my bed was an old, dusty print, depicting a knight's fight with a dragon. "Finis Terrae!" was its title, "The end of the world!" But I did not care. I could have shouted for joy. The illness of the winter was forgotten.

I felt like climbing a mountain or walking the ocean. Again a helping hand had reached out when I had needed it most, opening doors that appeared closed, guiding me onward when I thought the path had come to an end.

My thoughts turned to Gunnar. I had asked some of the prisoners if they knew where he had been sent. Nobody did. But at this moment I had no doubts. I would find him. I would see him again.

I tore open the window to let air into the stale, unheated room. The sky was black, without searchlights or flares. I could see only one star, but its light was very bright in the deep dark of the night.

◦

Back in Hamburg I resumed my efforts to get access to the remaining prisons and camps. Having been accepted in Dreibergen, I now had an example I could use. Soon all other doors opened, except one. A prison near Dresden cut me off with one sentence, "We only allow German spoken here." It was a prison notorious for its unbending rigidity. Not only did they bar any visits, they also insisted that all mail be written in German; they censored it themselves.

I did not give up. I sat down and addressed myself to the Department of Justice in Berlin.

If they had permitted Scandinavian prisoners to get visits, conducted in their own language, I wrote, how then could one prison refuse?

"After all," I argued, "a rule is a rule."

27

BY THE END OF MARCH my semester vacation started. Although two months without classes would leave me free to go on prolonged journeys, I could not completely forget my medical studies. Another exam lay ahead, and I was determined to set aside two hours each day for study. Now my luggage was heavier than ever. I carried my books along, reading in waiting rooms of railroad stations and in my hotel room at night.

We spent countless hours on trains and even longer waiting for them. The promptness of the German railroad had been shattered by the bombs of the American Air Force. The timetable existed only in print.

An order had been issued that no one could travel without a special permit; yet it seemed as if all Germany were on the move. Soldiers, Nazi officials, and civilians on special assignments like mine shared the trains with the refugees of the Third Reich — men, women, and children whose homes had been bombed. No train was long enough to hold them. Still, they were all granted permits — the local authorities being only too eager to rid themselves of the unwanted "have-nots."

Day and night they crowded the railroad stations, waiting to get away, hoping to find shelter with a relative or friend somewhere else. Huddled together in clusters on the platforms, they were surrounded by cardboard boxes and bundles containing the only possessions they had left, and they waited in a daze as hour after hour passed by. At the screech of the siren they reluctantly got up to be herded down to the catacombs under the railroad station, and, the alarm over, they slowly drifted back to the platforms where they resumed staring down the empty tracks — waiting.

The first sight of an approaching train sparked the listless mass into a raging mob. The station became one surge of people, fighting and clawing their way toward the train doors, pulling their last belongings and screaming children along. It was a war within the war, where I, too, learned to use fists and feet. Arriving on board was a victory in a battle where only the strongest had a chance to survive.

The train, ready to depart, groaned in protest. Its passengers were so tightly packed that it took the combined weight of several railroad officials pressing against the compartment door from the outside to shut it. Then, at last, a jerk. We held our breath, another jerk. The train moved. We sighed with relief.

The passengers stood swaying back and forth as one big body, or squeezed together on the seats until backs ached and seemed locked in a permanently bent position. Only occasionally did I catch a glimpse out the window; and, as we passed through North Germany's flatlands toward the hills and mountains of the South, I saw the patches of ice give way to the first green of spring.

We carried our suitcases over swampy marshlands and concrete roads. We walked over the cobblestones of small, sleepy hamlets and hurried over the asphalt streets of Berlin. The Scandinavian prisoners were now scattered in so many different places that we could not visit each group as often as before.

Some were always waiting, and, to make up for the lack of personal contact, I began to write greetings on their incoming mail. I used block letters, so that my handwriting could not be identified easily. Sometimes I wrote only a few words, sometimes a whole paragraph. Always they were meant to say, "You are not forgotten."

Each time we entered a prison I looked for Gunnar. Each time I was disappointed. When I came home after a trip, my first glance went to the bundles of letters on my desk. Hastily I leafed through them in search of his name, but weeks went by without any clues as to his whereabouts.

Soon my secret file on the locations of the Scandinavian

prisoners was up-to-date again — short of thirty men. I knew where they were, but we had no communication. They had been sent to the place near Dresden, the only prison which had turned me down.

Gunnar had to be one of them.

The Department of Justice in Berlin had not yet answered my letter, and one day I went to the District Attorney in Hamburg. But he shrugged his shoulders. "You must be patient," he said. "I've done all I can."

✿

I spent Easter at home. No trains for civilians were running during the holidays. In Hamburg the atmosphere was growing increasingly tense, with almost continuous alarms day and night.

Everyone was expecting the worst; and, in their fear, people began to talk openly about the war. The invasion from England was inevitable, they said; and what were they going to do if, one morning, they awakened to find British and American tanks in the streets? What would happen to their homes, to their belongings? Would the enemy loot and destroy? Would they take away their cameras and watches? What about the silverware and the china? One would have to find places to hide them. So the talk went, and everyone seemed far more concerned for their possessions than for their lives.

Rumors caught on like wildfire. One day we heard that paratroopers were landing near Hamburg; next someone claimed that burning phosphorus would be dropped from the skies at night. Our ideas of war focused more and more on our own immediate surroundings. No longer did we think in terms of soldiers fighting at the front lines. There was only one front that mattered, our own backyard. Our trenches were the holes we dug to hide our possessions.

People had begun to make extensive preparations for the invasion they were so sure would come. What they did made little sense; yet soon I found myself doing the same.

Chairs, even tables and sometimes a bed, were stacked up

in gardens in case the house was bombed or burned. Wires were strung from tree to tree — not to ward off the enemy, but to hang suits and dresses; and what we hoped to save from tanks or bombs often was spoiled by a drenching rain. More holes were dug, and each night we raced back and forth to fill them with suitcases and bundles.

It was like a game of musical chairs. Only those who still had something to lose kept running, while the boarders, the "have-nots," who had been bombed out, watched from the windows upstairs, their silent stares expressing a mixture of envy and satisfaction.

Good Friday there was a knock at our door. Outside stood the farmer who had picked up our lamb the day Mrs. Manning had died.

"I have something for you," he said, handing me a cardboard box and a bag of feed. "It will help you to get through next winter."

Against the palms of my hands I felt the scraping of tiny feet through the cardboard, and through the holes in the top came some excited peeps and a flurry of golden yellow.

We had a wooden shack in the back of our yard for our garden tools. It was without windows and not big enough to hold Mr. Decker's wagon, but it would do for our new boarders. The farmer helped us replace the door with a piece of board just big enough to keep the chicks inside. They were only eight days old, and all they needed to feel at home in our old shack was a little water and feed.

Early that day a few bombs had been dropped and at night we returned to the bunker. The floor was still covered with water; they had tried to clean up between two alarms. I had not been to the shelter for quite some time; still, it seemed unchanged. There on the bench was the young mother. She held the two older children on her lap while her foot rocked the carriage. The pale, weary face of the baby stared from the pillow; he was almost a year old now. When we first came to the shelter he had been only eight days old. Now his face had the look of all the other faces — the old women, the children, the "Hitler Youth" leaning against the railing, and the men in work clothes, worn with fatigue, sagging against the wall. In the bleak light of the bunker they all looked the same. Their skin had taken on a gray hue from lack of air and sleep. Their eyes stared into space, just marking time.

The American bombers droned over Hamburg without dropping their cargo. Their target was elsewhere tonight. "Thank God," we thought. But the alarm did not yet come to an end. Perhaps on their way back they would carry some leftover bombs; and, while we waited, a whole city prayed, "Please let them drop their bombs somewhere else!"

I prayed too.

The air was stifling. The two children on their mother's lap woke up and began moving around, climbing over suitcases and bundles, looking for playmates. Soon the concrete walls echoed with their high-pitched screams. The little one in the carriage got restless, stretching out his arms toward his mother, but she did not see. She had slumped forward in a stuporlike sleep.

The group of older children climbed their way back to the carriage. They pulled out the baby, pushed some bundles aside and placed him on the wet floor. Forming a circle around him they started to sing, "Ring around the rosie . . ."

Perhaps it was the staleness of the air combined with the dampness of the floor that made me nauseated. I had to get out. Abruptly I jumped up from the bench, stepped over bundles and suitcases, pushed past the people sitting on the floor and headed for the door. But it was locked and the air-raid warden had his hand on the latch.

"You can't get out," he said sternly. "You are in it with the rest of us," and, pulling his helmet down, looking over the bodies huddled tightly together, he triumphantly stated, "no, sir, nobody gets out."

°

I traveled all of May and did not come home until the first week of June. On the train I heard rumors about a heavy air raid on Hamburg, and I ran the ten minutes from the railroad station till I could catch a first glimpse of our street. My apprehension grew with each step, "Was our house spared?"

It was. There stood the hawthorn — in bloom, with its fiery red branches stretched wide like a sentry shielding us from the rest of the world.

Summer had come. Our rooms seemed much brighter. The windows, covered by cardboard, had been closed during the winter and the cool days of spring. Now they stood open, filling our living room with light. Again the sun found its way to the shiny black top of the piano — as it always used to do by late afternoon.

From the garden came the chickens' eager cackling. They had grown in size and taken over the yard, jumping over the wooden board which could no longer hold them back.

And, as darkness fell and the moon in its first reddish-gold shine, big as a wagon wheel, rose above our hedge, I thought how good it was to be home.

In the middle of the night our doorbell rang. I was half asleep and could not be sure because the rings were short and seemed hushed. Grabbing my robe, I ran barefoot across the hall to my mother's room. The two elderly sisters had turned on their light, and Mr. Mangold, in silk pajamas, stopped me outside his door. "Are they back again?"

With a quick glance I ascertained that the street outside was empty of cars. Half hidden by the hawthorn, a uniformed man stood at our door. He was looking up at our window.

"Willfried!"

He had come on furlough from Russia.

"How long can you stay?"

"Two weeks."

I looked at the calendar . . . it was the fifth of June.

The journey from the Eastern front had taken eight days and nights by train, and Willfried looked pale and worn, but none of us could think of sleep. With an air of happy excitement my mother prepared a midnight supper. I don't recall what was on our plates. Maybe oatmeal or turnips, perhaps even a cake? But with a white damask cloth, what was left of the good silver, a bottle of red wine, saved for a special occasion, and a twig from the hawthorn — it seemed like Christmas.

It was like magic: with the ring of the bell, the war had faded away. Willfried's presence had brought back the old togetherness, and the hope that one day life would resume again, leaving war and destruction behind like a bad dream of a night gone by.

Our laughter and happy talk was suddenly interrupted: the siren screamed . . . We heard Mr. Mangold and the two elderly sisters leave hurriedly for the bunker. But we stayed behind. Perhaps the wine had made us careless — we wanted to hold on to a midnight hour that had given us a glimpse of peace. We turned out the lights, opened the windows, and listened to the sounds of the night.

The music from the tavern had died down; there was no more stomping of feet. No sound came from the deserted houses nearby, not even the cry of a child or the bark of a dog. So total was the stillness that we could have heard a leaf fall to the ground. The skies remained quiet; there was not so much as the buzzing of a plane, yet, from the darkness outside war seemed to stare at us, drawing us back into its grip.

"Willfried, how is it in Russia?" my mother at last asked.

He did not answer at once; and his first words came haltingly, then pouring out of him as if the burden of his memories was too heavy to carry alone any longer. He was serving as a physician at the Russian front line; and, as I listened, I saw the war through his eyes — blood, stench, pus, infections, amputations, frozen legs, and open bellies; I heard the screams of the wounded and the sighs of the dying.

He told of the winter in the East, when the German troops still had been marching forward. Now they were in retreat — somewhere deep in Russia — leaving hate and destruction along their trail. Whole populations of villages were wiped out because of the resistance of a few.

Russian soldiers by the thousands had stormed the German trenches. Not even covered by their own artillery, they ran blindly, like a human wave, into the fire of the German machine guns. Yelling a battle cry which to German ears sounded like "Hooooraaaay!", the Russians were mowed down like grass by a sickle.

Willfried had gone into the field after that battle to render first aid to German and Russian alike, and there he came upon a Russian soldier, blood coursing from a torn artery in his leg. As Willfried knelt to apply a tourniquet, the soldier, hatred burning in his eyes, quickly pulled his knife.

I could not see my brother's face in the dark, but the bitterness in his voice made me shiver.

"Maybe the only good man is a dead man," he said.

I remembered the day when Willfried asked my mother why she had never told us that there are evil people in our world and she had replied, "Let us answer evil with good."

Willfried talked on, and as I listened, I began to realize that the war in Russia was not only a contest with the German aggressor over the right to a territory; rather, it was a clash between two systems, curiously alike in their glorification of collective thinking and action, and in their irreverence for the individual.

Still, the people caught up in this clash were human beings: men, women, and children who felt pain and joy, hate and love, who could cry and laugh, and who had that unique ability given to all people — an awareness of good and evil — and the power to choose between them.

It was dawn before the all-clear was sounded. I let our boarders in.

"Nothing happened," said one of the sisters looking around our hallway for a possible damage. "But you just wait . . . one of these days."

The sun was almost up before we got to bed, and we slept until noon. I arose before any of the others. Our house was strangely silent; but when I opened the front door, I saw a cluster of our neighbors gathered in the street. They were talking excitedly.

"What happened?" I called out.

"You don't know yet?"

I ran to join them; they were all talking at the same time.

"The Invasion!" "It started this morning." "They have landed in France." "Thank God, it is far away!"

They gave a sigh of relief.

I felt my heart in my throat, as I raced back inside to waken my mother and Willfried. "The Invasion has started!" I repeated it over and over again. The words sounded to me like the first hymn of peace. I thought of my prisoners, of Gunnar, and my hopes soared. Now surely the war would be over in less than a month.

A telegram arrived that same afternoon ordering Willfried back to Russia. The Invasion had canceled all furloughs. He was to report to the railroad station before midnight.

At dusk we went one last time into the garden. From the tavern nearby came the music. They were dancing again; only the immediate threat of the siren could bring their feet to a standstill. But the skies were quiet, unusually quiet. No alarms, no bombs. The chickens were lined up silently on the edge of Mr. Decker's wagon, contentedly soaking up the last light of the day.

We looked at the roses — the first ones were in bloom. They had come back after all. The roots, deep in the ground, had survived the last year's heavy bombing.

Turning toward the mountain ash tree, Willfried noticed the wagon and wanted to know how we got it.

"It's a long story," I replied vaguely, "and there is so little time left." I felt a lump coming in my throat.

Willfried stepped close to the tree, touched its trunk and looked up to the berries; it was only June, and they were still tiny and green. "The earlier they turn red, the harder the winter will be," he remarked.

There was a deep silence. At last Willfried spoke again. Lifting my face in his hands, he looked at me intently. "Take care of Mother!" he said, and in his eyes I read all those things he wanted to say but could not.

I tried not to cry.

"Don't worry, the war will end soon," I said.

He did not answer.

We took him to the station. He boarded and leaned out of

the window for a final farewell before the long troop train pulled out. Other soldiers were jammed in behind him, and many were shouting their last good-byes to wives and mothers.

I now realized that, during the long years of the war, I had barely given Willfried a thought, not taking time to write him more than a handful of letters. I had given all my time to prisoners of the Third Reich, the government I had come to hate — and I had failed to understand that Willfried and many others were also victims. Weren't they also prisoners, punished by circumstances over which they had no control?

Willfried looked pale and worn as he reached down to my mother. "Thank you — for everything," he said and took her hand.

"Willfried, don't give up serving life!" she replied in a low voice. "It is the only hope left."

The train moved, gained speed, and was in moments out of sight. I saw the sadness in my mother's eyes but did not know what to say; I turned away and stared into the darkness where the tracks lay empty. I had failed. I, too, had tried to serve life. But in helping the many, I had forgotten the one. And he was my brother.

○

With a magnifying glass I searched in my atlas for the place in France where the Allies had landed: Normandy. Measuring the distance from the German border, they seemed so near. For the next days I listened eagerly to the news from London, with my eyes glued to the map. But one week passed, and two — without so much as an "inch" of progress by the Allied troops. The war went on. The liberation — our liberation from the Nazis — seemed as far away as before.

People settled down again, no longer talking about the Invasion. After all, why should they be concerned about what had happened in France? In their minds France was as far away as Russia. What mattered was here and now. The lines in front of the stores seemed longer every day. They waited for the meat at the butcher's and wound up with bones instead. The pail of milk they brought home from the dairy was diluted to a light bluish color, and barely enough for an infant. After five years of war, rations had been cut down to the barest necessities. With the harvest still far away, vegetables were scarce. People spent hours in line for last winter's sprouted potatoes or the half-rotten remnants of turnips. And as they stood waiting, their eyes anxiously searched the skies for enemy planes, hoping, praying that their homes might be spared.

Their thoughts went back to the old, narrow circles of sustenance and survival, and I slipped into the same trap. That first week after Willfried left, I had written him a letter — and the second week, but the third week I did not find time and, within a month, I had forgotten.

I traveled again, read prisoners' letters, bundle after bundle, and studied my medical books two hours each day. As I went from one prison to the other, my thoughts always returned to the forbidding walls of the one from which I was barred.

Months had passed without an answer from the Department of Justice in Berlin. Would it ever come? Was there any hope left that I would see Gunnar again? I was impatient and restless. The war had forced all of us to live for today. I, too, wanted to live now.

But gradually my restlessness gave way to exhaustion, my impatience turned into resignation, and in the gray weariness of an almost robotlike existence I struggled through one day at a time, ceasing to hope for tomorrow.

°

But then one day in July something happened. We were again in Dreibergen. I don't know how the prisoners discovered it was my birthday, but all through the day, as each in his turn entered the visiting room, presents were pulled out of their hiding places in sleeves, leggings, and coats.

There was a letter folder made from boot leather. "From your friends in the cobbler shop." Scrapbooks and notebooks, bound in tin foil, from the bookbinder shop. A belt, bookmarks, and a small bell hammered in iron. The gifts had been made in secret from stolen material. A basket from the basket shop held a single rose and a note, "Stolen from the Warden's garden!"

Never had I received so many gifts. Never had I felt so loved. With a smile and a "Thank you," each prisoner shook my hand.

As we were trying to close my bulging suitcase before leaving, a final gift arrived. Dark green slippers, made of heavy felt. A small flag was in the package, Norway's colors, red, white, and blue. A note added, "For the last leg of your journey," signed by five prisoners. In peace time they had been a fisherman, an air force officer, a sailor, an editor, and a journalist. Now they worked in the tailor shop.

"Be careful," warned the Norwegian minister as we left the visiting room. "Don't let the guards see that you've had a happy day."

We were scheduled to leave Dreibergen early the next morning, but our train was delayed. When it finally arrived in the late afternoon, it was bursting with people. On board, we stood so tightly packed that my legs became numb.

Near midnight the train came to a halt, and the doors were flung open. The railroad official shouted commands, "Everybody out!"

Hamburg had been under a heavy air-raid attack, and the tracks had been ripped apart . . . the train could go no farther. We were still miles from the city, in open fields. There were no houses in sight. The crowd seemed bewildered, not knowing what to do.

Again orders were shouted, "Move on! Get going!"

We set out, cutting across the fields, and soon a path was worn through the trampled grass by hundreds of feet. The light of the moon lay cold over the pastures. The procession thinned out, as men, women, and children dropped from exhaustion. When we reached the edge of Hamburg, only a few still moved on.

The ruins began, but the bunkers were untouched. We walked until we reached the center of town.

"Fire." The Norwegian minister pointed in the direction of the port.

"Fire." I pointed toward my part of the city.

Then we separated. I was alone and my steps sounded hollow in the quiet of the night. Dragging my suitcase behind me I walked on past the empty shells of houses. But somehow in the maze of torn-up streets lined with ghostly façades, I lost my way, and, overcome by fatigue, I sank down on the curb.

There in front of a smoldering heap of ruins stood a soldier. I called out to him, "Can you show me the way?"

At first I thought that he had not heard me. Then he looked up abruptly. "Where am *I* going?" he asked.

"Where did you come from?"

His yell cut the silence of the night. "That was my home!" He pointed to the smoking ruins before him. Then he staggered as if he were drunk, slumped to a concrete block, and mumbled to himself, "I'll quit!"

Something scurried down the street, small fat creatures, moving about quickly. Rats, burrowing into the ruins.

I got up and hurried on, but soon my feet gave out and I sat down on the curb again. My shoes felt like a vise, tightly clamped around my swollen feet. I took them off.

It was near dawn. The first pink of the sunrise showed at the horizon — oddly competing with the glaring flames in the sky. It was then I remembered the green felt slippers in my suitcase, designated for the "last leg of my journey." Strength seemed to come from them, and I walked on with renewed vigor.

I walked and walked, until I arrived at the corner of our street. There I stopped. Ruins were all around me. One more step would bring me in sight of our house — if it were still standing. I took a deep breath and turned the corner. My eyes first fell on the hawthorn tree and — safely standing behind it — my home.

28

I HAD NOT YET EXCHANGED MANY WORDS with the two elderly sisters. The day they appeared at our doorsteps, we noticed the emblem of the Nazi Party on their coat lapels. They had been our boarders for more than six months and we did not feel they were a threat. They seemed to belong with the majority of Germans who, sooner or later, succumbed to pressure and joined the Party, not because of their convictions, but because they had none. I avoided meeting them. Perhaps I still remembered their prediction that disaster was on their trail; or was it a sense of guilt, the same feeling I had when the Deckers, after a long look at our living room, had glanced at each other and sighed.

Theresa and Irmgard Hedrich stayed to themselves. Their life appeared as gray as the sweaters they wore summer and winter, tightly pinned at the neck. It was difficult to tell one sister from the other except for Theresa's head, which was in continuous motion. At first her peculiar nod captured my attention whenever we were in the same room. The motion was constant and rhythmical like the pendulum of a clock. Irmgard confided that her sister had begun nodding after their first night of bombing, and now the nods would turn into a shake as soon as an alarm sounded.

Theresa had been a government employee and was drawing a small pension which together with her sister's earnings seemed just enough to get them by. Each morning Irmgard left for work at the crack of dawn, often after spending the night in the bunker. She returned home late in the afternoon, and we could set our clock by the time when she would pass through our hall like a shadow on the way to her room.

At suppertime she came to life, like a puppet set free for one magic hour. Then, even with our door closed, we heard her singsong voice from the kitchen, relating the news she had brought home from work. Stories were scarce, but she made them last by thrashing them over and over until they were worn to shreds. She relished tales about people who supposedly suffered from some fatal illness and were bound to die soon. She never tired of repeating their symptoms, even when Theresa, hard of hearing, constantly interrupted her. This monotonous singsong came to an end only with the scraping of their spoons, as they meticulously cleaned their plates.

At times I pitied them. Cheated out of a life of their own, they had to seek consolation in the mishaps of others. But one night I happened to be in the hall when Mr. Mangold came home. As usual he was loaded with packages; and, as he passed the kitchen, Irmgard looked up, stopping in the middle of a sentence. I did not like the piercing stare of her eyes, the quick glance at Theresa and the ensuing silence.

The only luggage the sisters brought the day they moved in was their radio. By good fortune it had been in a repair shop the night of their bombing. Now that they were confined to just one room, it became the center of their existence, their only link to life. At night, when they left for the bunker, they took it along, carefully holding it between them in Theresa's grocery net.

The radio was never turned off; it blared morning, noon, and night. Since Theresa, hard of hearing, always turned it up, the sounds drenched our home with military marches, battering our ears with the propaganda of the German newscasts, and even spilling it out into the street. We did not object, mindful of our own secret sessions with BBC; but when I studied or read, I covered my ears with my hands in a futile attempt to shut out the voice of the Nazis.

Yet, there came the day when I listened with sudden interest:

On July 20, 1944, I was home between prison trips. I was at my desk, reading prisoners' mail, when the pounding noise of a march was interrupted by the brief announcement, "This is a special news bulletin." At first I did not pay any attention and continued reading. "Special bulletins" were as frequent as our rations were scarce. They had been our daily food since the onset of war — only the announcements no longer concerned "victory," but "victorious retreats."

But something was different this time. Was it the voice of the announcer? He sounded strange; could he be drunk, or had he gone mad? I put my letter aside, listened intently — and felt my throat tighten.

"An attempt has been made on Hitler's life," the announcer shouted, stumbling over the words. "Early this morning a group of German officers tried to overthrow the regime!" His voice cracked with emotion.

I jumped up from my chair, pushing it back so hard that it fell to the floor. I rushed downstairs to the living room and turned on our radio. Impatiently waiting for it to warm up, I ran to the window and yelled out to my mother in the yard, "Come in — hurry!"

All we caught was the end of the newscast: "Der Fuehrer will make a speech late tonight."

He was alive after all. Our faces fell. I did not yet want to believe it. I closed the windows, locked the door, and tuned in BBC. But there was no news. I turned back to the German station. We stayed close to the radio and waited, waited for hours, still clinging to a hope which, for one brief moment, like the first rose at the horizon, had promised us dawn.

At last my mother got up, turned off the radio, and said with bitterness in her voice, "What a strange time for a rebellion. The officers waited till they saw that Hitler had lost the war. What did they hope to change if he had died?"

"It would have ended the war."

"The war?" she asked slowly. "Perhaps this one, but there will be another war and another as long as the spirit of Hitler is in the minds of the people."

The sun had set. It was dark when we went to the kitchen. It was long past the Hedriches' suppertime, but they were still at the table. They had not cleared away their empty plates, and there was some chicory left in their mugs. Irmgard's face looked flushed and Theresa's head shook more than ever. For a second I wondered which side they were on. But then Irmgard lamented, "Why would they try to do away with our Fuehrer? He's all we've got!" Her voice shaking with emotion, she began to tell what their lives had been like before Hitler had come to power. The picture was a sad and bleak one. Both their brothers had died in World War I. They had lost their savings during the depression of the Twenties. They had been without jobs. "Whom could we have turned to but *him?*" Her face lit up as if she were talking about a supernatural being. "He gave us work, an army, a Germany stronger than ever, and all he asked was that we give ourselves in return." She smiled. I had never before seen her smile and, for some reason, the sight made me ache inside. She rambled on, chanting the words with religious fervor, "He thinks for us, decides for us, knows what is best for us."

My mother, preparing our supper, had not looked up once. But at this point she quietly interjected, "Tell me, Miss Hedrich, what was your home like before it was bombed out?"

Mr. Mangold had joined us and was brewing his coffee. He coughed — he always coughed when he was nervous. He stood at the stove, taking quick sips from his steaming mug, and, as the aroma of coffee spread over the kitchen, I saw him glance sideways at the sisters, obviously impatient for them to leave.

But they did not move. Irmgard had ceased talking and I saw her look at Mr. Mangold with the piercing glare I had seen once before. None of us spoke. With a snort of angry disgust, Irmgard abruptly got up, took her mug and emptied the chicory into the sink. "Come on, Theresa," she said, "let's get out of here. We must turn on our radio and listen for our Fuehrer."

"Yeah, he sure is all they've got!" Mr. Mangold sneered behind them, as soon as they were out in the hall.

But Irmgard must have heard him. Quick as lightning she was back, her face purple and her eyes glittering with anger. "What was it you said?" she hissed.

Mr. Mangold, shrugging his shoulders, mumbled, "I don't know what you're talking about." But she did not give in. I had never seen her this way. She turned to me with fierce determination. "You heard what he said?"

"He agrees with you," I assured her. "The Fuehrer is all we've got."

"That was not what he said," she snapped.

"That's all we heard," my mother calmly intervened.

Irmgard was about to answer, but apparently changed her mind. She threw her head back and with a grim expression left the kitchen.

My mother glanced into the hall to make sure the sisters had gone, then turned to Mr. Mangold. "I wish you were more careful," she said.

He coughed and, shrugging his shoulders again, muttered, "I just could not help myself." He filled our mugs with coffee and said with a wary smile, "It was a bad day for you, too, I guess."

We did not reply, but Mr. Mangold, as if he suddenly had come to a decision, put his mug down, and began, "There is something I want to tell you . . ."

He did not get any further. At that moment the Hedriches' radio blared out. The volume on full, Hitler's voice rolled over us like an avalanche, cutting off our breath and choking Mr. Mangold into silence.

Whatever he had meant to tell us remained unsaid; before Hitler had ended the speech, he had left for his room.

Late that night we heard a knock at our front door, a familiar knock. "I was worried for you," Dr. von Berg said when we opened. He looked worn out, more tired than I had ever seen him before. Making sure that the door to our living room was closed and lowering his voice to a whisper, he turned to me. "I have come to warn you," he said. "You must be very careful. Many people will be killed in the days to come. Many more will be arrested. Don't travel. You will be safer at home."

"Safer?" I wondered.

I could not find sleep that night, although the sky remained empty and quiet. It was not so much the failed assassination I thought of, but what had happened in our kitchen. I tossed and turned, hearing again Irmgard's whining voice change in an instant into the shrill sound of fierce determination. Even with my eyes closed, I saw her piercing stare.

I opened my window and listened into the night. It was quiet outside, but from inside the house I heard Mr. Mangold's cough and wondered what he had wanted to tell us.

°

Only once more did I hear the attempted assassination mentioned in a German newscast. A brief statement was issued the following day that anybody directly or indirectly involved would soon be arrested and liquidated. No further details were disclosed, and the silence which followed was more threatening than any news.

During the early days of the Invasion the air had been buzzing with rumors. Now there were none, and people acted as if the 20th of July had never happened. But when I stood in the food lines and watched their masklike faces, I knew they only pretended. For the first time they had witnessed open rebellion by Germans. For the first time since Hitler had come to power their state of dull acceptance had been shaken. Yet even now they dared not form their own opinions. Their only visible reaction was fright and suspicion, and at night, when we were packed side by side in the bunker, the air was heavy with fear. Each spoken word was carefully weighed and the silence was filled with distrust.

Or did I only imagine that people had changed? At home everything went on as before. Mr. Mangold was as busy as always, carrying his shopping bags in and out and making his telephone calls. The two elderly sisters never so much as mentioned what had happened that night, and from the kitchen we again heard Irmgard's singsong voice dwelling on illness and death.

°

One week after the attempted assassination Reverend Svendsen and I traveled to Dreibergen. We arrived in the late

189

afternoon while the warmth of the sun still lay over fields and pastures. Stepping off the train, I recalled the day we had come here for the first time — the icy wind, the sleighs waiting near the tracks, the paths blocked by snowdrifts, and the toothless old woman.

Now the corn stood high and golden, swaying in the evening breeze, rippling in waves toward the horizon. Poppies, glowing red in the light of the setting sun, crowded the edge of the fields. Bluebells framed the paths, and, as we walked toward the town, war seemed far away.

It was dusk when we arrived at the first cottages. The evening was mild and people were still working in their yards. What little land they had was planted and well kept. The men wore the green uniforms of prison guards; but, tending their soil, they had cast off their green jackets. They smoked home-grown tobacco — I noticed patches of plants in their yards.

One guard stood in front of his cottage with a child on his arm. As we passed, he lifted the little boy above his head and asked laughingly, "Look! Who is taller than I?"

At the "German House" the innkeeper greeted us with a sullen, "You are late!" But having become used to our visits, he brought some supper. Fried potatoes and two slices of beets for each of us. And a mug of beer — its only resemblance to the prewar brew the foam and the yellow color.

The dining room was small and the air was as stale as our beer. There was one other guest, an old man who sat at the next table. He looked over at us, devouring the food on our plates with his eyes. Then stopping the innkeeper on his way to the kitchen, he begged, "Why can't I get supper, too?"

"We don't serve food to the public anymore," the innkeeper said; and, following the old man's eyes, he added, "They are on official business."

It was very quiet in the dining room. There was only the sound of our forks and knives, and the innkeeper, standing in the entrance to the kitchen, yawned, waiting for us to finish.

"I came a long way to see my son in the prison," the old

man broke the silence. "I went up there today, but they did not let me in. A new order, they say — no visits these days for anybody." He covered his eyes with his hand, mumbling, "I am an old man, sick, won't make it much longer. I wanted to see my son just once more."

He limped into the dark hall, and we heard him fumble his way upstairs. He had not touched his beer and some foam had spilled over on the table.

"My son is fighting at the front line. I can't see him either," said the innkeeper, wiping the table top clean and taking the mug away.

I stayed again in No. 12. On our first visit the innkeeper had said it was the best room in the "German House." I had stayed there so often that I no longer noticed the bleak light from the dangling bulb in the ceiling, the crack in the washbasin, or the falling plaster. I was even used to the dusty old print over my bed, the "Finis Terrae."

The day had been warm and I opened the window to let in the cool night air. Taking a deep breath, I knew I would sleep tonight — this hidden village had no alarms.

Only once did I awake and look at my watch. It was close to midnight; somewhere outside I heard the heavy rumbling of a truck as it passed through the sleeping town.

❉

When the prison gate opened the next morning, the courtyard was empty. Inside the prison we were met by a deadly silence. Halls and gangways were deserted. There was no click-clack of wooden shoes, and our own steps sounded hollow on the floors of stone.

Through my mind flashed the old man's words in the "German House" — "No visiting privileges these days" — and with growing tenseness I turned to the guard. "Where is everybody?"

"We had a lively morning," was his only reply.

Running more than walking to the Warden's office, I did not waste time with the usual "Heil Hitler," but yelled at him, "Where are my Scandinavian prisoners?"

He sat at his desk. A guard was just placing a mug of coffee before him; and, when the Warden looked up, I noticed that his face was unshaven.

"Your Scandinavian prisoners?" he slowly repeated. But then, apparently remembering who I was, he quickly got up. "They are here," he assured me. "You, of course, can conduct your visits as usual."

It was obvious: to him I was still a member of the Gestapo. He hurriedly explained that, due to "certain events," they had curtailed all activities and privileges and had locked the prisoners away in their cells. Motioning me to come closer he whispered, "We've got a special assignment."

"Dreibergen at last has been put on the map!" His voice was a mixture of pride and confusion. The Fuehrer had appointed his prison to participate in the executions of some of the conspirators of the 20th of July. The first truckload of German men and women had arrived shortly before midnight.

They had hanged them at dawn.

❖

The Scandinavian prisoners knew what had taken place. There was a cloud of apprehension over our visits, and they asked, "What will happen to us?"

I had no answer. Not until today had it occurred to me that Hitler in his madness might strike a final blow against all political prisoners. So far my Scandinavian friends had been under the jurisdiction of the German courts, and, while some of them had succumbed to illness and starvation, none of them had been deliberately killed as yet. But suppose one day the Gestapo took over the entire judicial system? Then there would be only one outcome: mass killing as it was practiced in the concentration camps.

For a moment I thought of my own safety. What were my chances? My odds of survival? The memory of the men and women who had died at dawn held me with a choking fear. I found it difficult to talk to the prisoners, and the day stretched on endlessly.

Shortly before the close of visiting hours, one of the Norwegian prisoners pulled a small package out of his sleeve. It was a bundle of closely written pages; and, handing them to me, he asked, "Will you carry it out?"

I felt myself going pale. It was hardly the time to take chances. Almost in a daze I heard the prisoner say, "It is my diary, my thoughts from behind the walls, written down as you once asked us to do."

Olav Brunvand was a Norwegian journalist. He had been sentenced to life for his resistance against the Nazi occupation. For years he had been in solitary confinement, locked in a cell, with only a bunk, a stool to sit on, a small basin in which to wash, and a bucket for a latrine. He could use the bunk only at night; during the day it was secured flat up against the wall. The only light came through a recessed window high up in the wall. The only life in the cell was his own. He had worn his fingernails down by scratching points, lines, and crosses into the wall, marking the days, weeks, and months gone by. It was his calendar, his cell had no seasons — it was cold summer and winter.

He had spent his years thinking out and committing a book to memory; and when I had brought paper and pen, he had begun writing down what he already knew by heart. The work had taken many months. He could only write for minutes at a time, always watching the hole in the door. He had carried the manuscript on his body, for they searched his cell each day.

I looked at the sheets. The paper was gray, tattered, torn at the edges. It was crowded with words. Not an inch was wasted, not a word was corrected, and its tightly written lines gave proof of what Gunnar had once said in only three proud words, *"I AM ALIVE!"*

I thought of the German prisoners who had been silenced at dawn. I opened my briefcase. My mind was made up. I had to give a chance to a voice which could still be heard.

I felt the piercing eyes of the guard at the gate, but we were not stopped for inspection.

Not until we boarded the train the following morning did

my tension ease. I stood at the window and noticed the patches of bluebells near the tracks. Once more I looked back as we gained speed. Dreibergen's station house had diminished to a small, black spot. Soon we were passing fields and pastures edged by poppies, looking like endless strings of red beads.

The air was pure. But my eyes were burning after a sleepless night, and closing them for a moment, I held my face toward the sun. Its touch felt like a hand.

We had comfortable seats in a compartment specially assigned for travelers on official duty. There were three or four others and directly opposite I faced a man in brown uniform with silver stripes. I glanced briefly at the button-shaped eyes in his round face and thought to myself, "Nazi district leader."

It would be a long journey. There were always delays. We might not arrive in Hamburg until late at night. I had no time to waste. Settling down I began studying my medical books, and later in the day I took out prisoners' mail. Going through the letters I forgot my surroundings.

I don't know how much time had passed — maybe only minutes — but I began feeling ill at ease, as if I were under observation. I looked up quickly and met a pair of button-shaped eyes.

He got up. "It's too drafty here," he muttered, placing himself next to me. Pretending not to notice I read quietly on. But my head started hammering under his persistent stare and the air got tense.

At last I heard his voice beside me, "What are you doing?"

My eyes stayed on the sheet of paper in my hand. I sensed danger ahead. Not because of the letters — I was allowed to read the prisoners' mail any time or anywhere I desired. But the briefcase with Olav's manuscript was on my lap.

"Didn't you understand my question?" said the polished voice. "What are you doing?"

"You have no right to ask," I replied calmly.

"We'll soon see!" he said triumphantly. "I thought you

looked suspicious the moment I saw you." And then quickly he fired at me, "Who are you? Where do you come from? What are you carrying? Your identification, please."

Should I give in to his demand? If he got my identification card, he would soon ask for the briefcase.

"You certainly ask a great many questions at once," I said coldly. "Please show me your own identification."

The Norwegian minister leaned forward in his seat as if he were about to enter the conversation, but a brief glance of warning from me sufficed. He could not help me. I was on my own. The less the Gestapo knew about my associations the better off I was. With expressionless face the minister turned to the window.

"She's asking for *my* identification! Did you hear that?" said the district leader to the other passengers, "as if my uniform wouldn't show who I am . . ."

"Anyone can wear a uniform," I interrupted matter-of-factly. I stole a glance at my watch. In a few minutes we were due in Luebeck, and I wanted to stall him until we arrived.

"So, let's see your credentials," he insisted brusquely. "Don't you know what's been happening in Germany over the last few days? You foreigners are . . ."

"Oh, I see, you think I am a foreigner?" I could not resist adding, "I suppose that's because I'm reading letters in a foreign language, and you can't imagine a German reading another language?"

Hidden laughter ran through the compartment. The district leader's eyes shot fire. Four men stared with sudden interest out the window. One suffered a coughing spell, then took out his handkerchief and wiped his mouth thoroughly. In the Third Reich, laughing could be a dangerous offense.

"You are under arrest." The Nazi put his hand on my shoulder just as the train rolled into the Luebeck station, which was jammed with people. He tore open the compartment door and shouted into the darkness, "Gestapo!"

Silence fell over the platform and a thousand pairs of eyes

turned toward us, hungry to witness an arrest. It was a common occurrence, but every new instance meant a welcome diversion.

"Get it over with in a hurry," I said. "I don't have much time. I must be in Hamburg tonight."

"We'll see about that. Who knows where you'll be tonight?"

He stalked ahead, yelling for the police, looking in vain for someone in uniform or a civilian with a magic badge and the word of power, "Gestapo!"

I was waiting as anxiously as he, but felt strangely calm. It had finally happened, now perhaps all was over. The Gestapo would not be satisfied with just looking at my credentials. They would search my briefcase, and my suitcase, too.

Hundreds of times I had tossed in nightmares, dreaming about the Gestapo. All I now felt was, "Let come what may."

But the miracle happened. In this huge Sunday evening crowd there was not one member of the Gestapo.

The staring eyes were disappointed.

"Follow me!" said the district leader finally.

I had luggage in both hands, and, handing him my briefcase I said lightly, "You may carry this for me. It isn't very heavy, but heavy enough for a woman."

Triumph burned in his eyes. I could read his thoughts, "Now you won't escape me."

We walked through the crowd, and for once there was no need to push our way through. For the first time in my life people stood aside to form a path for me.

The Nazi still looked searchingly around.

"No Gestapo on duty on Sundays, I guess?" I asked sarcastically.

"I'll take you to the railroad police." He sniffed angrily.

I glanced quickly back at the crowd. The Norwegian minister had stayed behind. I was relieved. With the district leader at my side I climbed the stairs alone.

"Heil Hitler!" he said, as we entered the police station. "I've arrested a woman who is highly suspicious. I want you to check her identification." He placed my briefcase on the desk.

"Now, wait a minute," said the stout policeman, looking from one to the other. The tone of his voice and the glance he gave the silver stripes told me a great deal. He was just lighting his Sunday evening pipe.

"All right, show me your identification," he said at last, surrounded by clouds of smoke.

I held up my green police card.

"Aha!" cried the policeman. "A colleague!"

He turned to the man in brown uniform. "Sorry, sir, nothing doing!" With his right eye he winked in my direction.

I could not miss the chance to turn the tables. "Why don't you check the credentials of this man? I found it highly suspicious that he refused to show them to me on board the train."

He *was* a district leader. Neither the policeman nor I doubted the validity of his papers for a moment, but the jovial policeman took his time scrutinizing them carefully, first holding them close to his eyes, then at arm's length, and finally upside down.

The uniformed man squirmed. He stepped closer and wanted to shake my hand, but I stared coldly ahead.

"You have no right to arrest people on the train without due cause," the policeman began sternly. "This woman is one of us and if she should report you . . ."

"I apologize, mein Fraeulein," said the district leader hastily. "I didn't mean any harm."

"It is not what you mean, but what you do that makes the difference," I said icily. "I advise you to stop bothering people traveling on the train. You are harming the Party image."

The policeman got a sudden coughing spell and leaned forward over his desk.

The Nazi district leader disappeared out of the office without saying, "Heil Hitler!" and, as I watched his stocky frame going down the stairs, he seemed to shrivel. Tomorrow I would barely remember his face, but only a few minutes ago he had held my fate in his hand.

29

I DID NOT ARRIVE HOME until late that night. My mother was still up waiting for me. I noticed the worried expression in her face. "Was everything all right?" she asked.

"Everything went fine — as usual."

"I must talk to you," she whispered and went back to the living room.

But numbed from fatigue I shook my head. "Tomorrow," I said and went straight to my room. Without taking off my clothes, I threw myself on my bed and fell into a deep sleep.

It was still dark when I awoke from a nightmare. I was bathed in sweat. I got up and opened the window. There was not a sound outside; it was the hour of the night when nature, at last at rest, is totally still.

I tried to go back to sleep; but I was wide awake and suddenly remembered my mother and her worried look. What had she meant to tell me? But the thought was replaced by another memory; and, without turning on the light, I fumbled my way to the briefcase and found Olav's manuscript. There was no time to read it; it had to be hidden, while it was still dark.

Cautiously opening the door to the hall, I listened: all was quiet and, stepping carefully, I sneaked down the staircase. With a flashlight, I found a glass jar in the kitchen, stuffed it with the bundle of pages, and screwed the lid on tightly.

Our garden tools were in the shack, but I dared not get them, afraid that the cackling of the chickens might betray me. Near the mountain ash tree I stopped and moved Mr. Decker's old wagon a few inches. With my hands I felt in the dark for the marks of the wagon wheels in the soil and dug with my fingers till the hole was deep enough to bury the jar. Then, replacing the loose soil, I rolled Mr. Decker's wagon back to its old spot.

With my mind at ease I returned to my room. There was a touch of dawn at the horizon — and as I lay down again, I thought of the "seed" hidden in the ground, biding its time to bear fruit.

❁

I must have fallen off to sleep again, and heard from somewhere far away the sounds of summer; the cackling of the chickens, the chirp of birds and the bumping of a ball against the sidewalk. A child laughed. I felt myself smile. Then a voice nearby, "I must talk to you, Hiltgunt."

Mother stood at my bedside. My eyes blinked from the bright sunshine on my pillow, and I mumbled, "I was dreaming of peace."

"I *must* talk to you," my mother repeated. There was something in her voice this time that made me listen. I was awake instantly. Shielding my eyes from the sun, I saw the piece of paper in her hand, blue, an envelope without a stamp.

I froze. My legs turned numb, and breaking out in perspiration, I whispered, "What do they want?"

"You have a summons for today."

My mother put the letter aside, bent down, and anxiously said, "I don't want you to go."

"I must. There is no way out."

"Yes, there is," she said confidently.

Dr. von Berg waited downstairs. "We want you to go into hiding," he began.

"No, my place is here," I cut him off shortly.

"You can't take any more chances."

"Suppose it is only another inquiry?" I argued, tense with a mixture of fear and resentment at finding myself caught in a trap.

"People are summoned and arrested by the thousands," Dr. von Berg pleaded. "Don't you realize what is happening these days?"

My temper suddenly flared, and I screamed at his kind, earnest face, "I think I do!"

"What if I took your advice? Where would I go?" I shouted.

"I have come to tell you," was Dr. von Berg's calm reply.

He gave me a slip of paper. "Leave at once for the railroad station," he urged. "Take the train to Berlin . . ."

"Berlin?" I interrupted. I stared at the paper in my hand. With his illegible doctor's writing he had jotted down an address. I was used to reading addresses, hundreds of them every day, and my mind mechanically recorded this one: Professor Ernst Reiner, Arnimstrasse 15, Berlin-Dahlem.

I looked up. "Who are these people?"

"Friends of mine . . ."

I glanced again at the address. Then crumpling the paper in my hands I asked quickly, "What about *my* friends in the prisons?"

"Is that all you can think of?" Dr. von Berg retorted. "Can't you think of your mother and brothers just for once? Did it ever cross your mind what would happen to them if the Gestapo caught up with you?"

Never before had I seen him angry. His words hit me like a slap in the face.

"They are on my side!" I shouted, infuriated. "They've always been!"

"Does that mean you need not consider their safety?"

I fell silent. His words had pierced deeply and hurt me — because I knew, deep inside, he was right. But I also knew I had to go on, at whatever cost. For me there was no return.

My eyes burned. I looked at my mother. Her face had turned ashen. Still, she smiled, sat very straight in her chair, and said slowly, "Do what you must."

"Then let me stay," I answered.

In a glimpse I saw her not only as my mother — but as my closest friend.

"You must go now," she said and got up. "Your summons is for noon."

✲

I changed from my white summer dress into a gray woolen suit and took a raincoat along. The day was clear and warm, but a summons to the Gestapo could mean a trip into the cold unknown. In my briefcase I had some bread, soap, and the Bible.

I went to the same place where I had been before, and, as I arrived, I looked at my watch. I was on time. It was precisely noon. Still, no bells were ringing, there was no strike of a clock. The church nearby had been hit in a recent air raid and all that was left of the clock in the tower was an empty hole. But the imposing mansion stood intact as before, not a brick was missing. I rang the bell; the buzzer at once responded, and the door, directed by invisible hands, opened on soundproof hinges, swinging outward like an arm reaching to enfold whoever came near.

I walked into the deadly silence inside. The only signs of life were the lines of footprints on the waxed floor.

I knew my way and went straight to the room behind the leather-upholstered door. I entered without knocking and mumbled my "Heil Hitler!" My eyes caught sight of the white door. Again I wondered where it led and whether they would make me go through it. The man at the desk barely looked up. I did not recognize his face and could not be sure whether or not he was the one I had talked to before. But, as he picked up a file from the desk, he curtly started, "This time you are prompt."

I did not wait until I was offered a seat, but sat down quickly, and, shielded by the desk, clutched my hands tightly together. Rigidly I waited for the man opposite me to talk. Instead he ignored my presence, opened the file, and began to study it. It was a thin file. Mine had been thick the last time, I recalled. Anxiously I searched his face for a clue and found none. He looked as blank as a sheet of unmarked paper and as smooth as the glossy white door behind him. The gray suit and black tie gave him the look of complete detachment, and for an instant I felt tempted to ask, "Have they ever called *you* in?"

He kept staring at the file, never turning a page. Remembering this prelude of silence from my previous visit, I now understood that it was part of the game. Minutes passed. Maybe they were only seconds. To me they seemed like hours. It was so quiet I could have heard a pin fall to the floor. Then the humming of a fly cut through the stillness. A summer fly, furiously hitting the windowpane, trying to get out. The buzzing roared in my ears.

"Why have you not yet sent us reports?"

I turned around quickly.

The Gestapo official had finished reading the file and the point of the pen he held was directed at me.

The game had begun. What I had experienced before happened again. Like an actor on stage suddenly facing the darkness of the audience I felt myself grow into the well-rehearsed role. Inside I was perfectly calm and free from all fear, as if someone — a director offstage — had taken complete control of the play.

"Your request is constantly on my mind," I cheerfully replied. "But then what is there to report when I only meet people willing to follow orders?"

He seemed surprised at my answer and angrily hissed, "Don't you know what's been happening these days?"

It was the second time today I had been asked this question, but this time my voice showed no emotion. "I think I do," I calmly answered.

"Well, then, you'd better start cooperating with us," he said sharply.

"I'll see what I can do," I promised.

"Today you'll be given a chance to prove it, the Gestapo official stated. Picking up a letter, he said, "We've a special assignment for you."

I held my breath.

"We received a report signed by two of your boarders concerning a Mr. Mangold," he began.

So that's what it was — Mr. Mangold! In a second it all came back to me: the day of the attempted assassination . . . the night in our kitchen . . . Irmgard Hedrich.

"What exactly did they tell you?" I quickly asked.

"Shouldn't you know?" he retorted.

"I don't," I said quietly.

"Well, what about his remark in your kitchen? You were present — you and your mother."

"How well informed you are," I said with a happy smile. "But then surely you'll know, too, that one of your informers is hard of hearing. How could she possibly have heard what was said?"

The Gestapo official, paying no attention to my words, continued that there was something more in the Hedriches' report. Why was Mr. Mangold not drafted, the sisters had wondered. What about that lesion on his hand — the right one to be exact? Did I know why there were two fingers missing? And what about his frantic activities on the black market?

The Gestapo official paused to light a cigarette. I leaned back in my chair pretending to be at ease, but inside I grew tense. Our silverware! The flour! The loaves of bread we baked! Were they also mentioned in the sisters' report?

I need not have worried. Actually, they were not really interested in his dealings on the black market, the man opposite me hastened to say. "The black market is as intricate a part of war as killing." He pulled deeply on his cigarette and expelled rings of smoke. "After all, where do you think I got this cigarette?"

"But then what is your concern?" I asked, no longer able to hold back.

"It's his name we don't like."

"His name?" I was startled, and almost laughed as something occurred to me. "Last time I was summoned because someone had objected to mine!" I exclaimed.

"That was different," he replied coldly. "Your name sounds foreign, but his is Jewish."

So that was it. But Mr. Mangold was not Jewish, and the Gestapo should know. They had us all in their files. Years ago each German citizen had to file proof of his Aryan descent. It was one of the first orders Hitler had issued after he came to power.

I had not forgotten the weeks and months my parents had spent writing letters, checking with churches all over Germany, trying to procure the required baptismal certificates of their parents and grandparents. It had been an elaborate task, and when they at last had turned in their papers, it again had taken months before they had been checked and cleared by the German authorities. We were found to be "clean." Since we had no traceable Jewish blood in our ancestry, we were pronounced Aryans.

Non-Aryans were people partly or fully Jewish. The ones who were fully Jewish were doomed, and, if they had not managed to leave Germany in time, they were later killed in the concentration camps. But there was also a large group of partly Jewish people. Many of them had not even known they had a Jewish grandparent. According to their ancestry they were graded 25 percent, 50 percent, or 75 percent non-Aryan. They were not deported or killed, but were treated like outcasts, condemned to a life of oblivion. In many instances they were excluded from institutions of higher learning and barred from any employment short of menial labor.

But what had this to do with Mr. Mangold? He was an Aryan like me. Only his name sounded Jewish.

"Suppose he is really Jewish?" suggested the Gestapo official in a tone as if he had mentioned the plague. "We will recheck his papers, of course, and trace each of his ancestors back to his great-grandparents." He looked up and grinned, "Everything has its price — falsified baptismal certificates are good black-market commodities."

Of course, they could arrest Mr. Mangold at once, he continued, but they had decided to hold off for just a little while. "Being Jewish classifies him as a subversive element and may give us a lead to others," he said. "We want to know whom he associates with — and this will be your assignment."

He did not give me time to answer, but jotted down his

telephone number and said abruptly, "Call us within one week."

Getting up I mumbled another dutiful, "Heil Hitler!"

"This time you'd better do your job," was his only response.

Casting a last glance at the white door behind him, I left hurriedly.

°

It had been cool inside the mansion, but on the outside I found myself bathed in perspiration, and I tore off my gray woolen jacket. I ran more than walked to the railroad station, as if by putting distance between the Gestapo and myself I might escape their request.

My mind was in an uproar. What was I going to do? Should I talk to Mr. Mangold? Should I let him know about the Hedrich report? What if the Gestapo found out I had warned him? But what if I did not tell him and just ignored their request? One way or the other — Mr. Mangold was doomed. Sooner or later they would come for him. Then they would make him talk. I knew he would talk. His breaking point was low. He would give us away, and they would find out about his dealings with us. One step would lead to the next . . .

I slowed down as I approached the railroad station. I felt trapped in my own indecision, dreaded going home, and was strangely relieved when I heard the scream of the siren.

It was early afternoon. The sun stood high, and as I came from the sunshine outside, the darkness in the catacomb below the platforms seemed even darker. Stumbling, step by step, along the sewer pipes, I was pushed onward by the crowd behind. Water was dripping from the walls, the ground was slippery, and from somewhere in the dark ahead of us came the stench of rotten garbage.

I heard heavy breathing beside me, then a choked voice, "For God's sake let me out!" From above came the roaring crash of a detonation, a hit nearby. Somebody sighed. The heavy breathing ceased. And in the silence that followed, my mind turned back to the room with the glossy, white door. I thought of the fly, the frantic buzzing as it tried in vain to reach the freedom beyond the glass pane — and then the realization struck me, "*I* got out!"

I was still free. They had let me go.

I suddenly felt very hungry. I had not eaten all day, and opening my briefcase, I fumbled for a piece of bread. Homemade bread. A slice from our own loaf. I chewed it slowly. My tension eased. I began feeling good all over, and no longer minded the stench around me and the rolling thunder above.

"*I AM ALIVE!*" I thought. Gunnar had used these same words, and now I fully understood how he must have felt.

"Yes, Gunnar," I thought, "I am alive."

°

It was late afternoon when I arrived at our local railroad station. Instead of walking straight home, I stopped across the street from the station. My mind was made up. I had to catch Mr. Mangold before he went home. It was the only chance to tip him off without being caught by the Gestapo. He kept irregular hours. Perhaps he was home already, but I dared not call to find out for fear our phone might be tapped.

I waited all afternoon, screening the crowd every ten minutes when a local train would arrive. Irmgard Hedrich came on the 5:48. I recognized her at once by the gray sweater, tightly closed at her neck. She looked neither right nor left, as if she saw nothing. But I knew better. She was an informer; our home would never again be the same. Not only would we watch out for every spoken word, but we would be suspicious of her every move.

The sun had set; it was dusk. Still, I did not give up, but continued waiting — trusting to luck.

It was almost dark when Mr. Mangold appeared at last. As he was leaving the station, I saw him loosen his silk tie and then light a cigarette as he headed home.

Quickly crossing the street, I caught up with him at the next block and, walking beside him, whispered, "I must talk with you."

We turned into a quiet side road with fences covered by hedges. Huge oak trees were shielding us from the houses.

"They are after you," I said. "You have been reported."

He dropped his cigarette, coughed, and his hands started to shake, as I told him about the Hedriches' letter.

"They don't like your name." I felt awkward and avoided his eyes. "They think you are Jewish," I said after a pause.

The match flickered in his hand as he lighted another cigarette, and again I looked away, gazing up into the tree. From somewhere out of its thickness came the song of a mockingbird. It was summer . . .

At last I heard Mr. Mangold. "Do you remember the night in the kitchen with the sisters? After they left, I wanted to talk with you, but then I was silenced by Hitler's speech." He shrugged and wearily added, "Actually, I was silenced a long time ago."

He had been only eleven years old when one day he came home from school to find his mother crying. His father was at his desk, bent over a piece of paper which had just arrived in the mail. It was the baptismal certificate of one of his grandfathers, procured to prove their Aryan descent. "What are we going to do?" his mother sobbed. His father had beckoned the boy to his side and yelled, "You are Jewish! As of today you are Jewish!" Tears had filled his eyes as he pounded his fist on the baptismal certificate.

The boy had not understood and wondered, "What difference does it make? Am I not the same as before?"

But the next day the father called him back and anxiously said, "You must forget what I told you!" He made him swear never to reveal what had happened. He had found a way out, he had said. They were Aryans after all.

"From then on my father pretended to be a Nazi," Mr. Mangold said, "and in living that lie he became more of a fanatic than Hitler himself."

The baptismal certificate which would have made Mr. Mangold partly Jewish had been replaced by another paper. "My father bought it from an SS–man and paid him off amply. But he came back for more." Mr. Mangold laughed bitterly. The blackmailer continued to come. When his parents were killed in an air raid and all their belongings were lost, he turned to the black market to go on providing what was demanded of him. He paused for a moment, then, shrugging his shoulders again, he said, "Don't you remember that I once told you everything has its price?"

There was one question left in my mind. Still, I dared not ask. But as if Mr. Mangold were guessing, he lifted his right hand. "See those fingers missing?" he whispered.

"I think I know what happened," I said quickly.

"I won't explain why I did it. You wouldn't understand. You never had to fear for your life because of something beyond your power to change. Fighting the Nazis was your own choice. I had none. Since the day I found out I was Jewish, all my actions were governed by only one goal: survival."

"What will you do now?" I asked.

"I don't know," he cried out. "I don't know!"

I took a piece of paper from my purse and wrote down an address, printing it in block letters, so that nobody would recognize my handwriting. I never forgot an address, and this one I had memorized only twelve hours ago. I handed him the paper and told him, "Leave at once. Go back to the railroad station and take the train to Berlin."

"But what will happen to you?" Mr. Mangold asked and for the first time I sensed true concern in his voice.

"I must stay and go on."

We shook hands — two strangers who had come to trust each other.

I should go up to his room, he said. In his desk was a gun. I should take it and keep it. Then we separated, and I heard his cough long after his steps were lost in the night.

∘

My mother looked worn out when I arrived home, and she anxiously asked what had happened.

"It was just a routine inquiry," I casually said.

But why then had it taken so long, she persisted, and why had I not called her before?

The interview at the Gestapo had been very short, I explained, and I had spent most of the day studying at the University library.

It was painful to lie. I had never lied to my mother. But Dr. von Berg's words stuck in my mind. He was right. By sharing my thoughts and work with her, I had endangered her life. The less she knew about any of my actions, the better her chances were if I got caught. I recalled the time when she had helped the Jews, and I remembered my resentment that she had done it in secret. How well I now understood what I once thought I would never forgive. She had wanted to protect me. Now it was my turn. I had to be on my own.

I stayed up late that night and, before going into Mr. Mangold's room to get his gun, I made sure that nobody was in the hall. When I returned, the gun weighed heavily in my hand; while I was looking around for a hiding place, it occurred to me that perhaps one day I might need it. If ever the Gestapo used their own special methods on me, how long would I hold out in not giving my friends away? The gun would be my only way out — everything had its price.

I slipped it into my purse; and, glancing at my police credentials, I smiled. It seemed long ago that I had signed my name there and noticed the line, "The owner of this card may carry a gun."

It was after midnight, but I did not go to bed yet. I was hoping for an alarm. I wanted the sisters to notice that Mr. Mangold had not come home. When the siren sounded at last, I made sure that we left for the bunker together. But nobody seemed to miss him.

The next day, however, my mother wondered, and in the evening she mentioned it to the sisters. Irmgard suggested that my mother should notify the police, implying that Mr. Mangold was just the kind of young man who would get in trouble.

I called the Gestapo.

"Did you talk with him after you saw us?" the Gestapo official inquired.

"How could I?" I replied. "He never came home."

Several days passed. My mother had given up on Mr. Mangold, the sisters had stopped talking about him, and I resumed my journeys.

When I returned two weeks later, I heard from my mother that the Gestapo had come one day and had searched Mr. Mangold's room. Then they had questioned her and had taken the sisters aside. Mother wondered about the sisters' great concern for Mr. Mangold. "Will you ever find him?" Irmgard had asked excitedly, as the Gestapo official had been about to leave.

"Don't worry," he had reassured her. "Nobody gets away from us. Nobody."

30

A FEW WEEKS LATER I passed my finals in all preclinical subjects. The same day it was announced that the University would close down; they said for an indefinite period of time — until the war was over.

The next day I was again on the train. "I am relieved," I said to Reverend Svendsen. "Now at last I can spend all my time working for the prisoners — until the day when they are free."

"And then?"

I looked up, but there was no time to answer. The train had slowed down and come to a standstill. Agitated voices were yelling outside.

"Dive bombers!"

We heard the humming in the sky, distant but clear, and swarmed off the train. Next to the track were fields of rye, recently cut and stacked up to dry. Only some bluebells were left standing along the edges. The train personnel were waving their arms and shouting commands, "Get away from the tracks! Hurry!"

Within seconds the crowd dispersed, running in all directions and throwing themselves on the ground. I lay down flat, covering my suitcase with my body as if it were most precious. All motion had stopped — people looked like small black dots across the yellow of the stubble field.

After a while the humming ceased. Deep silence hung over the scene. Turning over on my back I stared into the sky where a hawk circled slowly. The golden light of summer lay over the field. On the horizon was a narrow, dark line — pine forests. Near the road stood a mountain ash tree. Its berries were red. It was only the twenty-second of August; I thought of Willfried. "The earlier they turn red, the harder the winter will be," he had told me. I tried to envision his face, but it seemed far away, as if a haze would not let me see it, and suddenly I felt cold in spite of the warmth of the sun.

The dive bombers did not come. They called us back to the train, and we resumed our journey. The Norwegian minister did not repeat his question. What would I do after the war when the prisoners had left? I was glad he did not ask. I had no answer.

°

Now that Mr. Mangold was gone our supply of flour was rapidly dwindling away and I began to worry.

Then something unexpected happened. One day in September, the farmer who had brought the chickens was at our door again. He carried a heavy bag, and beside him stood a young girl with a suitcase. Her blonde hair was tightly held together in braids and her eyes looked red as if she had been crying. She was his daughter Lisa, the farmer remarked as he entered. As he pulled the heavy bag behind him, I noticed a small trickle of flour marking his way.

He was huffing and puffing when he sat down at our kitchen table; and, wiping his forehead, he told Lisa to go out into the yard and look at the chickens. He said he had stopped by to inquire how they were coming along.

As soon as his daughter left the kitchen, we found out the real reason for their visit. Lisa had taken a liking to the prisoner of war working on their farm. "After all," said the farmer, "she is only a girl. What does she know about war?" But fraternizing with the enemy was punishable by death. He paused for a moment as if there were another, more painful part to the story. Then, clenching his fist, he suddenly burst out, "The prisoner of war is a Russian!"

"What kind of man is he?" my mother asked quietly.

The farmer looked up in surprise as if wondering whether she had misunderstood what he said. "He is a Russian," he repeated.

They were in dire need of help on the farm, he said. Ivan was a hard worker, and, as they could not spare him, he and his wife had decided to send Lisa away. Would we keep her? And, patting the bag beside him, he added that we would not regret it.

"But what about the air raids on Hamburg?" my mother objected. "Lisa would not be safe here."

"I would rather see her killed by a bomb than let her love a Russian," was his stoic reply.

Would she stay with us, we asked Lisa, when she came in from the yard. She had stopped crying and quietly nodded her head. But then, turning to her father, hate was in her eyes. "You will never see me back on the farm," she said with determination. "I'll wait for Ivan; and, after the war, I'll go with him to Russia."

Her father was unmoved. "You'll never get there," he said. "The Russians hate us as much as we hate them."

"I don't hate the Russians," Lisa stubbornly replied. "They are not my enemies — you are!"

"I know what's best for you," he insisted. Then he left. Lisa did not bid him good-by.

Every month he returned with food. Flour, potatoes, and sometimes a side of pork. There was no gasoline left for his truck. An old horse pulled his wagon, and the long trip took the better part of a day. Yet Lisa never spoke to him, and she did not so much as look at the red ribbon he once brought for her hair.

We went to the housing authorities and asked the woman

with the horn-rimmed glasses to assign Willfried's room to Lisa. At first she turned us down. She said the city was closed to anybody coming from out of town unless there was a war-related reason — as if Lisa's reason for coming was not war-related! But how could we tell her? Yet, we found a way out and obtained a permit. A seminary in Hamburg, still open, was giving a crash course training young girls to replace teachers who had been sent to the front lines. Lisa applied and was accepted at once.

She settled down with her studies, but her heart was not in it, and she barely touched her food at mealtime. We treated her as one of the family, but she kept to herself. I never saw her laugh, and the deep shadows under her eyes bore witness to sleepless nights. At times she seemed so far away in thought that she appeared almost lifeless, only existing, waiting for a day which might never come.

Still, life went on and, in its own secret and indirect way, was taking care that the love she was not allowed to give one prisoner of war was passed on to many others. Because of her we had flour again and could continue to bake bread, to be carried in my suitcase to other prisoners.

*

True to the promise of the mountain ash, fall came early in 1944. The thick morning fog that usually arrives in October came with the first days of September.

The Norwegian minister and I were on another journey through Germany. One evening, as we were walking from the prison to our hotel, a gusty wind came up, whipping the first leaves from the trees. It took my breath away, seeming to choke me. I slowed down, thought for a moment I was taking ill, but then suddenly I knew.

I stopped in the middle of the street and said quietly to the Norwegian minister, "I've got to go home."

"But the prisoners are waiting."

"I know, but I've got to go home."

I took the late train and traveled all night. The windows

were broken and no attempt had been made to repair them. The wind whipped the rain into our faces and the wheels seemed to moan, "It can't be true, it can't be true."

Early the next morning I stood facing my mother. I drew a deep sigh of relief. Nothing had happened. "What made you interrupt your journey?" she wondered.

I had no answer.

A few hours later the telephone rang. Long distance — it was Guenther, calling from the Western front. I knew what he was about to say before he had spoken the words. I handed the telephone to my mother.

"I have waited so long for a letter from Willfried. Do you know anything about him?" I heard her anxious words.

The room was so quiet that I could hear Guenther's voice over the wire, "Yes, Mother — he is dead."

Since Guenther was a physician too, they had contacted him directly from the German Army hospital in Russia before sending an official letter to my mother. Willfried had died on the twenty-second of August — the day when I had been lying in the stubble field, trying to picture his face through the haze. His death had come after a battle, when he had been attending the casualties. A wounded Russian had shot him.

Mother broke down and cried. She went up to her room and locked herself in. I stayed downstairs and stared out the window. It had stopped raining. The winds had calmed down and the sky was turning blue. But the ground was red with berries from the mountain ash tree — silent evidence of the last night's storm.

Then I thought of my mother. It occurred to me that I had never before seen her cry.

31

ALL THAT IS LEFT to tell about the last months of the war could be expressed in a single word: waiting.

We were all waiting.

The broad mass of people spent their days in bread lines

and their nights in bunkers and waited with the vague hope that somehow, some day, this nightmare might come to an end; yet, they refused to consider what that end might be.

The active Nazis held out stubbornly. Still believing in the victory promised by their Fuehrer, they waited for a miracle which would turn the course of the war. With their minds blinded, they talked more loudly and were more aggressive than ever.

The "unknown soldiers," German men and women who had resisted Hitler's regime from the very beginning, waited, too. The world had not taken much notice of the hidden Germany; yet their wait had been the longest. Since 1933, German men and women had filled the concentration camps; many of them had perished.

Those who had as yet escaped the hands of the Gestapo had been forced into erecting barricades of deceit. The ordeal had lasted long — perhaps too long. I had been only seventeen when I first said, "No!" For more than ten years I had said "No"; and almost unconsciously I had come to divide humanity into two camps: those for and against Hitler. To me there was no in between.

But there came a moment when I saw that in the midst of the battle my sight had hardened.

It happened one day in a prison. I had stepped out into the hall and saw a guard standing by the door of a nearby cell.

"Do you know anything about art?" he asked and opened the cell door wide. "Come take a look."

I glanced quickly around to see if anyone were watching.

"Don't worry," he reassured me. "The prisoner is out in the yard."

I peeked in, then stepped back, startled by what I saw. The cell was an ordinary one, like the rest on the block; but the cold gray walls were covered with paintings: oils and pastels in colors ranging from the darkest to the most glaring.

I was stunned. "Are prisoners allowed to paint?" I asked.

"This prisoner is an exception. He has received a special permit from the Warden."

I looked a little closer and noticed something odd: all the

paintings portrayed the same subject: the ocean, the sky, a boat, and a fisherman. The moods of the pictures changed from raging storms to glimmering sunsets and quiet moonlit nights. But always the fisherman was there in his boat, surrounded by sea and sky.

The fisherman's eyes were fastened on a distant point, oblivious to the storm or to the set of the sails, and always fixed on an unseen goal.

"Who is he?" I tried to shake off the eerie feeling that was coming over me.

"He's a permanent guest."

He was a German prisoner. He had been a fisherman. Once, when a sudden storm had forced him back to shore early, he had found his wife in the arms of a lover. Later, calmly and deliberately, he had killed them both.

Premeditated murder! But the death sentence had been commuted to life in prison.

"When I came here," said the guard, "he had served twenty years. I was told to give him a piece of paper, so that he could write a request for parole."

"Why wasn't it granted?"

"He never wrote the request. He didn't want to get out."

Five years later he had been given permission to draw; then they gave him colors, brushes, and canvas.

"Take a close look," said the guard, pointing to a picture of a brilliant sunset: the colors which had looked just brilliantly glaring on closer inspection proved to be a distortion and perversion of nature. The ocean was violet, blood-red, and ochre; and the setting sun resembled a ghostly moon.

"He paints from memory," the guard said with an air of superior benevolence. "When you remain behind walls for such a long time, you forget."

I felt shaken. We had changed, too. Like the fisherman, we had lived so long behind walls that we could not see life as it really was. Our eyes were fixed on one goal, our minds possessed by one thought: to be free of Hitler.

We had lost everything that had once filled our lives with meaning: the aura of lightheartedness that only carefree days can give, the sense of security which comes with undisturbed sleep at night, the music we loved, colors that now had paled, and words we had once thought of as truth but which now were hollow to our ears.

Deep within myself I knew that all I missed still existed somewhere beyond our walls. And year after year, day after day, my mind hammered with one question: When? When would the Nazi regime end? My eyes were fixed on that one goal.

And when that goal was reached? Somehow I had never been able to see beyond it. I wondered if I could ever learn to see again the nuances of a reality now kept alive only by my memory.

The fisherman had reached the point of no return. Had I, too? Had I, too, lost touch with reality, seeing it only as my mind dictated? All my thoughts had been centered on the prisoners' welfare. My love had reached out to them, my hatred had focused on their enemies. Each day the faces of my friends looked more noble to me, while those of their oppressors looked more evil.

I glanced at the guard who stood dangling his keys and peering nearsightedly at the paintings. I noticed how his shoulders stooped, how aged and tired he looked.

"You'd better come now," he said finally, touching my arm lightly.

The German prisoner stood frozen at attention at the entrance of his cell. The guard shoved him in, and the cell door slammed shut.

"He's better off than I am," said the guard. "He's through with life. What more can happen to him?"

o

Over the years I had come to know many prison officials. To me they were representatives of a penal system, punitive and destructive; and, except for a few, I felt only fear, hate, and distrust. Then, one day, I pitied.

The camp where it happened had no barbed wire, for there was no chance of escape. The earth was gray with rocks as far as the eyes could see, and the cluster of prison barracks stood out like a dirty brown spot on the barren earth. This camp was a stone quarry.

It was late October, and the wind was gusty. Dust filled the air, covered my shoes, burned my eyes, and clogged my nostrils. As the Norwegian minister and I walked along the rim, we saw prisoners in the pit, hundreds of them; and in this vast desert of stones they looked as forlorn as the sage grass bent by the wind.

The only sound of life came from the barracks: the rattle of loose spouts and gutters in the wind, and the banging of doors flung open and shut by the coming storm.

One barrack had its door tightly closed. Its roof was tiled and its walls were brick. It belonged to the Commandant; and we had to pass a second door, leather-padded, before we entered his office. As I stepped in, my shoes sank into the thick carpet. Heavy silk curtains blacked out the windows and the heat of the room took away my breath.

The face of the man behind the desk looked flushed, and the veins of his neck and forehead swelled in anger when he heard why we had come. "Visiting prisoners?" he shouted. "Why? Nobody ever visits *me!*"

I showed him my credentials. "We have a right to see them," I insisted.

"A right?" he yelled, glaring at me incredulously. "What right? Out here *I* am the law!"

Suddenly we heard a peculiar sound. Whining yelps came from the depths of a large armchair in front of an electric heater. There, wrapped in heavy blankets, was a little brown dog.

I stepped closer and bent down to pet him. No sooner had I done that, than the Commandant stood beside me.

"Poor Nikolai is sick," he whispered.

I looked up, startled. Was this the same man? His voice sounded gentle. His face wore an anxious expression. "The dust of the quarry has made him sick," he said. "Everywhere dust. No way of keeping it out," and, petting the dog's head, he said, "We must get away from here, Nikolai!"

He had applied for a transfer, he told us, but the Department of Justice was slow. What if the dog did not last? He clenched his fist and pacing the floor, he resembled a prisoner himself.

We watched him in silence. Finally I remarked, "Your dog has a Russian name."

He turned around, his face lighted up. "I got him in Russia," he replied. "He's the only good Russian alive!"

Until recently he had been in charge of a prison in Russia, the Commandant said. It had been a special assignment given to him by the German Army. One day in Russia, searching a newly arrived prisoner, he had found a puppy hidden underneath his rags. "I took it," the Commandant said, "felt the warmth of its body, and decided to keep it for myself."

He leaned back in his chair, lighting a cigarette, and continued, "The Russian went down on his knees, pleading for his dog. I laughed. But then he beckoned to the puppy to come. It slipped away from me and ran over to him . . ."

The Commandant paused. His hand rested heavily on the dog, and he spoke more to himself than to us. "At that moment I saw something in his eyes which made me pull my gun, and fire."

He stared before him. The ashes from his cigarette dropped on the carpet. In the stillness I heard the sound of the fan of the heater. Outside the storm raged.

At last the Commandant looked up and glanced at the dog, which was licking his hand. "When the Russian fell over," he said, "the puppy came back to me. It wanted me after all!"

*

Fall 1944 was one continuous journey, but in my memory one event especially stands out.

In November I traveled for a day with an official from the Danish Consulate in Berlin who had obtained special permission for a prison visit. On the way to the prison we walked behind a prisoner and a guard. It was a chilly day with clouds hanging low and a drizzling rain. The prisoner's clothes were in tatters; he wore no shoes and the rags about his feet were wet and dirty. He staggered as he walked, but his body remained strangely rigid. His arms were raised; and, as we caught up with him, I saw that chains were fastened tightly around them, forcing him to hold them upward. The guard shouted at him, trying to make him walk faster; but the prisoner no longer seemed to hear his commands. Mechanically he walked step by step, with unseeing eyes, as if life had already departed.

Passing by, the Danish official cast a brief glance at him and remarked, "I hope he's not Danish!"

Something in me snapped. "He is a man in chains," I retorted.

That night going back to Hamburg, I sat in a train comparment which had no glass left in the window. The doorhandle was broken, and we had tied the door shut with a rope. Rain was seeping in and I pulled my coat closer. It was dark in the compartment and dark outside — with only an occasional strip of light coming in the window. Outside, an endless row of houses in ruins loomed like a giant shadow.

I buried my head into the collar of my coat.

"Finis terrae!" I thought, "the end is near. What hope is there for a new beginning if people do not change?"

32

WINTER CAME EARLY IN 1944. We were still in November when, late one afternoon, rain changed to snow; and by nighttime the ground was white. The skies, thick with snow, promised a quiet night. The sisters had gone to their room after supper, and we could hear the blaring of their radio. Lisa was upstairs, too.

My mother and I were still in the kitchen when a knock sounded at our front door. I ran into the hall, turned off the light, and peeped through the window. Outside stood a horse and wagon. It was the farmer.

"I must talk to Lisa!" he said as I let him in. Snow covered his cap and coat and hung in his hair and eyebrows; he rubbed his hands to warm them.

My mother started to put leftover soup on the stove, but he stopped her, "Don't, I can't stay. Where is Lisa?"

I went up to get her. The light in her room was still on, but she had gone to bed.

"Your father has come," I said.

"I won't see him!" She turned to the wall and would say no more. As I walked away from the door, I heard the key click in the lock.

The father was waiting at the bottom of the stairs, his fingers impatiently tapping the railing. Seeing me alone, his face flushed with anger. "She'll do as I tell her!" he exclaimed and shoving me aside, stamped up the stairs.

Lisa's locked door increased his fury; pounding with his fists against it, he commanded, "Lisa, open up!"

No response.

"Your mother has fallen ill!" he shouted. "I've come to take you home."

A few seconds passed. Then Lisa's voice, "What about Ivan?"

"We've got to get home!" her father urged. "We'll talk on the road."

There was another long silence. I suddenly realized that the whole house had become silent, listening. The radio was no longer blaring in the sisters' room, and their door to the hallway had opened just a crack. We could hear Lisa moving about, and at last the key turned in the lock.

She stood in the doorway, her pale face framed by a black scarf. She had on long boots, a gray woolen skirt, and a warm shawl wrapped around her shoulders. How much older she looked than the girl in blonde pigtails who had arrived at our door three long months ago.

A faint smile came to her face as she repeated, "What about Ivan?"

"Why do you keep asking for him?" her father retorted. "Why don't you ask about your mother? Can't you think of her for once?"

Lisa stopped abruptly and stared intently at him. "What

about Ivan?" she said slowly, a blush of anger coloring her white cheeks.

"All right, I'll tell you." Her father, in his heavy farm boots, shifted his weight uneasily from one foot to the other. "I've sent Ivan back to the camp. With winter here, I don't need him." He reached out to touch his daughter's arm. "Come now, let's forget about Ivan. Your mother needs you, and so do I."

Lisa's face looked ashen in the dim light, and the circles under her eyes seemed to have deepened. Yet her thin shoulders straightened as she slowly removed her scarf and wrap.

"So now you need me enough to want me back home!" She stared into her father's eyes. Her voice was calm, "Do you need me enough to want Ivan's child as well?"

Her father staggered as if struck by a heavy blow. "Are you . . . are you?"

"Yes, I am!" She lifted her chin and smiled.

The farmer clutched his throat. "I'll kill him. I'll kill you both!" he groaned.

"Oh, no, you won't!" Lisa scoffed at him. "You'd rather die than let it be known that your daughter is carrying the child of a . . ."

"Stop it!" he yelled at the top of his voice. Then, stepping back as if afraid to come near her he cried out, "You've shamed my name. I disown you!"

He seemed an old man as he slumped over the railing and walked heavily down the steps.

It was still snowing; and my mother called out, urging him to stay until morning. He neither answered nor looked back, but climbed on his wagon and commanded the horse, "Go!" But the wheels of the wagon were stuck in the snow and did not move.

"Please stay!" my mother called out once more.

He paid no heed. Getting off the wagon, he dug into the snow with his hands to clear the path. Then, fastening a strap to his shoulder, he took his place alongside the horse and pulled. Slowly the wagon began to move. As man and horse struggled together into the night, we heard him moan, "Oh, God, punish my daughter for what she's done to me!"

*

Irmgard Hedrich was waiting in the kitchen, dressed only in a nightgown with a coat thrown over her shoulders. "I just came down for a mug of coffee," she said; but the chicory was untouched on her shelf. She leaned toward my mother and whispered, "I couldn't help overhearing! Lisa is in trouble, eh?"

"It's still snowing," my mother said, warding off the question.

"Who's Ivan?" Irmgard tried again.

"The overcast skies will give us a night without an air raid," my mother observed.

Irmgard had no intention of giving up. "Ivan sounds Russian," she suggested. "Do you suppose Lisa was involved with a . . ."

I could feel the tension inside — the memory of the smooth voice of the Gestapo officer, "We've received a report signed by two of your boarders . . ."

"Shut up!" I interrupted her, suddenly overcome with rage.

My mother looked startled and Irmgard hissed, "How dare you!"

But I did not care. I saw before me Mr. Mangold's haunted face and clenched my fists behind my back. I wanted to hurl the word at her, "Informer!"

"Hiltgunt."

My mother's voice brought me back to my senses. In Irmgard's probing eyes I saw the new danger: she was about to write another report on Lisa.

I thought hard and fast; the old calm was returning. There was a game to be played and I knew my role by heart. "Please forgive me, Miss Hedrich," I smiled. "I guess I'm just upset about what has happened tonight."

"We are all upset," Irmgard nodded. "And now tell me: who is Ivan?"

"Ivan?" I shook my head in surprise. "You are mistaken, they are speaking about Ewald. The names are similar, aren't they?"

"Oh?" Irmgard could barely conceal her disappointment. "But who is Ewald?" she persisted.

"Ewald is a soldier," I informed her, this time at least coming close to the truth.

Irmgard was still suspicious. "Why, then, was her father so upset?"

"He's just old-fashioned," I said, shrugging. "Mind you, Lisa is not married."

"I'm old-fashioned, too. I think it's a disgrace," Irmgard retorted.

"Well, the Fuehrer is not," I quickly reminded her. "He wants babies for the Vaterland, lots of them — one way or the other."

"True," Irmgard hastily agreed; and, glancing at the clock in the hall, she exclaimed, "Oh, my, it's much later than I thought! I'd better give up my coffee." She made a hasty retreat.

My mother waited until we heard Irmgard close her door. Then she whispered, "Did she report on Mr. Mangold?"

I nodded.

She asked no more questions.

For the first time in weeks we spent a night without an alarm; yet no one seemed to get any rest. Lisa's light stayed on, but she did not answer our knock. From the sisters' room came the singsong of Irmgard's voice — obviously angry; but the radio drowned out the words.

Not until she was ready for bed did Mother mention my outburst of rage in the kitchen. Taking my hand in hers, she said quietly, "We can't keep away the bombs, yet let's pray that our home won't be destroyed by hate!"

I could not go to sleep. I lay still and listened. The sisters' room was next to mine, but their radio was off and Irmgard's voice had died down. It was dead still.

I looked about the room. On the wall above my bed was Eduard's painting — a reminder of long ago. I needed no light to see the Danish straw-thatched farmhouse with the sandy, uphill road, leading nowhere. On the opposite wall, Mrs. Manning's postcard; would I ever see the lady with the torch?

My eyes went to the desk. Barely visible in the dark were stacks of prisoners' letters. The memory and the promise faded. There was my *now*.

I got up and stepped to the window. It was boarded up, but there was one pane left; it was crusted with ice. Breathing on the glass I worked with my fingers until I had melted a small opening. The skies had cleared and the moon shone. Snow covered Mr. Decker's wagon, and the shack was stooping under its load. The mountain ash, tall and black, cast its shadow over the white ground . . .

I shivered. Everything seemed numbed with cold. Was there any promise of life left? The thought flashed through my mind: Lisa's unborn child.

°

In December fuel was scarce. We traveled in unheated trains, spent our days in cold prisons and our nights in chilly hotel rooms. At home I sat wrapped in blankets reading prisoners' mail.

Life in Hamburg had become one chain of alarms. As yet no allied troops had set foot in Germany, but their bombs seemed as thick as the snow flurries. I was exhausted from lack of sleep and had frequent nightmares.

In my dreams I was back in Dreibergen after the assassination attempt on Hitler. I again saw the guard who, after the execution of the alleged conspirators, had said, "We had a lively morning." Events of long ago came back — the small election booth, where I had given my first and last vote years ago, with two SS–men leaning over me to watch as I prepared the ballot with a trembling hand. Instead of the expected cross in the "yes" square I had put a timid line under "no." I no longer remembered what the question was. It was back in 1934, the last election after Hitler had come to power.

I relived in my dreams one incident from my schooldays: Over and over again I heard Miss Brockdorf's question, "Should we think subjectively or objectively about what concerns our country?" And I saw her lift her arm and tell me to leave the room.

But most often I dreamed of the crowded railroad stations, of the endless trains; and of the faces always pressed against the windows. Soldiers? Prisoners? I could not tell any more. But their eyes all seemed to say, "I'll never come back."

Then one day shortly before Christmas I received another letter in a blue official envelope without a stamp. I spotted it before my mother did and quickly put it aside before she could notice.

Why had they summoned me again? My mind refused to guess; and that night, at the scream of the siren, I thought, "If only it could be over now."

But the morning did come. I went. I arrived at the mansion on time, carrying my briefcase with some bread and the Bible, and this time, in my pocket, Mr. Mangold's gun.

Again I sat in the room facing the glossy white door. Again the man behind the desk kept me waiting. Yet I was calm from the very beginning. Touching the gun in my pocket, I felt peculiarly free.

"What do you know about the Norwegian minister?" the Gestapo official finally began.

So *his* turn has come, I thought; next time it'll be mine.

"Exactly nothing," I said. "He doesn't say much of anything during the prisoners' visits."

"Has he ever attempted to pray or read from the Bible?" the man opposite me persisted.

"Certainly not!" I retorted, pretending to be annoyed. "Don't you know that in the prison God is off limits?"

And thus it went. He asked many questions and I gave as many answers. It was obvious that he had nothing concrete to go on — at least, not yet; but it was equally obvious to me that in time he would.

Toward the end of the interrogation, the Gestapo official surprised me. "Why have you not yet sent us a report?" he asked; and, before I could reply, he added, "Well, what difference does it make? It'll soon be over, anyway."

I glanced quickly at him, then smiled and said vaguely, "With you or with me?"

"With both of us." His face showed no emotion.

He got up and looked out the window. Following his eyes, I saw the empty façade across the street. Below the gaping hole of a ground floor window were the last remains of a firm name, the letters "A" and "O".

"So let's enjoy what's left of the war!" The Gestapo official turned abruptly and gallantly held the leather-upholstered door open as I walked through.

Hurrying down the staircase, I was suddenly overcome by exhaustion. I stopped for a moment and held on to the rail.

✲

I was late getting home, but could not eat supper. All day long one alarm had followed the other. No bombs had been dropped; and toward midnight, when the siren screamed again, I did not go to the bunker.

The house was empty, and I wandered aimlessly through the rooms before settling in the living room with the prisoners' mail. The stillness of the deserted house began to close in on me, and I turned on the radio just in time to hear the announcement, "Heavy bombers are flying toward Hamburg."

I shut off the radio, turned off the light, and opened all windows. During raids I usually stayed in the hall; it was in the center of the house, yet allowed a quick exit if necessary. But that particular night nothing seemed to matter anymore. I stayed in a chair near the open window in the living room. Huddled under a woolen blanket, I waited.

Cold air filled the room. I could catch a glimpse of the sky; in the frosty night the stars stood out, brilliantly clear. There was silence. Then from far off came the familiar thin silvery hum . . . growing more intense . . . turning into a roar.

I stiffened. I was suddenly numbed with fear. Only moments ago I had not cared what might happen; but, with the engines thundering overhead, each fiber of my body seemed to scream, "I want to live!"

A whining sound pierced the air. I covered my ears, but the maddening sound increased. I pulled up my legs and bent forward. The air thickened in my throat. I fought for breath. Vibrations rocked the house, from the piano came a loud discord as if a madman had pounded the keys. Then a roaring crash, followed by another. My mind went blank.

When I opened my eyes, I was lying on the floor. How much time had passed? Seconds? Minutes? Hours? The silence was black and lifeless. There was a dull pain in my head; my nostrils were clogged and my lips parched. The air was full of dust. I moved my foot and heard the rustle of paper. I could lift my hand and touch the leg of the chair.

My eyes got used to the darkness, and I saw the prisoners' letters scattered among the debris on the floor. Plaster had fallen from the walls, and strips of cardboard were torn from the windows. Black paper hung in shreds from the frames and something silvery dangled from the piano, strings ripped loose by the pressure.

My forehead was sticky wet. Blood. I wiped it off, pulled myself up and fell back into the chair. I shook with cold and fatigue. I thought, "The windows must be covered at once." I got up and fumbled my way to the kitchen, opening and closing drawers as I tried to remember where I had put the hammer and nails I had used only the day before.

I tore off the loose shreds of paper from the kitchen window and glanced out into the yard. I stared long before I noticed . . .

Our shack was gone.

The kitchen door was stuck, warped by the pressure. I furiously pulled and kicked until it opened, and rushed out into the yard.

Where shack and chickens had been, there was now a crater with torn-up sods at the edge and splinters of wood strewn around. Nearby stood the mountain ash — unharmed

— and, underneath it, Mr. Decker's wagon, overturned, but whole.

I stared into the crater's blackness. All I could think was that I wanted to get away, and I slipped out into the street through the gate in our hedge.

The alarm was still on. The sky was glowing red and the sound of the fire engines shrieked in the distance. Our street was deserted, and the dark windows with their burned curtains and torn paper strips looked like black holes — like the hollow cavities of a face whose eyes had been gouged out.

I stopped on the sidewalk. In the silence I heard music — Mozart's piano concerto! In this night of destruction, the beauty of the tune seemed unreal, from a different world. "I am dreaming," I thought.

As in a deep sleep I walked up the front steps, past the door hanging on one hinge, into the cluttered maze of plaster, overturned furniture, and dust. There on a table stood a radio. I walked back outside.

The music brought back the memory of a summer day so long ago, when Elizabeth Levy had played that same concerto on our piano. The hawthorn was in bloom, the windows were open, and passers-by had stopped to listen . . . and Elizabeth's anxious whisper, "Pull the curtains!"

Stumbling over the rubbish on the sidewalk, I thought that tonight's horror had begun then. I stood still and listened to the Mozart again. My despair lifted and I gathered hope. Had not my own convictions proved strong and real? They would live on as long as I kept them alive.

All fear left me. I had dreamed of peace so often, but peace had always beckoned from somewhere in the distant future and far away. I had never reached for it in the present. I had to find it in the midst of the ruins, of the Gestapo, of bombs and war. I felt very calm, almost happy, as if I had discovered something I thought could not exist. "Peace comes from within," I mused, "Peace is *now*."

The sisters had returned from the shelter. "Now *your* turn has come!" Irmgard stated with a mixture of gloom and satisfaction as she surveyed the debris in our house.

"It's only the beginning!" Theresa wailed, and her head shook faster than ever.

○

A few days later the Norwegian minister and I were back on the train. We arrived in Dreibergen on Christmas Eve.

"If you wanted heat, you should have brought your own coal," said the innkeeper, when we checked in. His eyes were red and the kitchen was closed. "It's all over for the German House," he whispered. "My son fell at the front."

From the street came the click-clack of wooden shoes against cobblestones, but ice covered the windows and hid the view.

I was back in No. 12. The lightbulb dangled from a cord in the ceiling and shone dimly. By this time I knew every detail of the room by heart. The picture above my bed — how fitting, I thought to myself. The knight on his horse, struggling with the dragon, while the earth beneath split open . . . Finis Terrae.

I went to bed with my clothes on and spread my coat over the blanket for additional warmth. But the chill of the room kept me awake. At last I sat up and tried to jot down some of my thoughts.

"I haven't been able to sleep," I wrote, "thinking how in reality our efforts to help accomplish so little. Yet, in the darkest hour of our night I am coming to realize that the outcome does not depend alone on what we do. There is a greater power at work. And our helplessness and our prayers seem to release it."

○

The next day was Christmas, and we lit a small candle in the dim, cold visiting room of Dreibergen's prison. I saw its flame reflected in the prisoners' faces and wondered how the warmth from one candle could spread so much hope and light.

33

LISA'S FATHER NEVER RETURNED, and soon our supplies of flour dwindled to nothing. I began asking friends for bread, and I went back to Mr. Jenkins. Help always came from somewhere; my suitcase was never empty.

We traveled all of January 1945. During long hours in unheated trains we got used to watching for airplanes diving from the skies. As soon as the train would slow down, we would jump off and run for cover. I no longer counted fresh bullet holes in the windows and doors of our compartments after each attack.

Time stood still, caught in the icy grip of winter; but death marched on. Prisoners were slaughtered in the concentration camps. In the prisons they died of malnutrition. All over Europe people starved under Nazi occupation; and within the German borders, they perished in air raids.

For days at a time we were without gas, heat, or light. Sometimes we were without water. We were short of soap. We got no sleep. Life was decaying around and inside us. War was greed, envy, hate, and suspicion. War was frustration, fear, loneliness, and despair. War was waiting, always waiting for the day to become night and for the night to turn to dawn.

o

In the beginning of February a letter arrived from the Department of Justice in Berlin. Almost a year had gone by since I had written about the prison near Dresden to which I had been denied access.

"Your observation is correct," they wrote. "A rule is a rule. We have ordered the Bautzen prison to let you in."

I rushed to my file to prepare the list of the thirty prisoners I thought I would never see again. As I wrote "Gunnar Dal," winter suddenly seemed to give way to spring.

I phoned the Norwegian Church, but was told the minister was on a trip to Berlin. To save time I sent a cable, asking him to meet me at Bautzen.

I was at the railroad station before dawn. As we pulled into the Dresden station that evening, I stared around in amazement. Not a single windowpane was missing. The platform was clean and dry, without mud puddles and dirty snow. There was no antiaircraft artillery in sight. Dresden was the only large city in Germany not hit by bombs. There were no empty façades; the streets were tree-lined and untouched by war.

On the spur of the moment I decided to spend the night in Dresden . . . just to rest and forget the war, if only for one night. I would catch a train to Bautzen the next day and be there in time to meet Reverend Svendsen.

Eagerly I walked toward the exit. Suddenly the large loudspeaker crackled and a voice announced a train leaving immediately for Bautzen. I stood still — the thought of Gunnar rushed through my mind. I ran as if my life were at stake — up the stairs, over the bridge across the tracks, and down to the platform.

°

The guard at the prison gate glanced at my suitcase. But I had no need to worry. On this first visit to Bautzen I had made certain I carried only personal items. Still, his glance did not promise well for what lay ahead.

The prison tower rose above the courtyard. It resembled a church; but the narrow windows, black holes deep in the thick wall, were barred. The wintry morning was bleak, and I remembered my first prison visit in Hamburg. How many gates I had walked through since that time; how many barred windows I had seen.

Outside a closed door the guard turned to the Norwegian minister. "Wait here!" he said brusquely. Then beckoning to me, he ordered, "Come on!" For a moment I wondered whether I was still free and my pulse quickened as I passed through the open door to the office beyond.

"So you pushed your way in after all!" the Administrator bellowed, as soon as he saw me. He was a small, stout man with a head like a bulldog. I showed him my credentials and his eyes flickered with anger. "I can't stop you from coming," he said curtly, "but inside these walls I set the rules."

"One of my guards will be present and in charge of all visits," he informed me. "You will translate everything that is said, sentence by sentence." Dismissing me, he motioned for the guard to come in.

Reverend Svendsen had been taken to another room and I waited alone in the hall for the guard. I heard no sound in the big building, not even the echo of wooden shoes on ramps. I paced up and down restlessly. What should I do? Give in to the Administrator's demand, or take a chance and ignore it? I glanced down the hall and up at the stone walls, seeking an answer.

At last the guard returned; his face had a smirk. "There aren't many Scandinavian prisoners here," he said as we walked down the hall to the visiting room.

"You have thirty," I stated quietly.

"You can't see them all. Most of them are on a work detail in the munition factory."

"Then we'll wait and see them tonight," I persisted.

The visiting room was cold; the only light came from a small window, deeply recessed in the wall. There was just enough space for two benches. The guard sat on one facing me. On the wall above him Hitler's button eyes stared out from a large framed picture, and a poster proclaimed in fat black letters, *"THE VICTORY IS OURS!"*

The door opened and the first prisoner entered. His uniform hung in rags on his skeleton frame. His head was bent, and he walked slowly, painfully, his legs swollen with edema.

The Norwegian minister addressed him. The guard, staring at me, waited for the translation. I looked past him at those big, fat letters. *"THE VICTORY IS OURS!"* All doubt left me. I knew I would ignore the Administrator's order.

The guard looked at me expectantly and I returned his stare. The silence was heavy between us, but it was broken by the sudden scream of a siren.

Alarm.

The guard stood up. "End of the visit!" he shouted. "The prisoner has to go back to his cell."

The minister and I waited out the alarm in the visiting room. The hours went by and we stood at the window, watching the sky. Large formations of bombers followed one another in an ominous parade, and the intense hum of their powerful engines penetrated the thick prison walls. The air — the room itself — vibrated. Hitler's picture shook in its frame and the button eyes stared emptily.

Once I stepped into the hall and overheard a guard say, "So Dresden got it at last. They started last night, and now they are back."

"Thank God, we were spared!" answered another.

"Thank God!" echoed my own thoughts. "Thank God for getting me on that train in time!"

o

All afternoon the sky hummed with planes, and not until evening did the alarm cease. The guard looked at his watch and pronounced, "There is no time left."

"We'll be back tomorrow."

"No, it's against our rules. You can return only after four months."

"Then we'll see the prisoners tonight."

The guard disappeared. Obviously he was reporting to the Administrator; when he came back his face looked stony, as if he wanted to say, "We'll get you yet!"

But much to my surprise he nodded and said, "Follow me!" He marched ahead of us to the Scandinavian prisoners' barrack. There was a small office next to the entrance. "We'll conduct the visit here," he said and placed himself in the only chair.

It was nearly lights-out time. The prisoners had just returned from the munition factory, and from behind the thin plank wall we heard the clinking sound of utensils, stools scraping over the floor, and slow tired steps in wooden shoes. "Gunnar is in there somewhere," I thought.

The door opened and the first group of prisoners entered.

234

In the dim light of the single bulb hanging from the ceiling, they all looked alike. Their eyes, circled by deep shadows, resembled dark holes. Their bodies, emaciated from starvation, shook with cold. They swayed with fatigue. The bleak light accentuated the yellow of their skin. It was the color of death.

"You have three minutes." The guard looked at his watch.

They were the longest minutes I had ever spent visiting prisoners. The guard's presence seemed to contaminate the air and choke us. At last the minister spoke and the guard turned to me again, expecting a translation. Again I remained silent. But he let us go on. Sitting rigidly in his chair, he stared at me as if to register my every move.

I ignored him, remembering my first prison visit and the first prison rule I had broken. A prisoner had prayed in my presence and I had not stopped him. Now it was my turn to pray. Oh, for a way to give my friends a moment of hope.

The last group of prisoners entered and I looked into Gunnar's eyes. I felt the blood drain from my face; and, to conceal my feeling from the others, I turned quickly away.

"It is late," I said to the guard. I looked at my watch; and, pretending to tell the minister and the prisoners that we would have to go, I said in Norwegian, "We can't speak freely today, but we want you to know that you are not forgotten. Next time we meet, it will be to bring you home."

There was a deep silence, both in the room and behind the thin wall that separated us from the others. Perhaps they would hear us, too. I glanced at the minister and nodded. He opened his Bible and began reading aloud, "Herren er min hyrde, meg fattes intet . . ." — "The Lord is my shepherd, I shall not want . . ."

I looked at the gun on the wall, then at the guard's face. He sat motionless, but triumph gleamed in his eyes. I had played right into his hands. Yet, I felt no fear. As I listened to the ancient words of comfort and strength, I gathered hope.

In parting we shook hands with the prisoners as if the guard did not exist. For one moment I felt Gunnar's hand close around mine. "I'm alive," I heard him whisper, "and you are, too!"

○

Outside the guard turned brusquely to me, "I'll have to take you to the Administrator."

None of us spoke as he took us back. My own steps were the only sounds I heard in the dimly lit hall.

The guard went into the office alone. I was called in a few minutes later. The Administrator looked up from a paper covered with scribbled notes. "You didn't follow my orders," he began. "You didn't translate what was said. You let the minister read aloud from the Bible!" His fist pounded the desk. Continuing at the top of his voice, he shouted, "I'll notify Berlin; but, mind you, not your friends in the Department of Justice. I'll report you directly to Himmler!"

I did not attempt to defend myself. I felt strangely calm. My work was almost done and soon many helping hands would be waiting to get the prisoners home. For me the end was near, too — one way or the other.

○

"What will you do?" Reverend Svendsen asked on our way back to the hotel.

"Stay away from home for a while." We walked silently on. "I'll go to Berlin," I said at last.

"To whom will you go?"

"I think I know," I said, thinking of the summer night when I had given Mr. Mangold the address in Berlin. Only as I spoke did I realize that I no longer remembered the name of Dr. von Berg's friends. My mind was blank, perhaps because I had not eaten all day. My memory had never yet failed me. I would remember later, tonight or tomorrow.

The heavy smell of burned turnips filled the hotel lobby, but the dining room was closed. I went straight to my room and, without taking off my clothes, lay down, and fell into a restless sleep.

After some time I heard a siren — or was it just a dream? I

saw before me fat black letters, and I reached out for them. I tried to piece them together so they would form the address which had slipped from my mind. But, whatever I did, they always read, *"THE VICTORY IS OURS!"*

There was a hammering in my ears. It grew louder and more persistent. I awoke with a start. Holding my breath, I sat up and listened.

Someone was pounding at my door.

Yesterday I had felt so calm. Now perspiration broke out on my forehead. It was still night. Without turning on my light, I fumbled for my purse and took out my gun. What should I do with it — point it at the door or at my head? I tried in vain to steady my hand.

Then I heard from behind the door, "It is three o'clock!" It was not the Gestapo. It was the maid. "Get up!" she yelled, "or you won't catch your train."

I went limp. The gun dropped from my hand, and I broke into hysterical laughter, the tears rolling down my cheeks. I was alive. I was still free to go. All I had to do was to get on the train bound for Dresden and from there to Berlin.

A fine snow had fallen. It felt soft beneath my shoes as Reverend Svendsen and I walked. Perhaps Gunnar had walked this path yesterday, returning from his work detail, I thought. His footprints were now covered by snow and soon mine would be gone as well.

The railroad station was almost totally dark. Only a dim light burned in the ticket counter. A few people sat on their suitcases and knapsacks, waiting.

"When is the train leaving?"

"Who knows?" said the stationmaster, "Dresden has been bombed all night."

We waited. One hour, two hours, three hours? I don't know. Finally a conductor called out; "All aboard!"

"For Dresden?"

"As far as we can get."

The train rolled. I fell asleep. When I awoke, our train had come to a standstill. Beside us other trains had stopped, too: a freight train, packed with soldiers, and a train without any glass in the windows. Women buried their faces in scarves; children covered their frozen ears with their hands. Old men sat hunched on their suitcases.

Refugees.

We waited again. All that had happened yesterday seemed as unreal to me as what might happen tomorrow. I felt only the icy cold creeping up from the floor and deadening my legs and my mind.

At last we left the train and began to walk along the tracks. From time to time I turned to see if our train were moving. But it became a black dot in the distance and I stopped looking back. My feet were numb. I kept slipping and falling; and finally, no longer able to carry my suitcase, I dumped it somewhere along the icy tracks.

By noon we reached the "border." The ruins began. The streets were blocked off by rubble and fallen trees. The sky was black with smoke, in strange contrast to the white snow on the tracks. We had arrived in Dresden.

There was not one windowpane left in the railroad station. People, blindly pushing on, plied the railroad officials with questions. But they shrugged, "You'll just have to wait."

The crowd settled down. More than in any other place I felt the sinister mood of the times. The clatter of dishes — waiting. Eyes staring vacantly — waiting. The floor squeaking under boots and wooden shoes — waiting. The hum of voices which knew only one refrain — waiting.

The refugees sat on the floor, on bundles, on mattresses. Those who had come away with any belongings clung to them. A group of Ukrainians with long mustaches and tunics crouched in a corner, alongside a group of Hungarian soldiers in colorful uniforms.

Reverend Svendsen and I finally found a seat at one of the wooden tables. Beer dripped from its top. Next to us a soldier stood at rigid attention before an officer. The officer was demanding his papers.

"Just don't get the idea that you don't have to salute us anymore," the officer's face was an angry red as he made note of the soldier's name and company. "You will be reported — and you are aware of the consequences."

"But, Herr Major, I have . . ."

"Shut up!"

"Yes, sir."

Again I saw the Administrator's red face before me. "I'll report you directly to Himmler!" I thought of Berlin, of the address. Bending forward and covering my eyes, I tried to forget everything around me, so I would remember.

Workmen on tall stepladders hammered out the last of the glass left in the window frames. The bits fell tinkling to the ground. The loudspeaker crackled and a voice kept repeating, "Hello, hello!"

Each time I heard it, my heart beat a little faster. Would they announce a train for Berlin? Or any train, going in any direction? Just as long as it would take us away from here.

But I must go to Berlin. I must remember the name.

The voice over the loudspeaker said, "One — two — three — we're just testing the equipment."

Out of the corner of my eye I saw a hand rummaging through the ashtray looking for cigarette butts. There were none; but from the next table a woman's voice said, "Reiner, I got some for you!"

I looked up. Reiner! "Reiner," she had said. That was the name. Now I remembered. Professor Reiner. I saw the whole address before me as I had once scribbled it down. "Professor Reiner, Arnimstrasse 15, Berlin-Dahlem."

"I'm hungry!" I said to Reverend Svendsen. I elbowed my way to the counter, over mattresses and people, over stretched-out legs and sleeping children. I had rations cards for 200 grams of bread.

"Four slices, please."

A man stood next to me, filthy and shaking.

"Bread," he whispered hoarsely. "Please give me some. I'm starved."

But I turned my head the other way as if I had not seen or heard him. At the sight of the gray waiting room filled with

239

human want, I was overcome by a desperate fear. How much longer would we have to wait? Perhaps only a few hours — but what if it were days?

I wanted to live, I wanted to get to Berlin. All I could think of was the address that had come back to me. If only I could make it to Berlin, I would be safe.

Without looking back I hastily withdrew from the counter. Then I stopped short. I turned and looked for the man, but he was gone.

Through the broken windows I heard the sounds of fire engines, followed by ambulances and hearses. Out there, just a few minutes away, was a burning city with people buried in their basements, screaming for help, praying to be heard. But I prayed only for my own safety.

The day dragged on as endless as the twelve years we had waited. Finally word spread like a wave that a train was ready to depart. We jumped to our feet, plunged into the crowd, and pushed into the mad rush on the platform surging toward the door. We used our elbows and feet, kicked, cursed, and won. We got on.

The train moved.

Our compartment had windows. Snow fell outside and piled against the glass, making us an island of bodies rolling away from a city of death. My feet were no longer mine. They were lifeless. I was exhausted, ready to collapse; but we were packed together so tightly that no one could fall.

My mind began swimming. Suspended in a strange, timeless vacuum, I was neither asleep nor awake. And I was certain that the words I heard in the dark could only be a dream. They spoke of Leningrad, of a massive offensive by the Russians. They whispered, "We're nearing the end."

Close to midnight we arrived in Berlin. There were no signs, no glass in the station windows; and the platform, torn up by shells, was covered by crusty ice. Had it not been for the voice shouting through the loudspeaker, "Berlin — Anhalter Bahnhof!" it might just as well have been Dresden.

Reverend Svendsen and I were about to part. He would go on to Hamburg, but for one moment we stood together. As I looked at him, the moment when we first met flashed through my mind. I remembered his cold stare, how he had ignored my outstretched hand. Since that day we had come a long way together. Yet, how little we knew of each other. Always we had avoided personal thoughts, for always there had been the danger of listening ears.

Now he gave me his hand. "Take care, Hiltgunt," he said, for the first time addressing me by my given name.

I glanced over the tracks. Against the dark sky, empty façades stood like dead trees, and I asked something I did not mean to, "What will become of us when it is all over?"

For a moment he seemed startled; but then, smiling reassuringly, he said, "Don't worry! Our friends will be saved and get home."

I fell silent; I had not meant the prisoners. I had been thinking of myself — of all of us who would be left behind.

I walked out of the railroad station stumbling over rubble and sticks. With ruins all around, the street seemed wider than usual. I did not recognize my surroundings, but I knew that somewhere down the road was the Potzdamer Platz with a station for local trains. Others went the same way; the night's blackness made them and their luggage seem one. Snow had begun to fall, and soon it got so heavy that I could not see what was ahead.

"Where is the fatherland?" I heard a voice say through the darkness.

I stopped and looked up. "I don't know," I answered. "I don't know any more where the fatherland is."

"I haven't slept for three nights!" shouted the voice. "If they can't provide a roof over their soldiers' heads, they can go to hell!"

Then I understood. His "Fatherland" was not the fatherland I had thought of.

"Follow me," I said.

We walked on silently until, as if risen from the dead, a line of people stood before us. A beam from a flashlight shone through the snow and dimly lit their faces.

"Take it easy!" bellowed a hoarse voice. "Let's see your papers!"

We had come to "Café Fatherland," once a restaurant and dancehall, now a night shelter for soldiers on their way through Berlin.

○

It had stopped snowing when I got off the train at Dahlem, a quiet residential section. It was part of Berlin, but seemed untouched by war. Street signs were intact, and the houses, with layers of white on their roofs, resembled sleepy faces.

Arnimstrasse was a dead-end street; my footsteps were the first in the newly fallen snow. The moon was out and the trees lining the road cast long, thin shadows. It was past one o'clock. I was seized by fear. Suppose no one answered the door? What would I do? Where would I go? The last part of the way I ran more than walked.

The gate in the fence was locked. There was no name, just a number. Back from the street stood a villa of stucco. Part of the front wall was missing. All the shades were down, and there was no trace of life behind them.

As I rang the bell at the gate, I looked up at the house anxiously. Only seconds passed, but to me they seemed like hours. Then I thought I saw a glimmer of light — a curtain moved as if someone were peering out.

Before I could decide whether it was only my imagination, the house door opened. Steps came close — a woman. Underneath her coat I glimpsed the uniform of a maid, black and white.

"What do you want?"

"Let me in," I said. "I am a friend of Dr. von Berg's."

She unlocked the gate silently and led me to the house. "She's a friend of Dr. von Berg!" she called out at the front door.

A sigh of relief came from inside.

A tall, bearded man and a frail-looking woman stood in the dimly lit hall.

242

I introduced myself. "Forgive me for ringing your doorbell so late," I said and began to explain . . .

"Don't!" Professor Reiner quickly interrupted. "All we care to know is that you're Dr. von Berg's friend." He smiled and, stepping forward with his hands outstretched, he exclaimed, "His friends are ours, too!"

I saw that he limped, and, as if guessing my unasked question, he added, "Dr. von Berg saved my life in World War I."

The house was chilly; they wore coats, and they asked me to keep mine on. Only the night before the library next to their living room had been hit by a bomb. The carpets were rolled up and their pictures had been taken down. The walls were cracked and bricks lay strewn around. Dust was everywhere and icy air crept through the windows, which had been hurriedly covered by cardboard.

A woman in fur huddled on a folding cot near the cold stove and two men in heavy coats sat on stacks of books. They were refugees, Professor Reiner said, assigned to them by Berlin's housing authority; and, introducing me, he said that I was a refugee, too.

They asked no questions, and, making no comment about my late arrival, resumed their conversation without delay. They addressed each other with "Herr Professor," "Herr Doctor," and "Gnaedige Frau." They talked about books and paintings and ignored the chill and turmoil around them. Each time there was a lull in their polite conversation, someone quickly spoke up as if they dreaded the silence. Nobody mentioned the bombs or the state of the war. Did they not trust the intruder, I wondered, or was it their way of shutting out the present?

I sat apart on a sofa, sharing my seat with some broken library chairs. Its wine-red damask cover was torn. My eyes were heavy with fatigue; and, shivering with cold, I slid my hands into the sleeves of my coat. One of the guests was reading aloud from Goethe's *Faust*, but the words, once so familiar, now sounded like a foreign language to me — my ears still roared from the sounds of the fire engines in the burning city.

Then, after a polite knock at the door, Stella, the maid, came in. She wore a white starched apron over her black dress, and a tiny white cap was perched on top of her hair. She carried a tray with demi-tasse cups, carefully balancing them as she stepped over debris. The delicate cups contained chicory instead of mocha, and there was neither cream nor sugar. But the small silver spoon, neatly placed on the saucer, was like a flag of an undying past.

34

I STAYED TWO WEEKS IN BERLIN. They were the longest weeks in my life — not because of the endless alarms and air raids which turned day into night and night into day, and not because of the Reiners. They treated me as a friend when actually I had come as a stranger. They shared their rations with me and let me stay in the room of their son who was fighting somewhere at the front.

The unrest was in myself. I felt sidetracked in a world where I did not belong. Being away from my work was like cutting my life line. I wanted to leave, to go back to Hamburg; but I dared not take the chance.

The chilly sessions in the Reiners' living room continued. Each night the family and their guests sat huddled around the stove, losing themselves in discussions about literature and art of the past.

One day when we were alone, I asked Mrs. Reiner's permission to tune in the BBC. She did not object; but she remarked as she left the room, "What's the use of knowing about what can't be changed?"

Each morning I heard her pacing the floor, waiting for the mail. For weeks they had not heard from their son. At last a letter arrived from his captain. Their son was dead.

I was with Mrs. Reiner, saw her break down, and heard her cry out, "How could God let that happen?"

I wanted to console her, but what could I say? God did not

let it happen, I said to myself. We did. We, the human race. I had no answer for her, but I knew what I myself had to do. I had to go back to Hamburg.

Professor Reiner followed me to the station. There was a train scheduled for Hamburg — but when? Nobody knew.

"I'll wait with you," Professor Reiner said.

"Don't. You're needed at home."

But he lingered on; and at last he asked, "Why do you take so many risks? Why won't you stay in safety with us?"

Then I understood that he had known about my work all along.

"I must go," I replied.

He turned to leave, but I held him back. A question had been on my mind since the day I had come. "What happened to Mr. Mangold?"

"He died," Professor Reiner answered. "He was a sick man when he arrived. All we could do for him was to rush him to the hospital. Tuberculosis, they said. Far advanced."

He shrugged his shoulders; then as if remembering something, he looked intently at me and recalled, "Mr. Mangold told me about you. He said, 'I never was really alive; *she* was.'"

°

There was no official envelope in the mail when I arrived at home; and from the smile on my mother's face I knew that the Gestapo had not come for me. The report from the Administrator in Bautzen must have gone astray — the American bombs on Dresden had probably saved me.

I resumed my work.

Then one day a prison guard told me of a secret order from Hitler: all political prisoners in Germany were to be executed on day X, a day to be determined by the Fuehrer himself.

There was no time to be lost. We returned to Hamburg at once. The Norwegian minister used whatever contacts he had to send a message to Scandinavia. I rushed to the port to Mr. Jenkins, "We must send word to the Swedish Red Cross today — not tomorrow!"

The rest is history: Count Folke Bernadotte, the President of the Swedish Red Cross, and other Scandinavian officials intervened in Berlin. I don't know the details, but Heinrich Himmler released the Scandinavian political prisoners. One day early in April 1945 a fleet of Swedish Red Cross buses arrived and searched every German prison and camp. I had handed over my secret file to Reverend Svendsen, and whenever a prisoner could not be located, my file gave the answer. All of the Scandinavian prisoners were found and taken to neutral Sweden to await the end of the war.

My prisoner friends were safe when, only shortly afterward, thousands of political prisoners all over Germany were shot in camps, hanged, or loaded alive on ships that were sailed out to sea and sunk. Those who did survive owed their lives to an avalanche of events faster than death itself.

°

A few more air raids, and then the nights turned quiet. Only an occasional artillery thundered in the distance, and from the neighboring tavern came music, at first subdued, then louder, then the stomping of feet. They were dancing again.

Yet, the war was still on. During the day, the "People's Storm Troops" — old men and boys, Hitler's last brigade — dragged wearily through the streets. We stood in line waiting for either our ration cards or for supplies which did not arrive. Our stomachs were empty; our minds filled with rumors: "Hamburg will be surrendered without resistance!" "We'll be British — they'll get us food!" "The Russians rape and kill in Berlin!" and — a sigh of relief — "Thank God, they're not here!"

At home the sisters dwelt on the "tragedy" that had befallen our country; and I, listening to the BBC, no longer turned down the Levys' radio.

Only Lisa was silent. Her time was close. For hours she sat at the window staring into our yard, where lawn and rose beds were gray with dirt and rubble.

Then over our radio came the news of Hitler's death: April 30, 1945. For twelve long years I had dreamed of this moment; now that it had arrived, I felt no relief, no hate, no triumph — nothing!

I was alone with my mother; and, as we listened in silence, I saw her turn away and look at Willfried's photo on the wall.

That night I remembered the manuscript hidden in the ground under the mountain ash and I went out to dig it up. We had no electricity, but until the batteries in my flashlight were dead, I read — for the first time — what a prisoner had written while in solitary confinement. Once more, in my thoughts, I wandered along the gangways and bridges of a prison, where men had marked time by scratching points, lines, and crosses into the wall.

"Tear down the walls of your mind!" I read in the tightly written pages. "Free yourself of the prejudices that bar your view. Bury the hate that separates you from your fellow man."

I had to get that manuscript through the wall which now sealed Germany off from the rest of the world. I knew just where to go. Mr. Jenkins would find a way to get it to Sweden.

The next day I set out for the port. Again I passed Bismarck's statue. He stood unscathed amidst the ruins, his hand still holding the sword, but in my hand I carried a message of peace.

Returning a few minutes later, my steps were slow. Where Mr. Jenkins' house had once stood, I had found only rubble and ashes. "It was the last air raid," an old woman told me. "He never went to a bunker. He was buried alive."

I walked toward Reeperbahn. The purple sky turned gray and the silver stripes at the horizon faded. This was the hour of the day when the glittering lights of Hamburg's strip flashed on, when people crowded St. Pauli's block. Now they dragged past the empty façades, silent and withdrawn.

Only one place resounded with life. A wooden barrack, serving thin beer, had just opened its door. People pushed toward the entrance. Some soldiers jumped over a plank to get to the back door, but one of them had to stay behind. He had lost a leg and was unable to jump.

It was night and the moon was new. There was debris everywhere. I was twenty-eight years old, but at this moment I felt ancient. What was left for me? Gunnar had gone out of my life the day the prisoners had been released. He would return to his wife and child — to his own world.

Where was mine? Where would I go from here?

But then I remembered. I had made that decision long ago. As I walked on, at first slowly, my steps became firmer. One day I would be a physician. I would go on serving life.